This work is a re-examination of the decisions regarding the 1944 Warsaw Uprising made by the leadership of the underground Polish Army (AK), as well as the questionable attitudes of senior Polish commanders in exile in London. The questions raised are, was the uprising necessary and why was it so poorly conducted by a totally indifferent leadership?

The challenge is made that the Polish leaders in Warsaw and in London were clearly unfeeling. In Warsaw the uprising was allowed to happen and was doomed from the very beginning owing to poor generalship. The Soviets can be seen rather than to have betrayed the Poles, to have behaved in the same manner as they had always behaved to the Poles and Poland, that is underhanded and with great deceit. Therefore why did the Warsaw Poles rise up when encouraged by the Soviets? The Poles should have known that it was a trick. Despite plans laid down by the Allies to support such uprisings, as had been the case in Paris during August 1944, the Red Army watched the AK be destroyed by the Germans, to save themselves the same job. Once the uprising failed, the Polish leadership went into what could only be described as 'genteel' captivity, compared with the fate of hundreds of thousands of their countrymen and women who were herded out of Warsaw by German armed forces and sent to concentration camps, illegal prisoner of war camps or forced into slave labour.

In the West senior Polish commanders did not consider a 100% casualty rate to be unacceptable as they pushed for Allied flights to re-supply Warsaw. This callous disregard for life was part of the lack of understanding in the leadership of the reality of the Polish situation in 1944: the war was not about Poland but the complete defeat of Germany. If Polish freedom came out of this, then good, otherwise the Allies were not going to be diverted from the constant aerial bombardment of Germany, as the Allies swept eastward and westward towards Germany. This work is supplemented with Polish sources as well as interviews with five women who had been involved in the Warsaw Uprising as young women and girls in 1944. Now in their eighties these ladies kindly granted interviews with the author in Poland during 2012.

Evan McGilvray was born in August 1961 in Winchester, Hampshire. He is a graduate of the School of Slavonic and East European Studies, University of London (UCL). Following this he undertook post-graduate studies at the University of Bradford and the University of Leeds, where he researched the politics of the Polish Army from 1918 to date. He also taught at the two universities. Evan is quite happy to challenge the myths that Poles have created around the Polish Army and the role of Poland during the Second World War. He also has an interest in other militaries and their role in society – quite simply civil-military relations – Poland being one of the most interesting European examples.

Evan has written two previous titles – *The Black Devils' March – A Doomed Odyssey*. The 1st Polish Armoured Division 1939-45 (2004) and *A Military Government in Exile. The Polish Government in Exile 1939-45, a Study of Discontent* (2010), both published by Helion.

At present Evan is writing a new history of the 1944 Warsaw Uprising in readiness for its seventieth anniversary in 2014, as well as researching the military politics regarding the involvement of General Sir Ian Hamilton at the Dardanelles during 1915. He is also anticipating the opening of the archives relating to the Falklands War in 2012. To relax he has learnt to ignore the rest of the world, and notes, "Despite what Poles think, I am not a Scot, only in name!"

DAYS OF ADVERSITY

The Warsaw Uprising 1944

Evan McGilvray

Helion & Company

Helion & Company Limited
26 Willow Road
Solihull
West Midlands
B91 1UE
Tel. 0121 705 3393
Fax 0121 711 4075
Email: info@helion.co.uk
Website: www.helion.co.uk
Twitter: @helionbooks
Visit our blog http://blog.helion.co.uk/

Published by Helion & Company 2015
Designed and typeset by Bookcraft Limited, Stroud, Gloucestershire
Cover designed by Euan Carter, Leicester (www.euancarter.com)
Printed by Lightning Source, Milton Keynes, Buckinghamshire

ISBN 978 1 909982 95 6

British Library Cataloguing-in-Publication Data.
A catalogue record for this book is available from the British Library.

For details of other military history titles published by Helion & Company Limited contact
the above address, or visit our website: http://www.helion.co.uk.

We always welcome receiving book proposals from prospective authors.

Contents

List of illustrations and maps

List of Abbreviations

AAA   Anti-Aircraft Artillery.

AL   *Armia Ludowa* (Polish Soviet-backed Peoples' Army).

AK   *Armia Krajowa*.

BAF   Balkan Air Force.

CAS   Chief of Air Staff.

C-in-C   Commander-in-Chief.

CIGS   Chief of Imperial General Staff (British).

FO   Foreign Office (British).

MAAF   Mediterranean Allied Air Forces.

NIE   *Niepodległość* (Independence) Polish anti-Soviet underground movement, 1944-48.

NKVD   *Narodnaya Komissariat Vnutrennikh Del* (The Peoples' Commissariat for Internal Affairs). Soviet secret police, forerunner of the Soviet Union's KGB, or the present day Russian Federal Security Bureau (FSB).

NSZ   *Narodowe Siły Zbrojne*. National Armed Forces (Fascist-inspired Polish underground movement – very anti-Soviet and sympathetic to German aims, especially the Nazi hatred of Jews).

OSS   Office of Strategic Services.

PAST   *Polska Akcyjna Spółka Telefoniczna*.

PIAT   Projectile Infantry Anti-Tank (British Army issue hand-held anti-tank weapon).

PKWN   *Polski Komitet Wyzwolenia Narodowego* (Polish Committee of National Liberation).

POW   Prisoner of War.

PWE   Political Warfare Executive (British).

PWPW   *Polska Wytwórni Papierów Wartościowych* (Polish State Security Printing Works).

RONA   *Russaya Osvobodityelnaya Narodnaya Armya* (Russian National Liberation Army).

SOE   Special Operations Executive.

SZP   *Służba Zwycięstwu Polski* (In Service of Poland's Victory).

UB   *Urząd Bezpieczeństwa* (Polish Internal Security Force, 1945-1989).

WiN   *Wolność i Niezawislość* (Freedom and Independence) Polish anti-Soviet underground movement, 1945-48.

ZWZ   *Związek Walki Zbrojnej* (Union of Armed Struggle).

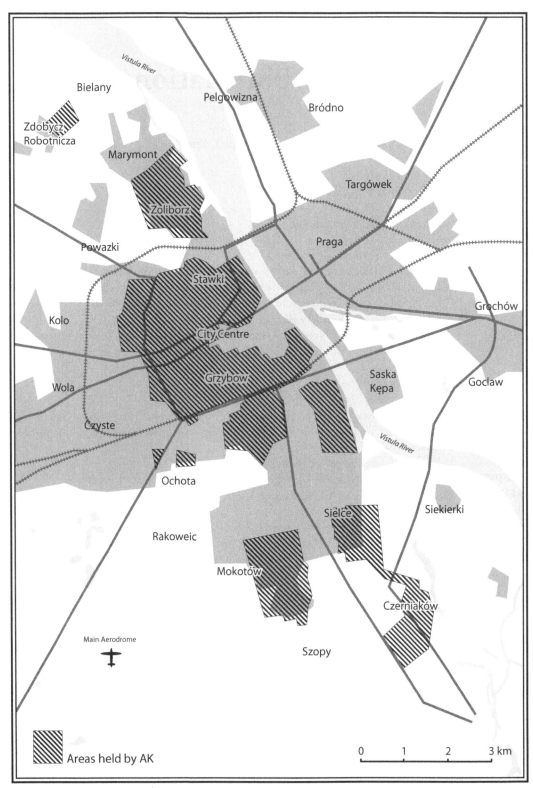

Map 1 Warsaw, 4 August 1944.

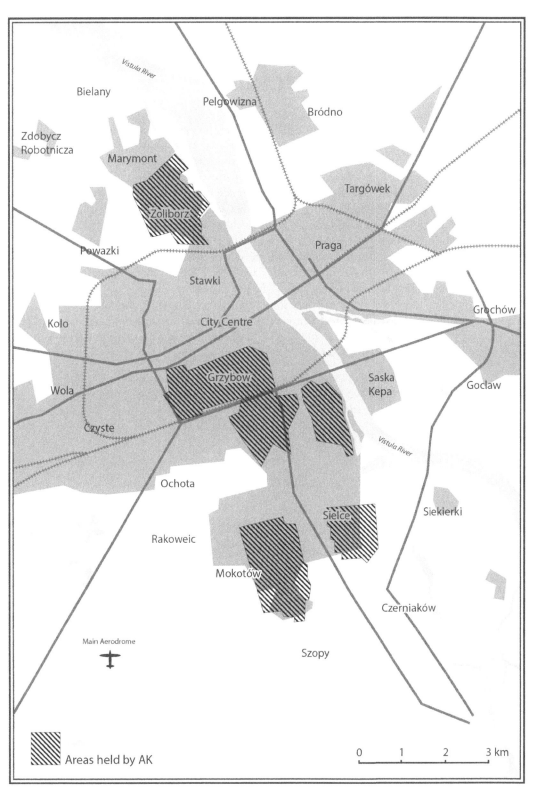

Map 2 Warsaw, 10 September 1944.

Preface

I wish to thank Duncan Rogers at Helion for giving me the opportunity of writing this history of the 1944 Warsaw Uprising, a subject which has interested me since my first visit to Warsaw in 1986. I would like to thank Dr. Barbara Dobrowolska: for graciously allowing me to use the tables from her book *Pielęgniarstwa Polskiego*; for allowing me to interview her and also for organising a visit to the Museum of the Warsaw Uprising, this made it possible for me to interview Barbara Matys, Barbara Gadomska, Stefania Hoch and Wanda Lesniewska in Warsaw in July 2012. I wish to thank the ladies for their time and for the artefacts they gave me. I would like to thank my wife Ela for her help in this exercise. I also have to thank the ladies at the Main Archive of the Polish Nurses' Association for organising hospitality on the day of the interviews.

For my trips to London I have to thank my daughter, Wioletta, for her hospitality and Ms. Shadia Khan for looking after me when I fell ill during one of the trips.

I hope that this work will help to dispel some myths about the uprising and the progress of the war in 1944, and cause people to focus on the news of today as contemporary uprisings play out their course on TV, the Internet and social networks. Try and look beyond what you see, remember and do not accept what you are told without good cause.

Introduction

This work is a re-examination of the failed 1944 Warsaw Uprising. It poses the question of not why it failed but why it went ahead at all, as it was quite clear that it was doomed before a single shot had been fired. The only conclusion that can be reached is that it was an attempted coup, led by an inept yet opportunist military clique. At the end of July 1944, it appeared that the occupying Germans were leaving Warsaw, but the Red Army had yet to cross the River Vistula into the Polish capital. The clique perceived a power vacuum, and hoped to take advantage of it. It was possibly the last chance for elements of the Polish military to seize power in Poland before the country was annexed by the Soviet Union.

The Polish Second Republic had been established in 1918, when Poles were at last able to restore the Polish state, which had been erased from the map in 1795. By 1944, a pivotal year for Poland, this old order had finally crumbled into dust and was scattered to the winds. The process of disintegration had begun in 1926, when after only five years of democracy Józef Piłsudski, the Polish amateur military commander; using Polish troops loyal to him seized power after leading a coup against the elected and legitimate Polish government. Piłsudski then ruled the country as a dictator until his death in 1935. Although ruled by a military clique between 1926 and 1939; Poland actually declined militarily as Piłsudski and his cronies saw little advantage in modernizing the armed services. Civil life also declined dramatically as the military took a leading role in society.

Professional soldiers and diplomats who were not approved of by Piłsudski and his followers became isolated and found their careers in tatters. This was probably one of the reasons why Poland became too close to Nazi Germany both politically and diplomatically as there were no dissenting voices to urge caution in dealings with Germany. This included participating with both Germany and Hungary in the dismemberment of Czechoslovakia during late 1938, However this did not prevent Germany from invading Poland on 1 September 1939 and Germany's new ally, the Soviet Union, followed this up with its own invasion of Poland on 17 September 1939. Once more, Poland was overrun and divided up between its two traditional enemies. September 1939 was to have long-term consequences for Poles as they had to endure the twin horrors of Nazism and Stalinism until 1945. After that date they endured Stalinism alone in various forms. It became watered down in stages, until the demise of communist rule in east-central Europe during 1989.

When in 1989 communism finally collapsed in Poland, a Polish communist military commander, General Wojciech Jaruzelski, was head of state. Historically, the Poles may have loved their military leaders regardless of their backgrounds, but from 1942 onwards it was clear that the British Foreign Office (FO) did not trust Polish military commanders to restore democracy in Poland when the war ended. Instead the FO considered that at least General Władysław Anders, Commander of Polish Second Corps, commonly known as 'Anders' Army' might try to enter Poland with "his" army and take power at the expense of civilian politicians. The importance of Anders will be discussed later in this work. There was also a suggestion that some Polish officers considered that Polish independence could only be restored with German help.[1] This has some credence, as Biddiscombe notes that after the failure of the Warsaw Uprising the Germans gave serious thought to encouraging existing pro-Nationalist groups, which had previously fought

---

1   Harvey Sarner, *General Anders and the Soldiers of the Polish Second Corps*, Cathedral City, Brunswick, 1997, p.56.

against them, to join them in an offensive to halt the westward advance of the Red Army. These groups included the *Armia Krajowa* (AK), awkwardly translated into English as "Home Army", and the leading Polish partisan group in Poland.[2] The concept of Poles wanting to fight the Soviets, even if they were supposed to be allies, is not ridiculous or shocking, as the Warsaw Uprising was to prove; it was the conditions of how this should occur that interested the Poles. However there is plenty of evidence that, despite the atrocities committed against Poland by the Germans and their allies, by the war's end many Poles were still inclined to support Germany rather than the Soviet Union. The British authorities were to discover this when they began to receive Polish refugees and Polish conscripts from the German Army. It is beyond doubt that after May 1945 General Anders, actively sought war against the Soviet Union. His agents caused mayhem in post-war Poland and in effect contributed to the civil war of 1944-1949.[3] It should also be borne in mind that during May 1945 Churchill considered that German forces might have to be retained. He feared that fighting might break out between the West and the Soviet Union as the war in Europe came to an end.[4]

The first piece of the puzzle of trying to make clearer the reason for the Warsaw Uprising is the fact that the Polish people had tended to regard the Polish Army as the most trusted institution available, owing to the misperception that the Polish military, rather than civilian politicians, was responsible for Polish independence.[5] To be fair, this probably had been the case in 1918-1921, but afterwards the claim was doubtful. Civilian trust in the military was a legacy of the lack of democracy in Poland; as a consequence of which Poles could only relate to the military running the country. However, doubts were raised when during the September 1939 campaign, Poland was comprehensively overrun by its enemies, and the military government fled into exile, even though the army was still in the field.

During September 1939 some Polish military commanders made a little headway against the German onslaught, but these were few and far between and their efforts were rendered useless once the Soviet Union attacked Poland from the east, in effect stabbing Poland in the back. In the event all the Polish Army could do was to withdraw from Poland (as ordered by the former government which had already cravenly fled), and try to make its way south and west, particularly to France, to continue the war from there. Many Polish soldiers headed towards France where General Władysław Sikorski, with French support had, following the fall of Poland, been able to establish a Polish government-in-exile based in Paris. Sikorski, a former Prime Minister, had been Defence Minister prior to 1926, but he was an enemy of Piłsudski and as a consequence had been outside Polish politics since Piłsudski's assumption of power in 1926. A Polish military force was also established in France but under the control of both the British and French High Commands. This situation lasted until the summer of 1940, when the German Army overran most of Western Europe, including France. Once more the Poles had to move their base, and made their way to the UK. Despite another Polish defeat as a result of the Fall of France during June 1940 Sikorski managed to maintain his offices and re-established the Polish government-in-exile in London. He was very lucky in that he enjoyed the support of Winston Churchill, the newly appointed British Prime Minister. However all of this was to change in 1941.

---

2   Perry Biddiscombe, *The SS Hunter Battalions. The Hidden History of the Nazi Resistance Movement 1944-45*, Stroud, UK, Tempus, 2006, p.32.

3   Evan McGilvray, *A Military Government in Exile. The Polish Government-in-exile, 1939-1945, a Study of Discontent*, Solihull, Helion, 2010, pp.157-76.

4   Frederick Taylor, *Exorcising Hitler. The Occupation and Denazification of Germany*, London, Bloomsbury, 2012, p.94.

5   Jerzy J. Wiatr, *The Soldier and the Nation. The Role of the Military in Polish Politics, 1918-1985*, Boulder, Westview, 1988, p.2.

On 22 June 1941, to the surprise of Jozef Stalin, the Soviet leader, Germany finally invaded the Soviet Union. The invasion was launched from German-occupied Poland into Soviet-annexed Poland. As far as the Poles were concerned this meant two things: all of Poland was now under German control, and what was the situation now regarding Poland and the Soviet Union, technically at war since September 1939? It was also known that the Soviets had deported hundreds of thousands of Poles to the wastes of the Soviet interior to be used as slave labour, as well as taking thousands of Polish prisoners of war. There was some talk of the Soviet government releasing these people. This was of great interest to the government-in-exile, for if Polish soldiers were released it meant that the Polish Army could be rebuilt after the disasters of 1939 and 1940 – this had included the internment in Switzerland of an entire rifle division.

However what followed was continuous obstruction by the Soviet government in discussions with the Poles in London. Sikorski frequently gave in to Soviet demands in order to keep the negotiations going. Furthermore the government-in-exile was under pressure from the British government to conclude a treaty with the Soviet government. The Polish-Soviet Treaty of July 1941 gave the Poles next to nothing except the ability to maintain talks with the Soviet government – or more realistically with Stalin and Molotov, his deputy and Foreign Minister.

There was one issue about which Sikorski did continue to badger Stalin, and that was the fate of thousands of Polish officers captured in 1939 by the Red Army: nothing had been heard of these men since spring 1940. Stalin prevaricated over this issue, but when in April 1943 they came across mass graves in the Smolensk area and in the Katyń forest, it was finally revealed by the Germans, that thousands of Polish officers had been murdered by the Soviets in1940. It was highly probable that the notorious Soviet security police, the NKVD, had committed the murders.

It was also certain that the Germans had prior knowledge of the mass graves, and had waited for an opportune moment to release the information at a time when Soviet-Polish relations were already at an all-time low. The fallout from the Katyń revelations was that after the Poles refused to accept Soviet assurances that they were not the culprits; the Soviet government broke off diplomatic relations with the government-in-exile. The Soviet government claimed that it was a German atrocity and was furious when the Polish government-in-exile demanded an International Red Cross enquiry into the mass graves. At least one historian has noted that the government–in-exile never recovered from Katyń once the Soviet government broke off diplomatic relations with the London Poles.[6]

The Katyń massacre had far greater consequences than that of the war period. This can be seen today by anybody who, in addition to being able to speak Polish, chooses to look beyond the elite hothouses of Warsaw and Kraków. In spite of the rhetoric of the official Polish elites and western bankers, Poland is still far from being a "normal" western democracy. This is because of the absence of an established middle class that could curtail the excesses and abuses being practised in Poland, notably in the workplace and in banking. Quite simply in the absence of such a middle class, a form of less conventional capitalism has become established. The lack of a genuinely educated and cultured middle class is because the people who would have formed it are long dead in Katyń, or from exile had settled in USA or the UK: now the third and fourth generations largely do not know or care about Poland. Katyń was more corrosive and destructive than most people have ever realised.

It was all too clear to the Allies that the Soviets were responsible for the murders. Even Churchill and his Foreign Secretary, Anthony Eden, had said so, but in private correspondence. They dare not say so in public for fear of damaging the Alliance against Germany, especially at a time when

---

6   Allen Paul, *Katyń. Stalin's Massacre and the Triumph of the Truth*, DeKalb, Illinois, North Illinois University Press, 2010, p.xi.

the Soviet Union was taking the war to the Germans and the British and American governments were being pressed hard by Stalin to open a Second Front in order to take some of the pressure off them.[7] The situation seriously weakened Sikorski's position as leader of the exiled Poles in the west, especially after Poles were released from Soviet captivity as this threw up a rival military leader to Sikorski in the form of General Władysław Anders.

Anders had endured the cruelties of Soviet captivity and so understood and shared the outrage of his compatriots: it appeared to them that Sikorski was making too many concessions to the Soviet government. Anders was also dangerous to Sikorski because not only did he have his own armed force: the so-called "Anders' Army" (correctly Polish 2nd Corps), but from his base in Iraq he was able to ignore or even defy Sikorski on the grounds of geographical distance and the vagaries of wartime transport, with its inability to reach remote and seemingly unimportant places until it was really necessary. However the greatest danger to Sikorski was that members of Anders' Army conspired against him. This group, the *Klimkowszczyna*, who took their name from Anders' aide-de-camp, Captain Jerzy Klimkowski, was about 400 in number. They wanted Sikorski removed. There were at least two known attempts on Sikorski's life by Polish officers while he was travelling by aircraft, so one can only speculate how and why he came to meet his end in an aircraft accident off Gibraltar on 4 July 1943, after visiting Anders and his men in the Middle East.[8] In 1944 Sikorski was dead and the troubles for Poland were about to multiply.

With Sikorski dead there was no longer a unified leadership in the exiled government in London. Stanisław Mikołajczyk, the leader of the Polish Peasant Party, became Prime Minister and General Kazimierz Sosnkowski became Commanding Officer, Polish Armed Forces. As we shall see neither man inspired hope amongst their British allies. Even through Mikołajczyk enjoyed the support of Churchill he never managed to get close to the British Premier in the manner that Sikorski had done. Furthermore, and even more damaging, Mikołajczyk and Sosnkowski could not stand the sight of each other and rarely conversed. Not only was there a lack of unity in Polish circles in London; the most powerful wing of the Polish military was no longer based in Britain but was to be found overseas under the command of a hostile General Anders.

The civilians amongst the exiled Poles were also increasingly becoming irrelevant, owing to the rise in prominence of the Soviet Union in the alliance against Germany. Many Poles failed to recognise this fact. Furthermore they did not understand that even though the British Government was behaving importantly within the Allied camp it was in fact becoming more and more irrelevant within it as the Americans dominated the western side of the alliance. The UK was still dining out at the top table but only out of respect for Winston Churchill and the fact that the British, with the British Empire, had been alone in the war against Germany between the fall of France in 1940 until the German invasion of the Soviet Union in 1941. Quite simply, the Poles had few friends within the alliance against Germany. Poland was not trusted and had no influence despite touting themselves as being the "First Ally"; a phrase which, in today's parlance, was a sound bite but was as ephemeral as all things of this nature.

In Poland itself there were further developments resulting from the political vacuum that was building, as it was becoming obvious that Germany was going to lose the war despite official denials from Berlin. It was only a matter of time before Germany would be forced to surrender. German troops would certainly have to leave Poland in order to defend their homeland. The problem for Poland was that its officially sanctioned government was in exile far away in London, while its main army was fighting in Italy alongside the Allies. However, the major obstacle to the exiled Poles was that, even on the eve of the Warsaw Uprising and in spite of the negotiations with

---

7   McGilvray, op.cit. pp.117-25.
8   Ibid. pp.90-2; 126-29.

the government–in–exile, the Soviet regime still would not recognize it as the legitimate Polish government. It was made quite clear that a post-war Poland would have to be Soviet-friendly. A communist, if not a Stalinist Poland, would be the only state that the Soviet government would recognise. It was against this background that the Poles took their greatest gamble to date in an attempt to liberate their own capital and country. The Warsaw Uprising was launched in an attempt to prevent the Soviet Union annexing Poland in the guise of liberation.

1

The Polish Underground State

To understand the Warsaw Uprising of 1944 fully it is necessary to have a clear picture of what had gone before the outbreak. During September 1939 twin calamities were visited upon the Polish state in the form of the Nazi and Soviet invasions. This should have meant that the Poland was finished and its people crushed but this was far from the truth. Even as the invaders set about the newly conquered nation's virtual destruction, its government administration and armed forces underwent a transformation and began to operate as underground organizations, and thus the Polish underground state was born.

This organisation should not be seen as only functioning between 1939 and 1945. It continued to strive for Polish independence until at least 1956. If we take Prażmowska's analysis as a guide, after the defeat of the Warsaw AK in October 1944, and after six years of civil war the final military defeat of the military underground in 1948 it operated under much reduced circumstances.[1] Of course another valid interpretation of the Polish underground or alternative state was the government-in-exile, which after 1960 continued to function unrecognised by any government, until the restoration of Polish independence in 1989. Once Lech Wałęsa was democratically elected as President of Poland; the Polish government-in-exile returned to Warsaw the Polish Presidential Seals of Office, which had been carried into exile in 1939. This was symbolism of the highest order as it finally put to rest the question of Polish independence, now restored after 50 years. It served to underline that no matter what the public thought, Poland had been invaded, annexed and illegally ruled by one dictatorship or other since 1939. The Polish Peoples' Republic was basically a satrapy of the Soviet empire, and left the Poles with an incomplete understanding of their own recent history. As Norman Davies comments, there were two taboos in Communist Poland when discussing recent history: do not speak badly of the Soviet Union and do not speak well of the Warsaw Uprising.[2] That is how myths begin which later people take as history and the truth; that is why events such as the Warsaw Uprising need to be re-examined and portrayed with facts and not beliefs.

In 1940 the Polish underground state should have been seen as complementing the Polish government-in-exile. Gross described the underground state as not primarily being an anti-German and anti-Soviet conspiracy but instead a substitute for Polish society and truly "an underground state".[3] Garliński wrote of the Polish underground state as a resistance movement and noted its activities: "It embraced not only political and military activities, but also, in the closing phases of the war,

---

1   Anita J. Prażmowska, *Civil War in Poland, 1942-1948*, Basingstoke, Macmillan, 2004. A groundbreaking work in English giving an alternative narrative to that of the Second World War finished in May 1945. This and others studies suggest that underground militaries in east-central Europe and the Baltic states continued to oppose Soviet occupations until at least the mid 1950s. The Hungarian Uprising of 1956, the best known, should be seen as evidence of the continued underground action of people whom the Soviet Union wished to colonize and suppress.

2   Norman Davies, *Rising '44. The Battle for Warsaw*, London, Macmillan, 2003, p.509.

3   Jan Tomasz Gross, *Polish Society Under German Occupation. The Generalgouvernement, 1939-1944*, Princeton, Princeton University Press, 1979, pp.172-3.

incorporated an underground, possessed a secret administration and judiciary, organized secret educational courses, both at secondary and higher levels, published journals and books, formed underground theatres, held illicit lectures, exhibitions and concerts, and preserved works of art".[4] The remit of the Polish underground state was clearly extensive.

The Polish underground state was loyal to the government in London but after the German defeat at Stalingrad at the beginning of 1943 and the Soviet counter-offensive that followed, ; an alternative version began to emerge from the wreckage of war. What the Soviets desired was a Communist Poland or rather a Stalinist puppet Polish government, loyal to the Soviet government and subservient to Stalin. The very existence of a Polish underground state complete with its own army, the AK, was a threat to Stalin and his ambitions for Soviet hegemony, at least in Europe. However it is obvious that Stalin was after more than Europe, given that the Soviet government made demands for the ex-Italian territory of Tripolitania in Libya either as part of the Soviet share of reparations or – quite simply – war booty.[5] Therefore it can be concluded that it would have suited Stalin if the AK and the Polish underground state were destroyed as it posed a threat to the Soviet doctrine of World Revolution.

Between August 1939 and June 1941Stalin and the Soviet government were in cahoots with the Nazis as they set out together to destroy Poland, its people and culture. However from June 1941 the Soviets were forced to be slightly more cautious in their approach towards the Poles, as from then on they were technically allies as a consequence of the German invasion of the Soviet Union. This reversed the previous state of undeclared war between Poland and the Soviet Union, which had existed since 17 September 1939. Basically the British Prime Minister, Winston Churchill, forced the Poles in London to forget this unhappy state and to move on. This led to a treaty of friendship between the exiled Polish government and the Soviet Union in an attempt to ensure unity was maintained in the war against Germany, and also to ensure that the Soviet Union remained in the alliance against Germany, as it was taking the brunt of the German military onslaught on the eastern front.

At this juncture it should be realized that having an underground state as well as an exiled government was bound to stretch loyalties. This was particularly evident later, given the suffering the Poles who had remained in Poland during the war were to endure. By 1943 the main question regarding post-war Poland was who actually deserved to govern Poland once the war finished. From exile in London, Edward Puacz, the veteran Polish Socialist journalist, warned émigré govern-ments in 1943 that they faced isolation as they had not faced enemy occupation of their homelands and should not assume that they were entitled to return home and take control.[6] This was without taking the Soviet challenge into consideration. Furthermore, those politicians who had remained in Poland were widely considered as being first-rate whilst those domiciled in London were largely politically second-class.[7] Therefore it should only been seen as fair that, if elected, first-rate Polish civilian politicians should have been allowed to govern post-war Poland. Applebaum asserts that if Poland had enjoyed post-war democracy, the AK would have been one of the political elites in Eastern Europe.[8] Their claim to governance was also more credible because they had also shared

---

4   Józef Garliński, 'The Polish Underground State (1939-45) *The Journal of Contemporary History*, Vol. 10, 2, April 1975, 219-59.

5   Geoffrey Roberts, *Stalin's Wars: From World War to Cold War, 1939-1953*, New Haven, Yale University Press, 2006, p.305.

6   Edward Puacz, *Problems of the Exiled Governments*, London, n.p.1943, pp.9-12.

7   McGilvray, op.cit. p.9.

8   Anne Applebaum, *Iron Curtain. The Crushing of Eastern Europe, 1944-1956*, London, Allen Lane, 2012, p.119.

the twin horrors of German and Soviet invasions and subsequent occupations – but all of this proved to be hypothetical as events in Poland after 1943 proved.

Towards the end of 1943 Jan Karski, a prominent agent and member of the Polish resistance escaped from Poland to the west in order to give to senior politicians, including Churchill and the American President, Franklin Roosevelt, evidence of German atrocities. He wrote an article explaining the *raison d'être* of the Polish underground state. This was published in the English language periodical *Polish Fortnightly Review*, issued by the Polish Ministry of Information, so the intention of the article is clear. Karski wrote that the most obvious aspect of the German occupation of Poland was that there was to be no question of official collaboration with the Germans: Poles had been put outside the law as exercised by the German authorities. He wrote "a Pole can obtain no legal redress against a German, in the sphere of criminal law or even that of civil law". The attitude of the Germans was, according to Karski, the root cause of the development of the underground state. As a consequence of this attitude, which gave no Pole protection under German law, it was deemed that in order to survive the Polish nation had to remove itself from the open and retreat underground, both physically and metaphysically,. Even if the Germans ruled the streets and could kill, kidnap and generally terrorise the Polish population at will; there was still an alternative authority available to Poles, the underground state which prevented them being left in a "state of chaos and internal lawlessness", and through which, therefore, they could prepare for the day when Poland would be liberated.[9] At times it must have seen to many Poles that German rule was just anarchy and bloodletting, but there was a definite purpose in the establishment of the underground state as an alternative government running parallel to the mobster rule of the German occupation authorities. It was proof that the Polish state still existed.

After the fall of Warsaw on 28 September 1939 it was decided by the Polish leadership that their chief objective was to prevent a de facto break in the continuity of Polish sovereignty. This was especially important in view of the official Soviet excuse for invading Poland ten days earlier: according to the Soviet government the Polish state no longer existed and the Soviet Union was intervening to protect the interests of non-Poles living in eastern Poland. Andrew Roberts observes that the Soviet Union invaded Poland "in order to restore peace and order", while the Soviet Foreign Minister, Molotov, declared that the Polish state had collapsed.[10] Of course this was a blatant lie and the government-in-exile needed to be certain that it was exposed as such. Furthermore it was also feared that either, if not both, the German or Soviet governments might try to produce puppet governments in Poland. However between 1939 and 1941 neither showed any inclination to pursue such a policy. It was only after 1943 that the Soviet government began to show an interest in such an idea, but the exiled Poles appeared to have little understanding, if any, of what the true situation was in Poland during 1943. This led to delusions about their real position and strength amongst the Allies, especially compared with the power – political, diplomatic and military – of the Soviet Union.

Karski may well have unwittingly contributed to causing the Poles to punch above their weight as he observed in his article, months before the Warsaw Uprising, that the AK was the second most powerful and well-organised branch of the Polish underground movement. Furthermore it was not merely an underground military movement (one of many found at that time in German-occupied Europe), but was in fact an official and legal Polish army. Karski considered that it was Poland's third army, with an equal status to that of the Polish armies found in Scotland and the Middle

---

9   Jan Karski, 'The Polish Underground State' *Polish Fortnightly Review*, 15 December 1943. Jan Karski, *Story of a Secret State: My Report to the World*, London, Penguin, 2011, Chapter 33, pp.411-21.

10   Andrew Roberts, *The Storm of War. A New History of the Second World War*, London, Allen Lane, 2009, p.25. Derek Watson, *Molotov: A Biography*, Basingstoke, Palgrave Macmillan, 2005, p.172.

East.[11] However this was only a Polish view. The AK might have had large numbers, at least in theory, and perhaps it was supported by the Polish people, but this ignores the fact that the AK was not an army at all. The most obvious thing was their supply of weapons, or rather the lack of a supply. The AK, unlike Soviet partisans for example, did not enjoy a regular supply of weapons or other material from the Soviet Union or any other source. As with many partisan units in occupied Europe the AK was chronically under-supplied; the weapons which they possessed were mainly light and they lacked armour, artillery and aircraft. As a result they were at a distinct disadvantage whenever they confronted the enemy.

A further disadvantage for the AK was their status as prisoners of war, which as with all partisans, was ambiguous at best. A Polish soldier from the Polish armies of Scotland or the Middle East, fighting in the uniform of the British Army, would be treated as a prisoner of war if captured and taken to a POW camp. The Red Cross would be informed of his capture and so on. An AK fighter, captured in 1943, was more than likely to be tortured and executed. It was not until the Warsaw Uprising before AK fighters were accorded the status of legitimate combatants and, if captured, were treated as POWs. This was the result of British and American diplomatic pressure on the German authorities via neutral embassies, as once the Allies realised that they were winning the war and the Germans began to suspect that they were not; the question of German war crimes was being aired. However this did not prevent the Red Army from killing AK commanders and then conscripting the AK ranks into the Soviet-friendly Polish Peoples' Army (or as it was known then, the First Polish Army, or colloquially the "Berling Army" after its commander Zygmunt Berling). This was to happen before, during and after the Warsaw Uprising. The status of the AK fighter was to become a political matter.

It should be recognised that even if the civilian arm of the Polish underground state was established reasonably smoothly; the setting up of the fighting arm of the movement was not so easily achieved. This was the result of the Polish officer corps, politicized in the interwar years, which continued to feud even in the face in the imminent destruction of Poland. The Polish leader, General Władysław Sikorski sought a clean break, both from this situation and from the pre-war military. He did so for two reasons: first, he was an enemy of the regime, and second, the regime had clearly failed in its duty to defend Poland. Its leaders were understood to have fled the country for Romania; this caused many Poles to consider that their military leadership had deserted in the face of the enemy.

As early as 27 September 1939, one day before the surrender of Warsaw, a secret military organisation was established. General Juliusz Rómmel, the commander of the Warsaw Garrison, authorized General Michał Karasiewicz-Tokarzewski to form an underground army. Rómmel had previously received his authorization for such a move from Marshal Edward Śmigły-Rydź, the Polish Commander-in-Chief (and virtual dictator of Poland from Piłsudski's death in 1935 until the invasions of Poland in 1939) who had already fled to Romania. Karasiewicz-Tokarzewski set about forming a military organisation and founded the SZP (*Służba Zwycięstwu Polski* [In Service of Poland's Victory]).[12] Sikorski did not trust Karasiewicz-Tokarzewski, whom he considered to be a political enemy, and in his search for a complete break from the interwar military regime he created the ZWZ (*Związek Walki Zbrojnej* [Union for Armed Struggle]) which took over the SZP and gave its command to General Kazimierz Sosnkowski who was in London and could be controlled by Sikorski.[13]

---

11   Karski, 'The Polish Underground State'.
12   Garliński, op.cit. p.221.
13   Ibid. p.223.

Sikorski's actions during November 1939 underline the problem he faced from within what should have been a totally loyal and focused army. Poland was facing destruction from east and west and still Polish military officers persisted in playing at politics – a game they were not even very good at. Sikorski could not trust senior officers such as Karasiewicz-Tokarzewski or the Chief of Staff of the SZP, Colonel Stefan Rowecki, as they had both supported the dictator, Józef Piłsudski. Furthermore he doubted if these two officers and others like them had any intention of restoring democracy to Poland after the war. Sikorski's position hardened once the commanders of SZP began to challenge his authority as Prime Minister and Defence Minister. It was considerations like this that led to the establishment of ZWZ and the appointment of Sosnkowski as its commander. It was a shrewd move on Sikorski's part. Even though Sosnkowski was opposed to Sikorski (as events after 1941 proved), by putting him directly under his own command, Sikorski had outmanoeuvred his political opponents while at the same time stamping his authority on the fledgling Polish resistance movement.[14]

During July 1941 Churchill bullied the Polish government-in-exile into signing an agreement – or more realistically a treaty – with the Soviet Union. As a member of the government-in-exile Sosnkowski was expected to accept the new situation but he refused and resigned in protest. Sikorski used this as an excuse to assume Sosnkowski's office as Chairman of Ministers for Polish Affairs. On 14 February 1942 Sikorski went further and issued a command that transferred the ZWZ into the AK with Rowecki, now a general, in command. Garliński observes that, following the German invasion of the Soviet Union, the activities of the underground army reached a new phase because the political situation changed as a result of the invasion. Poland was now totally occupied by Germany.[15] After 1942 the AK prepared for a general uprising. A further consideration was that once the Soviet Union became involved in the war against Germany, other underground groups, including communist partisan groups loyal to the Soviet Union, began to operate in Poland, especially eastern Poland.[16] This was to have implications for the future of Poland, and the consequences were to last until at least 1989.

---

14   McGilvray, op.cit. pp.26-7. *Generał Stefan Rowecki 'Grot' w relacjach i w pamięci zbiorowej*, (eds) Andrzej Krzysztof Kunert & Tomasz Szarota, Warsaw, Rytm, 2003, pp.18-19, 30-1, 56-7.
15   Garliński, op.cit. p.221.
16   Ibid. p.230.

2

Why the Rising?

By the summer of 1944 the war was going well for the Allies. The Western Allies had successfully landed in Normandy and were about to break out of Normandy, while the western advance of the Red Army, heading towards Germany, was relentless as if the mythical Russian steamroller of the First World War had been repaired and set into motion. This was to say nothing of the Anglo-American advance through Italy: Rome was liberated during June 1944. Furthermore in July 1944 in Germany there had been an attempt on Hitler's life. This bomb attack on him failed to kill him, while the perpetrators of the outrage and their families were savagely punished, but it revealed that there was some form of German resistance to Hitler and the Nazis. Indeed some premature reporting in the exiled Polish press claimed that this was the beginning of a possible civil war in Germany.[1] The reality was that disaffected members of the regular German forces sought to remove Hitler, but with the SS supporting him he remained all-powerful. However for the Poles in exile the war was slowly becoming a disaster for their ambitions.

The most obvious danger for Poland was the advance of the Red Army westwards. It became clear that far from liberating Poland, the Soviet Union was hell-bent on annexing the country and imposing Stalinism on as much of Europe as possible, thus making Stalin a neo-Tsar. The Polish government-in-exile in London sought to prevent this from happening but the western Allies had their own thoughts about the role Poland should play in 1944. The exiled Poles may have considered that during that year they had a major role but the Allies treated them as a minor ally and at times even considered them to be a nuisance, only consulting them when it was necessary. A perfect example of the Polish predicament was that during the Warsaw Uprising, General Sir Henry Maitland Wilson, Supreme Commander in the Mediterranean, told General Sosnkowski that the British no longer needed the services of Polish 2nd Corps in Italy and offered to have them flown to Poland to reinforce the Warsaw AK. Sosnkowski was unimpressed with this offer as it meant that his men would be flown to Soviet-occupied territory prior to being sent on to Warsaw. He feared, with justification that once on Soviet territory 2nd Corps might suffer the same fate as AK units which had fallen into Soviet hands: officers shot and the men conscripted into the Soviet-backed Berling Army.[2]

The Allies did consider that the Poles had a role in preparation for the Normandy landings but perhaps not the one which they may have desired, and as with other minor allies they were not privy to the timetable for D-Day – it was nothing to do with them. In the week which preceded D-Day (6 June 1944), the head of the Polish sector of Special Operations Executive (SOE), Colonel Harold Perkins, requested that the AK might disrupt German communications across Poland as part of an attempt to make the coming invasion of northern France as easy as possible.[3] Indeed,

---

1   *Dziennik Polski* (London) 22 July 1944.
2   Richard C. Lukas, 'Russia, the Warsaw Uprising and the Cold War' *Polish Review*, 20, 4, 1975, 13-26.
3   *Powstanie Warszawskie 1944: Wybór Dokumentów Vol. 1* (ed) Piotr Matusak, Warsaw, Egros, 1997. Hereafter referred to as *Powstanie 1*, Document 1, Letter from Harold B. Perkins to General S. Tatar, 31 May 1944. SOE was responsible for the co-ordination of underground activities from Britain and Tatar was Perkins' counterpart.

one of the major battles of the Warsaw Uprising, the series of assaults by the AK against one of the tallest buildings in Warsaw, the PAST building (Polska Akcyjna Społka Telefoniczna: Polish Telephone Joint-Stock Company), had the purpose of disrupting communications between the German eastern and western fronts; the Germans were desperate to hold this position.[4] However, on 20 August the Germans were forced to surrender it to the AK; the battle for the PAST building will be told later.

The Poles had already been threatened with not being allowed to go to Normandy unless the First Polish Armoured Division conformed to the British concept of an armoured division. The Polish version, which they tried to cling on to, was outmoded and unfit for purpose. The Poles intended to contribute two armoured brigades: this – as ever – had more to do with politics rather than the war with Germany. The British demand once more proved the overall lack of importance of the Polish Army to the Allies. Later, the fully armed and suitably deployed Polish First Armoured Division under the inspired command of General Stanisław Maczek, were instrumental in the Allied breakout from Normandy during August, as part of the second wave of the Normandy operation.[5]

The Polish Prime Minister, Stanisław Mikołajczyk, requested from Britain an increased supply of military supplies for the AK to support a rising in Poland. By disrupting communication lines between the German eastern and western fronts, this rising could have been of considerable military importance as part of the coordination for the invasion of Europe, as Perkins had already outlined. Mikołajczyk was also aware that Poles would pay a heavy price for such activities.[6] However the reality was that the AK was a very weak instrument for an uprising, and Mikołajczyk knew it.[7] During June 1944 the Polish General Staff in London estimated that the AK in Warsaw only had arms for 32,000 men, which meant that the vast majority had no weapons at all.[8] This should have had quite a sobering effect on those planning an uprising.

The main problem for the AK and any planned Polish operation in Poland was the advance of the Red Army towards Germany. As it moved across Poland, the Soviet government learnt that they did not really have to respect the London Poles, and the Soviet attitude began to harden towards them. This made it difficult to supply Warsaw from the west, as the last thing that the Soviet government wanted was a well-supplied and equipped anti-Soviet Polish military in their way. Also, the Soviet Union was now sponsoring a Soviet-friendly government in waiting, the Polish Committee of National Liberation (PKWN [*Polski Komitet Wyzwolenia Narodowego*]) and did not brook any interference for its plans to spread Stalinism across Europe. Even before the uprising had begun the problem of supplying the AK had been discussed by the Poles, the British and the Americans. During June 1944 Major S. Jędrzejewski discussed the problem in a conversation with General Donovan, the Head of American Special Operations (OSS – Office of Strategic Services) in Washington DC Donovan suggested that the Americans could supply a Polish uprising from Soviet airbases in the Soviet Union.[9] However this was to assume that Soviet Government would

---

4   Barbara Matys, nom-de-guerre 'Baska', interview with author, Warsaw, 16 July 2012. Barbara Matys, born in 1923, was a nurse but during the German occupation of Poland trained as a sapper and took part in the 20 day battle for the PAST building during August 1944 and was present when the building was surrendered by the Germans to the AK. Hereafter referred to as 'Matys'.

5   Evan McGilvray, *The Black Devils' March – A Doomed Odyssey – The 1st Polish Armoured Division, 1939-45*, Solihull, Helion, 2005, p.8.

6   Jan C. Ciechanowski, *The Warsaw Uprising of 1944*, Cambridge, Cambridge University Press, 1974, pp.9-10.

7   Ibid. p.55.

8   Ibid. p.115.

9   *Powstanie 1*, Document 8, Note of Major S. Jędrzejewski's conversation with General Donovan (Chief OSS) Washington D.C., 19 June 1944, dated 20 June 1944, pp.31-2.

allow the Americans to use bases on Soviet soil and the Soviets refused to cooperate with the Allies on this matter.

For the Polish government-in-exile the greatest concern was how to avoid outright annexation by the Soviet Union. Sosnkowski contacted General Kopański about the danger posed by the Red Army being so close to Warsaw and directly threatening to occupy the city. Sosnkowski considered that there were two routes the Poles might take. The first was the political route, with discussions and agreements with the Allies and the Soviet Government, but he had no faith in that. The second was to use the AK to act as a block to the Red Army advance, thus preventing them from completing the conquest of Poland, but he was careful not to mention actually fighting the Red Army.[10]

On the same day , 25 July 1944, the AK commander, General Bór-Komorowski, reported to Sosnkowski that the AK was ready for an uprising. He also made a demand for the Independent Polish Parachute Brigade, based in the UK, to be made available to support the rising as their deployment would not only provide military and tactical support but would also send a political message to those who wished Poland harm. In addition he requested aerial support, namely aerial bombardment.[11] This report would suggest that Bór-Komorowski was either a liar or a fool, as the AK was clearly not prepared to take on the German Army and far less the Red Army. He almost certainly understood his position and that of Poland when his request for Polish paratroopers was denied: they had already been earmarked for the ill-fated Arnhem offensive during the autumn of 1944. This made it quite clear that the Allies had tacitly given the Soviet Union an open hand in Poland.

Bór-Komorowski in his weekly military-political report for Poland, 18-25 July 1944, stated that the Germans were beginning to evacuate Warsaw.[12] However this report was made about a confused and fluid situation. Despite the perceived strength of the Germans in Poland, mainly owing to their brutal and murderous methods of keeping the population subdued, the reality was that by the end of 1943 the Germans only had a weak control of the countryside. Huge swathes of rural Poland were under the control of the AK.[13] This was an interesting situation for the AK to have been in, and it is worth considering whether the AK should have remained in the countryside instead of breaking itself by attempting to defeat both the Germans and the Soviets in Warsaw. Warsaw, despite being the capital and a trophy full of symbolism, was of no strategic value at all. It was a pity that the AK leadership failed to see the larger picture, because if the German hold on the countryside was weak; the Soviets would have had the same problem. They would have struggled to control Poland if a large military force operating in the countryside had opposed them.

The concept of a German withdrawal from Warsaw is extremely important. Without it the AK would probably have not risen up there. Alan Clark noted that the timing of the uprising looked perfect, as the AK appeared to have stepped into a vacuum created by the German withdrawal, but preceding the Soviet declaration of the liberation of Warsaw.[14] Bruce noted that until late July 1944 the AK Command had not intended the capital to be the scene of large-scale fighting. The original plan was that the Germans should be allowed to leave for the west, and the city's population was to have been guarded from last-minute atrocities with a small but adequate number of AK troops, very much like a Home Guard.[15]

---

10   Ibid. Document 46, p.75, General Sosnkowski to General Kopański, 25 July 1944.
11   Ibid. Document 55, p.83, General Bór-Komorowski to General Sosnkowski, 25 July 1944.
12   Ibid. Document 56, pp.84-6, General Bór-Komorowski to General Sosnkowski, Report on Military-Political Situation (18 July- 25 July 1944).
13   Jan Pomian, *Józef Retinger: Życie i pamiętniki "szarej eminencji"*, Warsaw, Pelikan, 1990, p.212.
14   Alan Clark, *Barbarossa: The Russian-German Conflict, 1941-1945*, London, Cassell, 2005, pp.390-1.
15   George Bruce, *The Warsaw Uprising, 1 August 1944 – 2 October 1944*, London, Rupert Hart-Davies, 1972, pp.70-1.

It was planned that a well-armed AK force of about 4,000 in number was to leave Warsaw in secret once the front reached the city, assemble some distance from the city and then launch a strong attack on the "retreating and presumably demoralised Germans". The problem was that preparations for this action would have removed a majority of weapons from the city and would leave it dangerously under-armed if fighting was suddenly to break out. The change of plan, to a revolt in Warsaw itself, came about on 21 July 1944 at a meeting of AK senior commanders in the city. It was concluded that if there was a sudden German collapse there; a revolt in the capital would be required in order to claim the independence of the Polish Republic ahead of the arrival of the Red Army.[16] The political motivation of the Poles was clear and perhaps, if well supported, they might have successfully concluded this venture, because (as Clark wrote of the rising) "all the same, the Poles very nearly brought it off. By 6 August they were in control of almost the whole town, and had greatly enlarged their armament with captured German material."[17] The problem was; what was the situation in Warsaw during the last week of July? The AK commanders in the city certainly did not know, and their actions were to expose their ignorance.

By the summer of 1944 the situation in Warsaw was confused and altering from day to day. Even the Germans were not certain about what was really happening; it seemed that only the Soviets had any real degree of certainty. The Poles in Warsaw must have realised that the Germans were nervous, if not scared, of the possibility of defeat as indicated by events during the previous months. From 16 October 1943 until 15 February 1944 the Germans had carried out a very public reign of terror, with mass executions in the streets. On average 280 people a week were being murdered. This came to an end on 15 February 1944, probably as a result of the assassination of the Warsaw District SS and Police Commander, SS Brigadenführer and General-Major Polizei, Franz Kutschera, by the AK. It was Kutschera who, after taking up his post in Warsaw on 25 September 1943, orchestrated this relentless butchery. After his death on 1 February 1944; the street executions stopped: killings in Warsaw continued but in secret. Between October 1943 and 31 July 1944, 8,400 Polish men, women and children were murdered there by the Germans.[18]

By 22 July 1944, as the Red Army approached Warsaw, the Germans in the city began to panic. Thousands of German civilians, especially those Germans born in Poland who had sided with the occupying Germans by taking the privileged statuses of *Volksdeutscher* or *Reichsdeutscher* began to flock to railway stations seeking tickets for an exit to Germany.

Zenon Kliszko, who was later part of the Communist ruling elite in Poland between 1956 and 1970, was present in Warsaw during the uprising. He noted that between Monday 24 July 1944 and Tuesday 25 July, German institutes in Warsaw were closing down as rumours began to spread that the Red Army was already in Praga, the suburb on the eastern shore of the River Vistula. However by 26 July, the Germans were already taking back control of the city after this short period of panic.[19] It should be noted that another group of people who would have been filled with dread as the Red Army approached were Polish traitors who had sided with the Germans when they were in the ascendant but were in a dangerous position once the tide of war turned against Germany. They were not as enthusiastic in 1944 as they had been previously for Germany and

---

16   Ibid.
17   Clark, op.cit. pp.390-1.
18   Bruce, op.cit. p.68.
19   Ibid. p.73. Zenon Kliszko, *Powstanie Warszawskie: Artykuły, przemówienia, Wspomnienia dokumenty*, Warsaw, Książka i Wiedza, 1967, pp.64-5.

Nazism.[20] This part of Polish historiography is generally ignored in Poland, as it is a rather inconvenient truth.[21]

An understanding of the last week of July 1944 is seminal in the understanding of the Warsaw Uprising and its outcomes. The most important factor is that the Poles, including the AK in Warsaw, really did not have any real idea of what was happening in the city. Eventually they made the wrong call for a localized uprising within a major urban area, hundreds of miles from any realistic chances of support, resupply and reinforcement. The AK commanders in Warsaw did not know that as early as 21 July 1944 Hitler had decided to defend Warsaw. The German leader ordered General Heinz Guderian to take command of the Eastern Front, reorganise it and halt the Red Army advance. In turn Guderian appointed General von Vormann to take command of the German 9th Army, located in the middle of the Vistula area that included Warsaw. By 26 July these two commanders had halted the German rout while ominously to the south of Warsaw, fresh from murder in Italy, the Herman Goring SS Panzer and Paratroop Division had arrived, and the SS Viking Division were also training in the area. The omens were not good for the Poles.

Earlier in the week that the Germans were reinforcing Warsaw, Bór-Komorowski toured Warsaw in disguise and had seen the Germans apparently fleeing the city. At the time he did not call for an uprising: however during the plenary meeting of the Warsaw AK Command on 26 July it was realised that the Germans were in fact reinforcing the city, and doing so swiftly. Polish room for manoeuvre was limited. They had no intelligence reports regarding Soviet intentions in the immediate future, while the shortage of weapons and ammunition continued to remain a problem, reducing the ability of the AK to fight. Furthermore tensions were also growing within Warsaw as half-starved Polish civilians, who had anticipated a German collapse in the city began to loot German shops and warehouses and were shot down by German military police. As this was taking place units of the Herman Goering Division marched across Warsaw in full battle order while the 73rd Infantry Division detrained outside the city and began to man the Praga defences.[22]

Contemporary German Army reports help to make sense of the confused situation in Warsaw during the period immediately before the Polish revolt as orders from the Chief of Staff of the German 9th Army issued on 24 July 1944 are basically directions and methods for leaving Warsaw.[23] The German document is confirmed by a Polish source, in which Bór-Komorowski reported to Sosnkowski that the Germans were evacuating eastern Poland, with a complete abandonment of the city of Białystok and its surroundings as well as the town of Dęblin.[24] This, of course, served to convince the Warsaw AK commanders that the capital was about to be evacuated by the Germans. Without the aid of German military and political intelligence the picture in Warsaw at street level is confusing because, as Pomian observed in the dying days of July, the Germans had almost completed their evacuation of Warsaw while the beginning of "the evacuation of certain Wehrmacht and certain police units" seemingly signaled the completion of the entire operation. At the same time the Soviet armies under the command of Marshal Rokossovsky advanced towards the city. It seemed as if the liberation of Warsaw was at hand.[25]

---

20   Peter Caddick-Adams, *Monty and Rommel: Parallel Lives*, London, Arrow Books, 2012, p.343. See also McGilvray, *A Military Government in Exile*, p.175, regarding the pro-German sympathies of Poles serving in the Wehrmacht; their pro-German stances continued even after capture by the allies and continued on after the war.

21   Gordon Corrigan, *The Second World War: A Military History*, London, Atlantic Books, 2010, p.2.

22   Bruce, op.cit. pp.73-8, Jerzy Kirchmayer, *Powstanie Warszawskie*, Warsaw, Książka i Wiedza, 1959, pp.109-10.

23   *Powstanie 1*, Document 43, 24 July 1944, pp.72-3.

24   Ibid, Document 56, 25 July 1944, pp.84-6.

25   *The Warsaw Uprising: A Selection of Documents*, Andrzej Pomian (ed) London, n.p.1945, p.vi.

A report from the Socialist Party in Poland described the situation in Warsaw at the end of July: "The Soviet Armies were forcing the Warsaw suburbs from the south and the east. On Saturday, 29 July, they were already in Otwock. On Sunday, the 30 July they had taken Świder and advanced to Anin. They were already in Milosna and had taken Wolomin and Radzynia. Strong Soviet forces were already crossing the left bank of the Vistula below Jeżiurna. Every evening the Soviet Air Force dropped flares over Warsaw and bombed German military objectives in Praga and eastern districts of Warsaw. The German Armies were continually retreating. At night, exhausted, miserable-looking units of Wehrmacht passed through the city – betraying German defeat."[26] It seemed almost certain that the Germans had been defeated in the Warsaw area but it should be noted that these were Wehrmacht units; regular German army units. However the Germans had other units to hand, irregular and ruthless, if not lawless units; police units usually used for hunting down Jews in the countryside.

A dispatch from the Polish underground authorities in Warsaw, sent at 13.00 hours, 30 July to the Polish government-in-exile, reported that guns could be heard and that all Germans who could leave the city had done so; only the army and the Gestapo remained. There was a sense of unease in the message as it also reported that after several days of "confusion" the Germans were now "calmer", although the Red Army was only twelve miles away. An indication to some that the German hold on Warsaw had lessened was that the AK underground newspaper, *Rzeczpospolita*, was widely sold by some 600 newsvendors without any hindrance. At the same time Poles were waiting for the results of talks being held in Moscow between Stalin and Mikołajczyk. The following day, 31 July, German newspapers in Warsaw were not published.[27] It seemed to the Poles that if they rose up and were supported by the Allies; the Germans in Warsaw would be comprehensively defeated. They were due to be disappointed at all levels.

As already discussed, the Poles in London failed to recognise just how far their stock with the Allies had fallen, especially compared with the Soviet Union. Mikołajczyk discovered that the British Government expected him to compromise on four points in order to reach some kind of an agreement with Stalin. He was expected to remodel the Polish Government in London so that there were no anti-Soviet elements within that body; accept the annexation of eastern Poland, including the city of Lwów, withdraw the suggestion that the NKVD was responsible for the murders of thousands of Polish military officers and others at Katyń as well as reaching some form of working arrangement with the Polish Committee of National Liberation, the so-called "Lublin Committee". Mikołajczyk was not prepared to do this and was disturbed that the British Government supported the Soviet Government to such an extent.[28]

The British Government was already aware that Warsaw was on the verge of rising. The diplomat Edward Raczyński had informed the British Foreign Secretary, Anthony Eden, as he passed on Bór-Komorowski's request for western aerial support. Also requested was a warning to be sent to the Germans, via the BBC, that they must treat the AK as legitimate combatants and not murder them upon capture. Raczyński also drew Eden's attention to the fact that the Red Army, as it approached Warsaw, was disarming AK units, arresting its members and executing the officers. Raczyński requested that the British Government should make approaches privately to the Soviet Government in an attempt to prevent this continuing.[29]

The Poles were very clear why they wanted an uprising: "we wanted to be free and owe this freedom to nobody".[30] Wanda Lesniewska, a nurse during the Warsaw Uprising, echoed this

---

26   Ibid. p.vii.
27   Ibid. pp.53-71.
28   Ciechanowski, op.cit. p.65.
29   Ibid. p.49.
30   Robert Forczyk, *Warsaw 1944. Poland's Bid for Freedom*, Oxford, Osprey, 2009, p.26.

sentiment in an interview with the author. She said that the uprising had to be fought as the Polish people, Polish society and its culture had been undergoing systematic destruction by both the Germans and the Soviets since September 1939 and that by 1944 all that was left was "honour, and honour counted".[31] The objective of the AK, the Polish underground and the Poles in the West was more than an aspiration; it was a plan for survival. It was obvious that Poland was extremely vulnerable to annexation by the Soviet Union which had already swallowed up a third of Poland as a result of the joint German-Soviet invasion in 1939. As a consequence of Soviet aggression, plans for a future uprising were drawn up and considered. The AK had planned for a national uprising against Germany as early as 1941. Such an uprising would not have been feasible unless Germany was close to collapse. By November 1943 three variations of the plan had been formed:

1. A general uprising throughout Poland in the event of a complete German collapse. This had been the case in 1918, when Poland had been able to snatch independence as the occupying Germans withdrew.
2. Operation *Burza* (Tempest), an AK operation originating from eastern Poland.
3. "*Battle for the Capital*": a plan for a major operation but only in Warsaw. Originally the AK had sought to avoid fighting in cities, as there was a strong chance of civilian casualties. They had intended to operate only against German lines of communications.[32]

On paper *Burza* looked the most promising prospect for Polish liberation. It called for local actions which should have had the effect of assisting the Soviet advance into Poland, but it also demanded that the Red Army should work with the AK. However the Red Army only had ill intentions towards the AK and Poland in general. As a consequence the AK reverted to a policy of Piłsudski: the traditional mantra of the *Doctrine of Two Enemies*; the two enemies being Germany and Russia. By July 1944 the AK was not only trying to prevent the Germans from destroying Warsaw as they retreated but also trying to prevent the Soviet Union from imposing a puppet government on Poland. Equally, it was just as important to the AK that it should demonstrate to the world that it was able to participate in the liberation of Poland and not rely on the advance of the Red Army. Therefore a two-headed plan came into being: a military campaign against Germany and its allies and a political campaign against the Soviet Union.

Bór-Komorowski intended that any uprising should have the effect of driving out the German garrison at Warsaw followed by the reorganization of local government prior to the arrival of the Red Army. But all of this depended on outside aid, including aerial support from the West. If such an uprising was successful it was hoped to present Stalin with a *fait accompli*: Warsaw liberated solely by Polish effort and sacrifice. If the AK had been able to survive the war intact; Polish independence might also have been able to survive the war. Even if the Red Army remained hostile to the AK, it would have been difficult to arrest 40,000 members of that body without comment from the West. It would not have been Katyń, where Poles were led away into forests and murdered by the NKVD with a shot in the back of the head. AK members wanted to resist Soviet aggression but with some reservations once the vulnerable civilian population was considered and the distinct possibility of civilian casualties if fighting broke out between the AK and Soviet forces.[33]

Sosnkowski considered that the plan was doomed without Soviet support but Mikołajczyk was willing to run the risk of an uprising in Warsaw rather than have a Soviet puppet government

---

31   Wanda Lesniewska, (born 1924) interview with author, Warsaw, 16 July 2012. Hereafter referred to as 'Lesniewska'.
32   Forczyk, op.cit. pp.33-4.
33   Waclaw Zagorski, *Seventy Days. A Diary of the Warsaw Insurrection, 1944*, London, Frederick Muller, 1957, translated by John Welsh, p.18.

installed in the capital without putting up a fight. As there was no united thought or clarity amongst the Polish leadership about the start of an uprising it was left to Bór-Komorowski, as the AK Commanding Officer in Warsaw, to announce the timing of the uprising. "W"-Hour (*Wybuch* – "Wakeup") was chosen – 17.00 hours on 1 August 1944. However for many reasons the plan was totally and utterly flawed.

The main reason for the failure of the Warsaw Uprising was the unfathomable trust that some Poles had in the Soviet Union, even though the overall feeling amongst Poles was that the Soviets could not be trusted. Another reason for the failure was the very poor planning of the revolt and its lack of preparation.[34] The timing of the rising was appallingly bad. Bór-Komorowski believed that it was easier to assemble his troops using rush hour as cover but he ignored the fact that it was a limited window, as curfew was only three hours away at 20.00. The original time for the uprising, midnight, might have had an element of surprise and confusion for the Germans. As a result of Bór-Komorowski's decision to begin the uprising in late afternoon, orders to mobilise were not completed before curfew and some units did not receive their orders until the following morning. The result was that at W-Hour less than 20,000 soldiers out of a possible 40,000 AK fighters were available. Two years of planning, which might have provided a viable operational plan, was replaced by last-minute improvisation. The entire arrangement was based on the delusion that the Soviets would respect and assist it.[35] The Polish problem was that neither the Germans nor the Soviets respected them or their uprising.

The Germans had been aware for a while that something was afoot in Warsaw but when it finally broke out had underestimated the size of the uprising. Much of the German knowledge about a possible AK insurrection had been gleaned from the interrogations and torture of thousands of captured Poles, including the former AK leader, General Rowecki, taken and held in the notorious Warsaw prison, the Pawiak. Rowecki was deported to Germany and murdered there once the AK rose up, probably on 2 August and at the express command of Himmler. From these brutal interrogations the Germans were able to assemble pieces of information about what might happen and make preparations to counter any rising in Warsaw. Many key German buildings, barracks and places were transformed into heavily fortified positions that could hold out against sustained attacks. By the end of July most German-held buildings contained machine-gun positions near entrances complete with barbed wire obstacles and sentries on rooftops. These measures were complemented by a network of Gestapo informers roaming around Warsaw, while a series of street checkpoints deployed around the city made it very difficult for the AK to move personnel and equipment.

Despite all of Hitler's posturing, holding Warsaw during the last week of July 1944 was not an easy task for the Germans. For example there were no German defensive lines in Praga, on the eastern shore of the Vistula, where Soviet armour was already probing. Lieutenant-General Reiner Stahel, who was briefly responsible for stopping the Red Army as it advanced towards the capital, had few troops available to man such lines. In addition to a scarcity of resources, German plans for defending Warsaw against the AK and the Red Army were hindered by a lack of a unified command system between the Wehrmacht, the SS and various German civilian officials. Once the

---

34 Robert Fisk notes that nearly 50 years later during 1991 American organised appeals for an insurgency against the Iraqi dictator, Saddam Hussein, which led to a wholesale slaughter of the rebels by Iraqi forces as western forces stood on the sidelines as the chance for an Islamic republic were dashed only for the Americans to invade and conquer Iraq and install an American friendly regime 12 years later in 2003. Fisk compares this to the 1944 Warsaw Uprising and the Soviet betrayal of the AK. Robert Fisk, *The Great War for Civilization. The Conquest of the Middle East*, London, Harper, Perennial, 2006, pp.812-3.

35 Forczyk, op.cit. pp.34-5.

uprising began, Hitler demanded that the Luftwaffe carpet-bomb the city– only to be told that local units lacked the fuel to do so.

Himmler, however, considered that the Warsaw revolt was an opportunity to further his murderous anti-Slav stance and a chance for an independent combat mission for his SS troops. He volunteered Obergruppen Fuhrer Erich von der Bach-Zelewski and his anti-partisan group for the job. Bach-Zelewski took over from Stahel, who only held command in Warsaw from 28 July to 4 August 1944, when he found himself and his headquarters surrounded by AK units. Bach-Zelewski and his men had a brutal reputation and their murderous reputation preceded them. Snyder observes that the death camp at Auschwitz was Bach-Zelewski's brainchild, while Hitler himself said of Bach-Zelewski that he was a "man who would wade through a sea of blood" in order to see the Jews exterminated.[36] This suited Hitler who wanted the entire population of Warsaw dead, while demanding "Warsaw to be levelled and in this way a terrifying example for entire Europe to be created". However the use of non-military units had a serious consequence for the Germans, as Bach-Zelewski's men relied on firepower rather than conventional military tactics. This allowed the lightly armed AK to hold on longer than might have been anticipated.[37]

The Soviet offensive against Warsaw was much subtler: Stalin could afford to wait and see. It is clear that Stalin, via the Soviet High Command, the *Stavka*, ordered 2nd Tank Army to attack towards Warsaw, but he did not mention a direct attack into the city. It was also unlikely that the Soviet Commander, Marshal Rokossovsky, would have wanted his armoured units to enter Warsaw itself, especially the narrow streets of the Old Town. Once the AK rose up in Warsaw the Soviets initially seemed confused about the situation, but once it became clear that the AK had seized the initiative, Stalin ordered the suspension of all Soviet offensive operations around Warsaw. In this manner Stalin had begun his policy of wait and see, as he correctly considered that the Germans, once they recovered themselves, would be able to destroy the AK. Quite simply Stalin allowed the Germans to do his dirty work, thus preparing the way for the establishment of Stalinism in Poland.

Stalin was not the only ally who did not necessarily totally endorse the aspirations of the London Poles. The Allies also acted in a way which – even though Polish actions in Warsaw were helpful for winning the war against Germany – indicated that Polish interests were not necessarily theirs. An early indication of just how Poland was to be treated on liberation became clear when the American Secretary of State, Cordell Hull, announced that Poland (and other liberated countries) would be administered, like Italy, by the Allied military authorities. This meant that Poland would in effect be treated in the same way as a former enemy.[38] It was also becoming clear that the Polish government-in-exile could not assume that it would be able to return to Poland and assume power. Mikołajczyk was particularly incensed with this.[39]

The exiled Poles considered that the AK had been taking the fight to the Germans to such an extent that by the summer of 1943 there might have almost been an insurrection in Poland. The British government must have been aware of this, because Eden had already told Churchill that AK activities had caused the occupying German Army to suggest that the Gestapo was completely ineffective in maintaining order there. These complaints were made so strongly and so often that Himmler was forced to go to Poland in order to restore order and unity within the German armed forces.[40] This surge in AK activities was questioned by the British government, which suspected that the AK was being used to oppose Soviet partisans being parachuted into the

36   Timothy Snyder, *Bloodlands: Europe between Hitler and Stalin*, New York, Basic Books, 2010, pp.150, 206.
37   Forczyk, op.cit. pp.35-7.
38   NA: PREM 3/355/6, Eden to Churchill, 23 November 1943.
39   McGilvray, *A Military Government*, p.141.
40   NA: PREM 3/355/6, 23 November 1943.

country.[41] Mikołajczyk assured Eden that this was not the case but he did explain that there were Polish concerns about Soviet activities there. He told Eden that underground communist newspapers were suggesting that the Soviet authorities were planning to take "reprisals" against "Polish patriots" once the Red Army entered Poland.

Despite this provocation, Mikołajczyk assured Eden that the Polish authorities had not issued orders to either the Polish military or civil authorities which could be interpreted as orders to resist Soviet guerrilla fighters in Poland. He also asserted that in the event of a German withdrawal he hoped that the Polish authorities already there would be able to assume power while a passage across the country was arranged for the Red Army on its way to Germany. He declared that both he and General Sosnkowski sought an early entry of Polish troops into battle and an uprising should coincide with the Red Army advance into Poland.[42] This was a rare meeting of minds between the two Polish leaders, who generally disliked and distrusted each other.

Mikołajczyk made it quite clear to Eden that if the Red Army attacked the Polish underground the Poles would defend themselves. He asserted that Poland was the real test of Soviet intentions: he claimed that for Stalin the Polish Question was not one of frontiers because his ambitions were global. Mikołajczyk feared that once the Red Army entered Polish territory the country would be reduced to a vassal state – or, as he expressed his fear, it would be the "… seventeenth republic of the Soviet Union". Eden denied that anything of this nature would happen. In the same meeting, Edward Raczyński told Eden that he did not want to see Poland become part of the Soviet Union's *Lebensraum*.[43] A clear reference to Nazi Germany's policy of imperialism, it also revealed that the British government was losing the support of moderate Polish figures such as Raczyński. The disgraced Marshal Edward Śmigły-Rydz, the military dictator who had fled into exile in 1939 (but had the decency to die in 1941), had said "with the Germans we risk losing our freedom. With the Russians we shall lose our souls."[44] These attitudes made it even more difficult for the British government to try to persuade the Polish government-in-exile to take a more conciliatory tone towards the Soviet Union, but as Applebaum remarks, the international revolution or the Leninist doctrine of "world revolution" had not been abandoned by Stalin, as many had thought. It had merely been postponed: after 1943 it was very much back on.[45] There were further indirect diplomatic clashes between the Soviet government and the Polish government-in-exile, using the FO as an intermediary. Much of this had to do with the question of partisan warfare in Poland.

The Soviet government claimed that Polish partisans were resisting the Red Army and were even collaborating with the Germans. This was denied by the FO, on behalf of the Poles. The indiscriminate use of Soviet agents led to the Germans taking severe reprisals against the Polish civilian population. Raczyński told Eden that in the past the AK had restricted its activities to more targeted operations such as the assassination of prominent Gestapo agents and leading Nazis. Right up to his death Sikorski had suspected that the AK had been penetrated by the Soviets while SOE, responsible for guerrilla warfare in occupied territory, commented that the Polish government could not be expected to hand the AK over to the Soviets or, as SOE wrote of the Soviets, "a thinly-veiled enemy" whose only interest was self-interest.[46] Paul notes that in Soviet-occupied Poland the Polish underground state was virtually non-existent owing to the complete penetration

---

41   McGilvray, *A Military Government*, p.141.
42   Ibid.
43   NA: FO 954/19C13543/1265, Eden to O'Malley, 12 November 1943.
44   Paul, op.cit. p.15.
45   Applebaum, op.cit. p.44.
46   NA: HS4/144MP/PD/4455, 13 August 1944.

of society by the NKVD; the assumption is that the Gestapo was nowhere as effective as the Soviet secret police, which allowed the Polish underground state to function.[47]

By 1944 it was quite clear what Soviet policy was regarding the AK. Mikołajczyk told Eden that he had received a telegram from Bór-Komorowski which was a copy of an order sent from Moscow to Soviet partisans operating in eastern Europe. This order was brief and to the point ' … all partisans are ordered to disarm Polish attachments. Those resisting will shot on the spot. All Polish underground organisations are to be exterminated and their leaders executed.'[48] It was as many Poles feared; conquest by liberation. Therefore the most obvious method left to the Poles for fending off unwanted Soviet attention to their sovereignty was to keep the AK intact, ready to resist with the Polish people any attempt by the Soviet Union to annex Poland. This raises the question of whether the AK deployed sensibly during the summer of 1944 or was it wasted while at the same time the Polish Government-in-exile was duped by the Soviet Government?

47   Paul, op.cit. p.69.
48   NA: PREM 3/335/7, Mikołajczyk to Eden, 17 January 1944.

3

The Military Aspect

The last chapter discussed how difficult it is to understand why the Poles, using the AK, rose up against the Germans just as the latter appeared to be withdrawing from the vicinity of Warsaw. This chapter will demonstrate that the Poles felt that, as usual, they were trapped between their two traditional enemies, Germany and Russia. Even though these two countries were at war with each other, they still presented a significant threat to Poland and its intention of regaining independence after the war. The Poles feared that the Germans would destroy Warsaw as their record for destruction and mass murder whenever they withdrew from a position was appalling. The Soviet record, whether withdrawing or advancing, was no better.

Since the Red Army had first crossed into Poland during 1944 in its advance towards Germany; the AK had cooperated with their Soviet allies, despite claims to the contrary from the Soviet government. Indeed it was the Soviets who were showing bad faith as after joint operations during July it became increasingly routine for them to disarm AK fighters, arrest them, conscript them into the Soviet-friendly Berling Army, deport them to the Soviet Union – or simply murder them. Usually AK officers were murdered by the NKVD, while on 31 July 1944, the eve of the Warsaw Uprising, the Soviets arrested around 30 senior AK officers after inviting them to a conference.[1] The British War Cabinet were aware of the Soviet attitude towards AK officers, as Polish generals recently returned from Poland had clearly stated that AK leaders fighting the Germans had been arrested and imprisoned by the Soviets.[2] Soviet involvement in the disarming and murder of AK members by their security forces was raised in a dispatch from the Polish diplomat, Edward Raczyński, to Sir Alexander Cadogan, Permanent Under-Secretary at the FO, as he sought protection from both the British and American governments from these outrages. He begged the two governments to declare the AK to be legitimate combatants in the service of the Allies and thus to be treated with the honour and dignity befitting prisoners of war.[3] Raczyński was seeking protection for the AK from both the German and Soviet armed forces.

The Polish demands were extremely damning as one ally was asking for the intervention of two other allies in order to prevent a fourth ally from destroying the first ally. It was obvious that the Soviet Union was hell-bent on destroying Poland and then annexing the country, and the Germans were the perfect instrument to do this for them. It was almost as if the Molotov-Ribbentrop Pact was still active. However there was just one chance, albeit a small one, that if the AK revolted against German rule; it might embarrass the Allies, principally the Soviets, into supporting the action.

Sadly this proved to be an extremely naive tactic because even though the British, American and South African air forces, together with their Polish counterparts, tried to aid Warsaw, flying long and hazardous missions to the Polish capital from either the UK or Allied bases in Italy, there were

---

1   Chris Bellamy, *Absolute War: Soviet Russia in the Second World War*, London, Macmillan, 2007, pp.616-7.
2   NA, PREM 3/355/12 W.M. (44) 95th Conclusion, Minute 3, Confidential Annexe, 24 July 1944.
3   *Documents on Polish-Soviet Relations, 1939-1945. Volume 2, 1943-1945*. London, Heinemann, 1967, document 176, p.306. Hereafter referred to as *DPSR 2*.

no large-scale attempts to help Warsaw. The Allies took a pragmatic view: they looked at the high casualty rates amongst aircrews and were appalled. As a consequence the flights were suspended. Weather was also a factor in the cancellation of the flights. The London Poles also demanded that paratroopers of the Polish Independent Parachute Brigade be made available for Warsaw. This was never going to happen for two reasons: it would have been impossible to drop them over the capital, and they were needed for the Arnhem offensive during September 1944. The Poles also learnt the hard way that the Soviet government could not be embarrassed into helping them until it was too late. When Soviet aid did finally arrive it was superficial, but enough for it to be said that the Soviet Union had helped at Warsaw.

Even though the 1944 Warsaw Uprising is condemned as being ill-conceived, there are a few considerations which need to be discussed before any narration of the actual fighting. The most obvious is the question of what the Red Army might actually have done once it arrived at Warsaw? Without doubt many Poles, especially senior commanders and politicians, were quite rightly afraid and suspicious of Soviet intentions once the Red Army was in full possession of the city. Soviet propaganda broadcast into Warsaw urged Poles to rise up against the occupying Germans. This message was reinforced with the dropping of leaflets, purporting to have been signed by Molotov himself, suggesting that any rising would be backed by the Red Army.

Prior to the uprising there were a number of mixed messages, but the one which had the most influence on the population was the German demand at the end of July 1944 for 100,000 Poles living in the capital to assemble ready to dig anti-tank ditches around the city, in anticipation of the Red Army's approach. Even though this order was ignored it did cause great anxiety throughout Warsaw as it raised the fear that the Germans were about to deport the entire male population. Later, during September, the chief organ of the AK, *Biuletyn Informacyjny*, wrote of those uncertain days of July 1944:

> In the last days of July there was a very considerable increase of arms dumps liquidated by the Gestapo and arrests of men responsible for the organisation, which clearly pointed to preparation for a large-scale German police attack on Polish military formations. Three days before the uprising, machine gun posts were simultaneously set up at various points in the streets, while at key points, like the Zoliborz Viaduct, tanks drew up in position. These preparations gave grounds for the statement that the German authorities were on the point, any day, of putting into execution their long contemplated but hitherto not implemented plan for the wholesale removal of the male population of the capital.[4]

This statement was made during September, when it was obvious that the uprising was about to become yet another glorious Polish military failure. It may have been an attempt to justify the revolt. However, overall it should be seen that German actions had pushed the Warsaw AK Command into a corner. This caused them to rush decisions as they tried to work out what German intentions really were, as well as trying to second-guess Soviet designs on Warsaw. Under these difficult and trying conditions Bór-Komorowski made his decision at 17.30 hours, 31 July for an uprising to begin twenty-three and a half hours later at 17.00 hours on 1 August 1944. He then received information which suggested that the arrival of Soviet armour in Praga would not be as soon as previously thought, but Bór-Komorowski declared that it was, 'too late. The order is given, I will not change it."[5] The die was cast.

---

4   Pomian, op.cit. p.ix.
5   Forczyk, op.cit. pp 13-4.

From an AK intelligence report for the morning of 31 July, it was clear that the Germans and Soviets were already engaged in armour and artillery duels throughout the Praga area. The civilian population had already left as the fighting had begun when the Germans opened fire on Soviet positions at 06:00 hours that day. This thirteen-point AK report concluded with a request for orders.[6] Not to have taken this report seriously was reckless and ignored military professionalism and training (although this – to a quite breathtaking degree – was never a strong suit with the interwar Polish Army). However the political pressure from the Poles in London on the Warsaw AK to do something, anything to reassert Polish sovereignty was so extreme that a revolt had to be in the offing during the summer of 1944. The Polish supreme commander in London, General Kazimierz Sosnkowski, would have liked to see Warsaw liberated by the AK but even he had his doubts about it actually happening.[7]

Bór-Komorowski stuck to his decision for an uprising and he based it on three assumptions: the Germans were about to abandon Warsaw; the Allies would provide vigorous support; the Soviet offensive would continue. He was wrong on all three counts. His military-political immaturity gave him no real sense of proportion of where Poland was in the real world of inter-Allied politics and the prosecution of the war against Germany. The country was not at the top table: indeed it was a minor ally of no real consequence to the Allies. Even if some senior British officials disliked the situation there was nothing that they could do about it except to wait until the war ended and then try to salvage Polish independence – but not before.

The brutal suppression of the Warsaw Uprising is another example of the lack of Polish perspective regarding their foes. In the British National Archives there is a striking photograph from a collection of captured German documents, dated 5 May 1941. The image is of a banquet at which Nazi and Stalinist officials are celebrating. What they are celebrating is unclear but of course by this date Hitler and his cronies had already decided to invade their ally, the Soviet Union.[8] Given the odious nature of the Molotov-Ribbentrop Agreement and how the Soviets and Nazis had behaved towards each other, both before the signing of this agreement and then again after 22 June 1941, the duplicity of these two regimes should have been in no doubt. To have had any faith in the Soviet Union should be seen as a further example of Polish wishful thinking. It would seem that the Warsaw AK leadership had not thought through the response of the Germans, from Hitler downwards, to a revolt in Warsaw or anywhere else in Poland, nor of the consequences of any such rebellion.

The Nazis saw any revolt by the Poles as a challenge on racial grounds. The war in the east was one of annihilation and extermination of both Jews and Slavs: principally Jews, but according to Nazi doctrine Slavs also fell into a category of racial inferiority. Warsaw had already provided an example of how inhumanely the Germans would put down any revolt when the Jews of the Warsaw Ghetto rose up during April 1943. This rising was put down with the greatest brutality by SS-General Jürgen Stroop, using SS and police units normally deployed in the guise of anti-partisan warfare in Poland and western areas of the Soviet Union, in the hunting down and mass murder of Jews. Snyder observes that: "German anti-partisan operations were all but indistinguishable from the mass murder of the Jews."[9] With the use of mass murderers and of fire, Stroop was responsible for the systematic destruction of entire families, as well as buildings in Warsaw. He considered that his methods, which he described as being the "toughness of our operation in the former Jewish residential areas" as being highly successful and thought they had impressed the

---

6   *Powstanie 1*, Document 163, Intelligence Report, AK in Praga on German and Red Army Activities, 11:30, 31 July 1944, p.213.
7   Ibid. Document 105, Sosnkowski to Bór-Komorowski, 28 July 1944, pp.105-6.
8   NA, GFM 33/681, Serial 1699.
9   Snyder, op.cit. p.240.

Poles living in Warsaw.[10] If Stroop considered that he had overawed the local population and that they would be afraid to revolt in the future he was clearly mistaken.

The Warsaw Uprising became the only German ground operation of World War II that, with the blessings of both Hitler and Himmler, relied almost entirely on the SS. Initially both men viewed the German counter-offensive as a "special operation" on a countrywide scale: Nazi-speak for extermination. If Hitler and Himmler had their way, there would be no prisoners or survivors. It was only when it became obvious that the SS and the special police units were not adequate for real urban warfare, as opposed to their usual task of slaughtering unarmed civilians before more conventional German military units were deployed in Warsaw. The lack of high-quality infantry meant that the Germans were forced to rely on firepower, rather than skilled military tactics.[11]

However, the beginning of the uprising began badly. Barbara Gadomska, who served as a nurse during the Warsaw Uprising, told the author that the timing of the uprising was not well organised and many units started prematurely, including her unit on Mokotówska Street.[12] In other areas action started as early as 15.05; nearly two hours before "W" hour.[13] These premature attacks basically gave the game away and so the rising began "as a spluttering of small-scale attacks rather than a coordinated assault upon the German power in Warsaw". By "W" hour the Germans were more or less waiting for the AK.[14] Furthermore, German armoured units had began a counter-offensive against the Soviet 2nd Tank Army at 06.00 hours, 1 August, a full eleven hours before the beginning of the Polish offensive and so were already on alert.[15]

Therefore, despite the gallantry of the ordinary AK fighter, the Warsaw Uprising was doomed to fail from the very beginning, as can be seen from the first reports received from various AK positions dotted around the city. An early intelligence report suggested that generally there was a lack of clarity in the orders received by commanders, in addition to the lack of planning by the AK General Staff. Furthermore it was reported that ordinary people were furious about the uprising and lacked enthusiasm for it. Warsaw citizens were unimpressed with the revolt and did not support it.[16]

Hanson comments that Warsaw did not fight as a solid, single unit but as isolated districts cut off from one another. This was instrumental in creating different and conflicting results.[17] However during the first days of the uprising AK action could not have been totally ineffective, as some commentators suggest. Bartoszewski notes that during the first week of the Warsaw Uprising entire German units were destroyed by the AK and were "never mentioned again".[18] The problem is that the contemporary reports of the initial days of the insurrection destroy two long-held Polish myths about the Warsaw Uprising.[19] The best that could be said about the opening of the Warsaw Uprising was that the situation was mixed. In his reminiscences a young AK fighter, Ralph Smorczewski, considered that the atmosphere was such that "everybody knew that soon the town would rise up against the occupiers".[20] On the other hand, Dr. Barbara Dobrowolska, then a

10   *The Report of Jürgen Stroop concerning the Uprising in the Ghetto in Warsaw and the Liquidation of the Jewish Residential Area*, A. Rutkowski (ed) Warsaw, Jewish Historical Institute, 1958, pp.40-74.
11   Forczyk, op.cit. p.26.
12   Barbara Gadomska, (born 1927) interview with author, Warsaw, 16 July 2012. Hereafter referred to as 'Gadomska'.
13   BR. Żuławski, *Powstanie Warszawskie*, Łódź, Wojska Polski, 1946, p.16.
14   Forczyk, op.cit. p.39.
15   Ibid. p.48.
16   *Powstanie 1*, Document 194, Warsaw, 1 August 1944, Intelligence Report no. 9, Warsaw Area, pp.239-41.
17   Joanna K.M. Hanson, *The Civilian Population and the Warsaw Uprising of 1944*, New York, CUP, 1982, p.3.
18   Władysław Bartoszewski, *Abandoned Heroes of the Warsaw Uprising*, Kraków, Biały Kruk, 2008, p.9.
19   Hanson, op.cit. p.205.
20   IWM: 12787/03/41/1, Ralph Smorczewski, Reminiscences.

seventeen-year-old girl on the fringes of the AK, was shocked when her father told her hours before the rising that a revolt was about to happen: she told the author that she had no idea that there was such a conspiracy afoot.[21] Sadly, later that day her father was killed in the fighting, and her home, which was close to SS barracks, was set alight by the Germans. Gross is also observant of the civilian situation in Poland in 1944 because as he noted " … the underground was a substitute for an entire society rather than its military or political organization only. Its foundation was a citizen rather than a politician."[22] This meant that even if the Poles were willing to accept or tolerate German protection against the Soviets, they were unwilling to join the underground unless they were driven by desperation to "go to the forest".[23] This suggests that civilian support for the AK was tacit rather than active.

By the evening of 1 August the first reports of the fighting began to arrive at the Staff HQ of the Warsaw AK, as unit commanders assessed their situations and options after the initial few hours of the revolt. At 21.00 hours the commander of the city centre (Śródmieście) area reported on the military situation in the Żoliborz region (in the northern sector of Warsaw) as well as on communications from the Praga area across the Vistula. Even if the Polish offensive for Warsaw did not begin officially until 17.00 hours, operations, not including the premature attacks discussed earlier, began earlier than "W" hour. A report stated that at 15.10 hours a German patrol complete with an anti-tank gun had been moving towards an AK position. This led to a short fight, which saw the elimination of a group from XXII Platoon from the Żoliborz region. The report already noted how the Germans were able to dominate the situation, as they had plenty of artillery and tanks, predominately the Panther (a medium tank with a 75mm main gun) and the Tiger I (a heavy tank with an 88mm gun). Further reports also indicated that the beginning of the revolt is not going to plan. Captain Kamiński (Żaglowiec) reported at 18.35 hours that the territory, which he described as "Objective 15", could not be captured owing to the failure of an offensive from the west. At the same time Squad 23 was already fighting a defensive action against the enemy.

The premature beginning of operations at 15.10 hours made it impossible for Squad 23 even to have a decent basis from which to withdraw: heir position was in extreme danger. Another report, by telephone, from "Kucharz", Commander of Otwock region, not only gave news of fighting in the Międzylisia area but also reported the presence of 160 Soviet tanks in the Otwock area.[24] This is an example of the resources available to the Soviets but which they failed to use to support the Poles in their struggle against the Germans. However it must not be forgotten that the Red Army had been fighting the Germans since 06.00 hours that same day and it might be reasonable to suppose that they wished to preserve their resources. There were other considerations: the Red Army was apparently unaware that the revolt had started but also it was exhausted and at the end of a 400-mile supply line.[25]

In an interview with Alexander Werth on 26 August 1944, the Soviet Commander at Warsaw, Marshal Konstantin Rokossovsky, was quite evasive about the Warsaw Uprising. When Werth asked if Rokossovsky could have taken Warsaw within a few days of 1 August, as had been suggested by the Soviet newspaper, *Pravda*, Rokossovsky replied that the Red Army could have done so if the Germans had not thrown so many tanks into battle. He added that he would not take the city with a frontal assault and that there was on a 50-50 chance that the Red Army could

21   Dr. Barbara Dobrowolska, interview with author, 18 July 2012, Łódź. Hereafter referred to as 'Dobrowolska'.
22   Jan Tomasz Gross, *Polish Society under German Occupation. The Generalgouvernement, 1939-1944*, Princeton, Princeton University Press, 1979, p.279.
23   Ibid. pp.279-84.
24   *Powstanie 1*, Document 206, 1 August 1944, p.253.
25   Brian Taylor, *Barbarossa to Berlin: A Chronology of the Campaigns on the Eastern Front, 1941 to 1945. Volume 2. The Defeat of Germany, 19 November 1942 to 15 May 1945*, Staplehurst, UK, Spellmount, 2004, pp.209-11.

have captured Warsaw in early August. When Werth asked Rokossovsky if he considered that the uprising was justified in such circumstances, Rokossovsky replied, "No, it was a bad mistake", and that the insurgents (as he referred to the AK) had started "off their own bat", without consulting the Soviet High Command. When Werth observed that the Soviet government, via broadcasts, had urged the Poles in Warsaw to revolt, Rokossovsky denied that the broadcasts from Moscow were alone in this and claimed that both the BBC and the AK radio station, *Świt*, had done the same. For the remainder of the interview he was evasive on the subject of Warsaw and the Allied use of Soviet airbases.[26]

The Poles were not only deceived by Soviet broadcasts but also by the appearance of Soviet armour on the east bank of the Vistula at Praga. This was very suggestive because as Sydnor writes: "the Russian reach for Warsaw, which prompted the tragic and ill-fated uprising by the Polish Home Army of General Bór-Komorowski on August 1, marked the high point of the summer offensive". Sydnor notes that the Red Army had advanced over 400 miles in a little over a month but had outrun its supplies, exhausted its men and had worn out its tanks and vehicles. It then had suffered badly from strong and concentrated German counter-attacks on 2 and 3 August. The effect of this was to bring the Soviet advance briefly to a halt. It was the first time that the Germans had been able to stop the Soviet advance and the German Commander, *Generalfeldmarschall* Walter Model, swiftly brought in the Waffen SS to try to bring the Red Army to a total halt at Warsaw.[27]

However it was not all bad news, as Captain "Sępa" reported the capture by the AK of Czerniaw to the commander of Area V in Mokotów. "Sępa" also said that his people were in good spirits but were already requesting more ammunition as they were short of all types.[28] An audit of fifty-four fighters and their arms illustrated just how badly armed the AK were. This group was armed with a single Sten sub-machine gun, three pistols with ammunition, two Czech pistols without any ammunition and 200 homemade grenades. By contrast, the enemy, in addition to their standard issue weapons were supported by a battery of anti-aircraft guns (no doubt the iconic and versatile 88mm anti-aircraft gun, which could also be deployed as an anti-tank gun and as a standard artillery piece). This mainstay of the German artillery was considered to have been extremely formidable by all those who came up against it.[29] Standard German artillery was supported by multi-barrelled rocket launchers, mainly the swG 40, which could rapidly fire a series of rockets, either incendiary or high explosive. It was nicknamed "the bellowing cow" by Poles, because of the noise of the rockets just before they exploded. However Gross notes that AK commanders were frequently not truthful about the true state of their units and tried to cheat in order to get extra supplies and men allocated to them at the expense of others.[30] Kochanski observes that a major problem concerning arms for the AK was that two large arsenals were on the wrong side of the River Vistula in Praga. Others were positioned with such secrecy that their locations were lost. In 1947 an AK weapons dump was found which contained 678 machine pistols and 60,000 rounds of ammunition, while another found in 1957 took two weeks to empty.[31]

---

26   Alexander Werth, *Russia at War, 1941-1945*, London, Barrie & Rockliff, 1964, p.877.
27   Charles W. Sydnor Jr. *Soldiers of Destruction. The SS Death's Head Division, 1933-1945*, Princeton, Princeton University Press, 1977, pp.305-7.
28   *Powstanie 1*, Document 207, 19:45 hours, 1 August 1944, p.254.
29   The author's grandfather, Frank McGilvray, who served in the Royal Artillery during the North Africa campaign often spoke of the German 88mm gun with admiration enough for this author to take notice even before he really understood exactly what his grandfather was talking about. Later the author's Housemaster, WTR Roberts, also a Royal Artillery veteran of the North Africa and Italian Campaigns made a similar impression regarding the 88mm flak gun.
30   Gross, op.cit. pp.42-3.
31   Halik Kochanski, *The Eagle Unbowed: Poland and the Poles in the Second World War*, London, Allen Lane, 2012, p.404.

To the south-east of Area V in the area known as Krajewski 2a, rocket launchers also supported German artillery, which was to have consequences for an AK group trying to operate in the same district. Furthermore, the Germans had installed extra searchlights as they sought to detect and destroy any AK offensive. An AK reconnaissance patrol operating in the same neighbourhood towards the Traugutta Fort discovered that there was no suitable cover to conceal any movement, and so an order was given that the enemy in that vicinity was to be destroyed and arms and ammunition in the fort was to be captured.

The group selected for this operation had been waiting for orders since 29 July. Despite the preparations the group had tried to make, such as being certain that they were well equipped when the orders did arrive, they were not always clear. The problem for the AK was that as an underground conspiracy; secrecy was paramount. Therefore its members had to maintain a sense of normality, including mundane things as holding down a job. The AK lacked a large dedicated military force, such as that of Tito's guerrilla force in Yugoslavia, so AK members had to lead a deadly double life. Because of this, it was not easy for the AK leadership to coordinate operations, as its members had to be contacted discreetly in order to assemble at a given point. Even getting to an assembly point required great guile so as not to attract the attention of the enemy. Furthermore, in the face of constant and hostile Gestapo vigilance the AK, especially in an urban environment such as Warsaw, had great difficulty in collecting weapons and moving them around the city ready for distribution. Even, so it should be noted that the AK did its best to fulfill its orders.

The commander for the operation around Krajewski 2a received his orders for the uprising at 09.20 hours on 1 August. Clearly this gave him little time to collect the personnel necessary for the offensive but he managed to do so, and had already organised patrols ready for "W" hour. At around 16.30 hours he received a report from his sappers that the Germans had established a post at Krajewski 2a. This was a huge problem, as they had a weapons dump nearby. However in a grenade attack the Polish sappers managed to destroy the German position and a communications post which had been set up there. The sappers reported that in their attack they had also destroyed a German power substation: this attack coincided to the very second with the beginning of the Warsaw Uprising.

Further confusion in the coordination and communication of AK offensives is illustrated by an operation against the Warsaw Citadel and the area to the south-east of this position. The Adjutant of the group chosen to attack the Citadel, Captain "Zagłowa" (2nd Lieutenant Stefan Szuba) reported that since 14.00 hours there had been no contact with the commander, Captain "Jur" (Captain M. Kamiński aka "Zagłowiec") supposedly already in position waiting to attack the Citadel with his men. The lack of real planning is further illustrated by the fact that there were only 130 AK fighters in the area, which lacked adequate communications. This is to say nothing of its missing commander, who had apparently gone out to try to see if he could improve on his group's situation, but had failed to return.

This situation clearly throws up a number of questions. What to do? And when? Should a localised offensive begin at once, or should such an operation only begin at "W" hour? "Zagłowa" took control of the situation, assuming the post of temporary commander and starting to issue orders. He and his men began to take up positions ready to attack German gun crews, including an anti-aircraft machine gun post. The Poles took every rifle they had, six in number, and moved to the windows of the third floor of the block of flats at Krajewski 2, ready for action. At 17.00 hours, they attacked the German positions.

Under the command of "Bundara" (2nd Lieutenant J. Krzywnicki), 209 Platoon moved up from the Citadel side to the Krajewski block of flats using the cover of a heap of concrete debris. Their movement drew fire from enemy artillery and from the anti-aircraft gun as the Poles attacked from the direction of the Citadel. Several AK fighters became pinned alongside the heap of concrete debris by the German artillery fire and became isolated from their comrades, who had been able to push ahead. At a stroke this AK offensive had been cut in two owing to superior enemy weaponry.

Under the command of "Maja", 207 Platoon moved from the right-hand side of Krajewski 2a, crossing domestic gardens towards nearby concrete walls. The first squad moved swiftly towards the grounds of the History Faculty of the University of Warsaw. From there they came under heavy automatic fire as well as being shelled by an 88mm anti-aircraft gun being used as field artillery. Another squad, Lunicz Squad, only had two sub-machine guns to reply to such devastating enemy fire-power and only one magazine between the two guns. The commander of the squad only realised this when after the first burst of automatic fire; the gun did not fire any longer. It had run out of ammunition. What happened afterwards to Lunicz Squad and the remainder of the first squad is not clear. Only the casualty rate gives some idea what probably happened, with one dead, five wounded and nine missing, three of which did return unharmed. "Maj", commanding 3rd Squad, which consisted of twelve "adventurous" people was under the shelter of concrete walls by a carpenter's workshop. They managed to creep forward, throwing grenades as they advanced. However they soon discovered that they could not leave the shelter of the walls owing to heavy machinegun fire and shelling from the 88mm gun. From statements made by the wounded and riflemen from 3rd Squad, who eventually managed to withdraw under the cover of darkness from their exposed position, it was learnt that a platoon commander had been killed along with a rifleman, while two had been wounded. Nine riflemen eventually returned unharmed.

The casualty rate for the first day of the uprising should have caused alarm bells to sound. It was quite obvious that they were unsustainable, especially once it was clear that the Soviets were actively preventing Warsaw from being reinforced by the AK. Poles claim that the opening days of the uprising were successful but it was all relative and at times quite delusional, as so many small skirmishes with very little gain was at the cost of an average 59% casualty rate. The injuries received were often extremely serious and again could not continue in the long term. For example, a platoon commander was wounded in the lungs in a failed operation to link up units. This was catastrophic not only because of the nature of the wound but because experienced field commanders could not easily be replaced.

The Warsaw AK simply did not have the necessary medical equipment to deal with such serious injuries and to lose commanders on failed and possibly unnecessary operations was to become a serious problem. By 21.20 hours it was quite clear that operations in the area of the Krajewski block of flats were failing. The problem of lack of weapons and soldiers when faced with a heavily armed enemy complete with artillery support meant the AK units in the area were obliged to withdraw or face annihilation the next day. Just before midnight they withdrew, taking their wounded with them. These they left under the care of Dr. Sosna before taking up a new position at 35 Śmiały Street.[32]

A report from the commander of 207 Squad, after the first day of fighting, was critical of the poor organisation of the uprising. From the very outset of his report this commander condemned the whole uprising as being insufficiently prepared: as well as being expected to fight with many of his men being more or less unarmed, orders and decisions from Warsaw AK Command lacked any coordination or purpose.[33] However at first the Germans did not take such a view. SS-Obergruppenführer and Police General Ernst Kaltenbrunner reported to Himmler during the early hours of 2 August that the uprising was extremely dangerous, while referring to the AK as "bandits".[34] Kaltenbrunner, a fanatical Nazi later hanged as a war criminal following the

---

32   *Powstanie 1*, Document 210, Warsaw-Żoliborz, 1 August 1944, pp.255-8.

33   Ibid. Document 212, Warsaw-Żoliborz, 1 August 1944, pp.260-3.

34   Ibid. Document 223, Berlin, 00:30, 2 August 1944, p.276.

Nuremburg Trials, was reacting to the first German reports coming from Warsaw and as he sat at his desk in his Berlin office was trying to judge what might happen next. At that point Soviet intentions were unclear. It might have been reasonable to suppose that the Red Army would try to cross the River Vistula and support the uprising, or at least provide aerial and artillery assistance, in addition to allowing Polish infantry reinforcements into Warsaw. A further consideration for the Germans was that the British and Americans might do something to support the uprising. During the first few days the Germans could only wonder what might happen next.

The Germans were right to consider what the Allies might do in response to the Polish rising: but putting aside all political concerns, between 20 July and 30 July the Soviets had suffered heavy casualties in fighting along the route to Warsaw from the east. A report from the Chief of Staff of 2nd Soviet Army recorded that this body had suffered 582 dead, 1581 wounded and 452 missing, while 130 tanks and armoured guns had been destroyed or damaged. The Germans had also suffered an appalling casualty rate, with 19,566 dead, wounded, captured or missing. In equipment terms the Germans had lost 73 tanks and armoured guns, 16 large artillery pieces, 9 tank transporters, 102 motorcycles, 82 lorries, 3 armoured trains, 477 smaller artillery pieces, 67 anti-tank guns, 242 mortars, 1,238 machine guns and 2776 smaller vehicles, destroyed, damaged or captured.[35]

Taylor notes that by the end of July the Soviet 2nd Tank Army had reached Praga but had encountered strong German resistance there from the 3rd SS Panzer Division *Totenkopf*, the Hermann Goering Parachute Panzer Division and the 19th Panzer Division, which all attacked "the depleted 2nd Tank Army".[36] This suggests that despite the huge amount of German equipment destroyed or captured by the Red Army and the high German casualty rate; the Soviets had been badly mauled in the fighting for the eastern approaches to Warsaw. In short, ten days of heavy fighting had taken a huge toll of the Red Army. While the Germans and the Soviets pondered their next moves, General Bór-Komorowski, the AK Commander in Warsaw, reported to the western Allies that after two days of fighting there was a "catastrophic shortage of ammunition" in the city.[37]

German intelligence reports also give an interesting and often accurate picture of what was happening during the uprising. An *Abwehr* officer's report, in which he considered intelligence gathered by German reconnaissance patrols reporting to the staff of the 9th German Army about the situation, made several observations on the uprising. The most striking was that at night all was quiet; the Abwehr officer considered that perhaps the AK lacked the confidence to operate at night.

The reluctance of the AK to fight at night was probably due to its lack of ammunition: nocturnal operations would be considered a waste of ammunition. The Germans were also aware of Polish objectives, which included the main railway station, the east railway station and their marshalling yards, the main telephone exchange, municipal offices and the cavalry complex near Szwolezerów Street, as well as the police buildings of both criminal and political investigation forces. This was quite an ambitious list of objectives for such a poorly armed and badly coordinated offensive; equally they had underestimated the German response.

The report noted that on the whole the Poles did not have proper uniforms and that many wore on their arms a brassard sporting the Polish national colours, red and white, emblazoned with the white Polish eagle on the red section. Others wore German uniforms with Russian helmets and a large number wore German helmets. The Germans were also quick to note just how poorly armed the Poles were but made the point that even so they were well trained and had been able to defeat

---

35   Ibid. Document, 231, Battle Report, no: 099, 2 August 1944, p.282.
36   Taylor, op.cit. p.208.
37   *Powstanie 1*, Document 235, p.284.

smaller German defensive positions. This should be treated with caution, as during the opening days of the uprising the Poles, having largely caught the Germans off guard, were quite successful, and no doubt this report was being economical with the truth. However Barbara Matys outlined to the author that she and her female colleagues had received quite detailed and lengthy training in bomb-making and sabotage from Polish military engineers.[38] They were indeed the famous women sappers or *minerki* who fought so bravely in Warsaw. This reinforces the German assertion that the Poles were adequately trained, but lacked the resources to do better. Even so, the German report does record the fact that at least one of the Polish attacks was so strong that even with armoured support the Poles were still able to eject the Germans from one of their positions. An increased use of petrol bombs (often referred to as Molotov cocktails) thrown from well-constructed and stoutly defended barricades around Jerusalem Avenue (Reichsstrasse in the German report) gave the AK a distinct advantage as long as they remained intact and in Polish hands, as they had long and clear views of the fighting in Central Warsaw.

The German intelligence report remarked on the good organisation of the Poles and the intelligent way in which they had been deployed. This caused the Germans to consider that some of the Polish commanders had received formal military training, especially as at one stage they had out-thought the German tactic of trying to block Warsaw in from the rear (that is to the West). The German report took account of the fighting in the forests to the north-west of Warsaw, from the north of the bend in the River Vistula as it flowed through the city where there was a strong presence of about 300 AK fighters. The report admitted that on 1 August the Germans had been driven from the forests and had had to withdraw to the nearby town of Modlin. There had also been an AK attack using 200–300 soldiers on a German communications position to the south-east of Pruszków on 2 August. This attack left three Germans dead, including two officers and six wounded. There were no AK dead but the Germans did manage to take sixty prisoners.

As already mentioned the Germans were unsure how to react to the uprising in Warsaw: they were not certain of its nature and where it was going. Reports from German agents (V-Mann) suggested that the uprising was the work of many different Polish Nationalist resistance groups in Warsaw and throughout Poland. The Germans then decided to suppress the revolt in Warsaw totally, as a warning to others who might be considering such an action elsewhere, either in Poland or anywhere within German occupied Europe.[39] Erickson observes that during the early days of the Warsaw Uprising the AK had been able to capture enemy strong points and instillations lightly guarded by the Germans and then spent the next two days and nights trying to capture more heavily guarded German positions, but they then split into smaller groups throughout the city and lost contact with each other.[40]

In a report dated 2 August 1944,14.15 hours, to the commander of the German 9th Army, Lieutenant-General Reiner Stahel, the German commander of the Warsaw Garrison, said (as in other German reports), that Polish attacks, despite being lightly armed were well executed, suggesting that the revolt was better led than the Germans might have expected. The German response was to deploy "storm sappers" who were to burn down buildings in an attempt to counteract the well-fortified Polish barricades and defensive works.[41]

As an interesting note to this method of waging warfare, Bór-Komorowski himself wrote in his autobiography that a few days before the uprising the Germans withdrew all Polish fire-fighting crews and their engines from Warsaw. This alarmed Poles, especially those who were aware of

---

38   Matys.
39   *Powstanie 1*, Document 265, pp.306-7.
40   John Erickson, *The Road to Berlin: Stalin's War with Germany, Volume 2*, London, Cassell, 2003, p.272.
41   *Powstanie 1*, Document 271, pp.312-3.

the coming revolt, and they correctly concluded that the Germans were about to fire the capital. Bór-Komorowski was struck by the presence of a German fireman captured by the AK. During his interrogation this fireman told his AK inquisitors that Himmler had personally ordered a large section of the Koepenick Fire Brigade (from near Berlin) to be sent to Warsaw on the second day of the uprising, not to extinguish fires but "as specialists to organise the firing of the city proper and large built-up areas".[42]

A report from within Warsaw sent at 10.00 hours, 2 August, revealed just how badly the uprising was going for the AK. Almost from the beginning of his observations, its author "Gromski" wrote of the military situation as being dire. The revolt at Żoliborz had been liquidated; operations at Ochota were still ongoing while the offensive in Mokotów had run into difficulties, as the enemy there had strong armoured support. Gromski further reported that communications with London were not working. In the larger scheme of things in Warsaw this was an irrelevance but it does show where the loyalty of the Warsaw AK lay, even if the exiled Polish government was very much out of touch with reality and exercised very little overall influence in their occupied homeland.

However, despite the overall lack of coordination and commands for the Warsaw Uprising, there were many examples of individual bravery and sacrifice among AK fighters. Gromski reported that when the first German tanks arrived on the streets of Warsaw; AK fighters attacked them, destroying the lead tank with explosives while its crew fled the scene. This AK counter-attack prevented German forces from continuing their offensive in the area at that time. The AK had to rely on improvisation, limited owing to the lack of weapons and ammunition, but even so the AK continued to fight on.[43] They had expected to receive outside support within seven days, if not reinforcements: instead they found themselves stranded with enemies all around, with the broad, deep River Vistula to their rear: between the devil and the deep blue sea.

At the time of Gromski's report another report was received at the Warsaw AK HQ one from Lieutenant-Colonel "Sławomir"(Lieutenant-Colonel E. Pfeiffer) who was in Central Warsaw (Środmieście). The report concerned the situation there and how the battle for Warsaw was progressing. He said that the Old Town had been captured and barricaded against the Germans by Polish civilians. At the same time a Polish offensive against the second highest building, the PAST building, began at 08.45 on 2 August. The PAST building was the telephone centre for German-occupied Poland and linked the German eastern front with their western front. It became a prime objective for the AK. The Germans had already deployed four tanks in the area around the PAST building and in fighting for it the AK managed to capture a German armoured car. A further report for the same day, made at 11.00 hours from IV Region, noted that the objective of its offensive, 2 Gorski Street, had been captured by the Kiliński Battalion, commanded by Captain Leliwa-Roycewicz ("Leliw") and the commander of IV Region, Major S. Steczkowski ("Zagończyk").

There was further action towards the main Post Office with the principal Polish objectives being the corner of Chłodniej Street. However realising the AK plans was proving to be difficult, as the defending Germans had a tank supporting their position. At the PAST building, the AK captured three vehicles as well as destroying a tank and a lorry. The Germans moved eighty men in two groups from Woła to be used in an attack upon the Łukasiński Company. Both of these groups were destroyed by the AK in the fighting which caused Polish morale to soar. They had only suffered two wounded, as well as capturing a tank that had held the corner of Chmiel Street and Marszałkowska Avenue.

---

42   Tadeusz Bór-Komorowski, *The Secret Army*, London, Victor Gollancz, 1950, p.236.
43   *Powstanie 1*, Document 274, Report from 'Gromski' to AK Staff, Information on the Situation in Wolna, 2 August 1944, 10:00 hours (Warsaw-Wolna) sent 13:45, 2 August 1944, pp.315-6.

At 11.35 it was reported that German position at Warsaw University was being heavily defended by the enemy while an offensive by 2nd Group, AK, on Plac Marszałska was being repulsed. At the same time it was reported that all bridges over the Vistula remained in German hands. 3rd Group, AK, was given the task of attacking German positions at the hospital on Solcu Street where the Poles ran into heavy enemy infantry fire. Despite suffering two dead and two wounded, Polish morale remained very high, as for once adequate supplies were actually reaching them. Further reports concerning AK attempts to seize the bridges over the Vistula were tales of frustration. At 12.50 hours reports on the fighting around Plac Marszałska claimed that German units had withdrawn from the area. In the square itself there were still German vehicles, but none of them were armoured.

At 14.45 hours reports were received from AK units already suggesting the changing nature of the fighting, as a lightly armed AK unit had attacked areas on Dąbrowski Square and at 146 Marszałska Avenue and had destroyed two police vehicles. The report of this incident highlighted the fact that five of the police had been killed and two Kalmucks (Soviet citizens from Asia who were anti-Soviet and fighting for the Germans) had been captured. The Poles were also able to capture two rifles and 200 rounds of rifle ammunition. By late afternoon came a most disturbing report from the 2nd Region concerning the use of Polish women as human shields in front of seven tanks as the Germans advanced into the area; the women ran towards the AK barricades when the AK fighters opened fire on the tanks from upper storey windows. This was the beginning of the unreserved German brutality used during the Warsaw Uprising.

Since invading Poland in September 1939 the Germans had consistently used brutality against the population. During the previous year, 1943, they had put down the Jewish revolt in Warsaw using horrific methods, including setting fire to buildings and allowing people either to jump to their deaths or be burnt alive. AK commanders should have realised that the same would happen to them, as the Nazis viewed Poles in much the same way that they viewed Jews: they hated them both. Ten minutes later, at 16.40 hours, a report came from the 4th Region. The Chrobry Battalion, commanded at this time by Major L. Nowakowski ("Lig") was on the corner of Chłodna Street fighting off an enemy attack coming from the direction of Wola. This enemy offensive comprised about fifty soldiers supported by five tanks; the situation was described as being "very dangerous". There was a further assault on the central Post Office, which had been reinforced by the enemy. By 17.00 it was reported that the Post Office had been captured by the AK. While this was happening the Germans had reinforced their garrison at the PAST building with two tanks, and the AK was once more attacking the building.[44]

A report dispatched at 05.20 hours, 2 August, from Region 4 stated that the enemy had attacked a Polish position on the corner of Chłodno and Leszno Streets. The attacking group consisted of German military gendarmes, heavily supported by about twenty tanks. Amazingly this attack failed, owing to the stout improvised Polish barricades, which blocked main thoroughfares in Warsaw. They caused armoured vehicles to filter into narrow sections, where they were easily ambushed by AK fighters armed with petrol bombs. The barricades were made up of paving slabs ripped from the pavements and built up to over head height. They stopped German armoured attacks dead: enemy infantry feared to clamber over such obstructions when they would be faced in a confined space by grim and determined AK insurgents.

At 06.30 there had been a German attack on Kredetowa Street which consisted of about fifty gendarmes with armour support. The AK in the area was able to beat off this attack. Fifty minutes later the commander of 4th Region reported the presence of six enemy tanks and several armoured cars, heading towards Jerusalem Avenue from the main railway station. From the PAST building

---

44   Ibid. Document 275, pp.316-8.

there was continuous enemy fire, which was growing in intensity along Wielka Street. At 08.40 a further report from 4th Region read that objectives on Górski Street had been taken, as well as about 200 prisoners, a mixture of Germans and Kalmuks. 2nd Company, Kiliński Battalion was responsible for the taking of these prisoners as well as the capture of military equipment. In addition, they provided reconnaissance to support the Polish garrison now at the Central Post Office. Ten minutes later, the commander of 2nd Region reported that 23 Ujazedowski Avenue was clear of the enemy.

Throughout the Warsaw Uprising the question of enemy armoured support remained a problem for the AK, and was probably the determining factor for the failure of the uprising. However during the early days of the rising the AK seemed quite able to deal with armoured attacks using quite unsophisticated tactics. These included allowing the Germans to draw near, in fact too close, before opening fire on them with rifles and throwing grenades. This tactic caused panic amongst the enemy and caused them to withdraw. In one attack on an AK position at 2/4 Plac Dąbrowski the defending Poles used such tactics and fought off three tanks and two armoured cars. One of the retreating tanks gave off such thick smoke that the AK believed the vehicle had been wrecked. However in other parts of Warsaw the AK was beginning to struggle with unrelenting armoured attacks.

A telephoned report from the AK position at the Warsaw Polytechnic illustrates the problem of armoured attacks on AK positions. Lieutenant Wagner reported that since the evening of 1 August he and his men had been under sustained attack, which had continued through the night. Wagner stated that if he was expected to execute his orders successfully he would need reinforcements. Clearly there was a limit to what the under-armed and outnumbered AK units could realistically do. Fighting continued, at the PAST building, with German infantry as ever supported by armour. It was also reported that the buildings opposite PAST were on fire. A further report, received at 10.50, announced heavy fighting towards Plac Dąbrowski as enemy tanks moved up from Napoleon Square. At 2/4 Plac Dąbrowski mixed units of Germans and Ukrainians attacked the post there, but the offensive was badly conceived, sloppily delivered, and as a consequence easily repelled by the defending AK.[45]

Fighting between Poles and Ukrainians should be seen as more antagonistic than that between the AK and the regular German Army. This was all to do with the baggage of interwar history. There was bad blood between the two peoples, owing to territorial disputes and the disreputable way that interwar Polish governments and their military treated the Ukrainian minority.[46] All of this played into the hands of hard-line Ukrainian nationalists. They sided with Germany primarily as part of an anti-Soviet crusade, which at times manifested itself as an opportunistic anti-Polish campaign. This part of the Warsaw Uprising is quite ironic, given that much of it had to do with an attempt to prevent a Soviet annexation of Poland. In the short term both the Poles and Ukrainians failed to win their individual battles for national determination and were swallowed up by the Soviet empire. Both states had to wait until the early 1990s before they could re-establish sovereignty and independence.

Fighting in Warsaw continued unabated throughout 2 August, with the AK frequently taking the fight to the Germans. A report from 1st Region received at 21.45 hours reported that an AK offensive had begun earlier that afternoon at 14.00 hours, against German positions at the Brühlt Palace, the City Hall (*Ratusz*) and the Blanka Palace. It was noted that not all of the AK units involved in this offensive were sufficiently armed: however these units maintained a sustained attack on these German positions. Despite using heavy artillery, fired directly at the attacking Poles, the Germans were unable to prevent the AK from ejecting them from their positions.

---

45   Ibid. Document 276, pp.318-20.
46   Kochanski, op.cit. p.29.

There were other AK successes reported on 2 August, as at 18.10 hours a report from 4th Region gave the excellent news that the Kiliński Battalion had captured 2 Górski Street as well as the central Post Office, and were once more attacking the PAST building. The Chroby Battalion had isolated a gendarmerie unit located on the corner of Chłodna Street, while an offensive from Wola involving an entire company of SS troops supported by five tanks, was being held in check by AK units there. Further good news came in: the Łukasiński Battalion had captured three sub-machine guns, thirty-three rifles, nine hand-held anti-tank weapons, several cases of 9mm ammunition and 900 litres of petrol.

The Tłomacki Post Office fell to AK units and nine prisoners were taken; the Czarniecki Unit brought in twenty-six prisoners. It was reported that twenty-two more barricades had been built to hamper German operations while 10th Group AK had been able to advance further towards Leszno. However there was another side to the campaign, as heavy enemy machine gun fire prevented communications between 176th and 169th platoons who were trying to operate together. Furthermore several squads of German gendarmes, armed with automatic weapons, were beginning to surround Polish units in the orchards in the Leszno area. Things were beginning to look bad for the Poles but on 2 August their morale was high. There were further successes against enemy armour: AK fighters destroyed three more tanks while a fourth was very publicly ablaze on Marszałkowska Avenue, a main thoroughfare. This vehicle was able to withdraw but did so with smoke billowing from it.

At 19.50 it was reported that the telecommunications building at 45 Nowogordska Street, which AK Commanders were considering attacking, was well guarded and therefore a difficult objective to try and capture. At the same time reports were also being received to the effect that AK attacks against the two main railway stations, the central railway station and the Post Office railway station, were being repulsed and impossible to complete owing to heavy enemy fire. One bright area for the AK, though, was that communications were beginning to improve even if they often only seemed to bring bad news.

The commander of 3rd Region reported that for the first time he was able to communicate with "Golski" (Captain S. Golędzinówski) the commander of 4th Region, who reported the following: 1st Company had failed to take Fritschkaserne and so had withdrawn from the area. The report had further news, mostly mixed in fortune and confusing: there was a lack of any information about 1st Company's offensive in the Filtrów area but it was assumed that this area had been captured by the AK, however a more reliable report, not based on assertion noted that Second Lieutenant "Pługa" (Second Lieutenant J. Piętowski) the commander of 4th Company, defending the Filtrów region could not remove the German Command Post there. 1st Company under the command of Second Lieutenant J. Zborowski was attacking the Ministry of Communication buildings but could not capture it. Reports, often unreliable streamed into the AK Command Post in Warsaw. To date this offensive had cost the AK one officer killed, two fighters wounded and ten missing. The AK Group Commander, gathering as many men as possible, planned a strong offensive against the Department of Architecture building at Warsaw Polytechnic, with a battalion covering the area from Mokotówska Street to Emilia Plater Street, Lwów Street with Śniadecki and Noakowski Streets.

At 20.00 hours a further attack was launched using 2nd Platoon under the command of Lieutenant Szar, reinforcing Second Lieutenant "Andrzej" (Lieutenant K. Czyż) commander 1114th Company, at the central Post Office. They were responsible for its capture. At 22.00 hours an AK offensive was once more launched against the PAST building. The Polish attack was two-pronged: one attack by 1st Company went in via the Saxon Gardens and a second was mounted from Zielna Street. The enemy robustly defended the building, supported by three tanks, and the attack was stopped before it could gather momentum.

Polish success came from other quarters. At the same time as the attack on the PAST building was made; the Chroby Battalion stormed German gendarme units at 75a Żelana Street and forced them to withdraw to a wrecked house, which lacking a roof, was exposed to the elements. The Germans maintained their sense of discipline and so they still posted sentries around their demolished redoubt. At 02.50, in the early hours of 3 August, a report from 2nd Region (originating from 20.15 hours, 2 August) requested assistance, as the Germans were attacking a Polish position at the site of the pre-war Polish State Securities Printing Works, PWPW (*Polska Wytwórni Papierów Wartośiowych*), the site where prior to the outbreak of war important Polish documents such as passports, I.D. cards, share certificates etc were printed. Overall the situation was quiet with occasional rifle fire and German tanks patrolling enemy-held areas. Polish morale was once more reported as being good but many AK units continued to lack sufficient ammunition.[47]

Other reports received during 2 August indicated that despite the suddenness of the Polish uprising; the Germans were already beginning to understand it and work out how to respond to it. A report from 23rd Region, Mokotów Fields, concerning the progress of an AK offensive there clearly showed the use of SS troops: once the offensive began; the AK ran into heavy fire from SS troops supported by tanks and by German 88mm guns. An AK attack in 26th Region also ran into heavy enemy fire and quickly became bogged down. The fighters were left to hug the ground, unable to move either forward or back owing to the presence of enemy armour.

At 22.00 hours on 2 August the enemy went onto the offensive, coming southward from the directions of Narbut and Kazimierzowski Streets. During this time AK units such as "K" Battalion operating from the Warsaw racetrack, had not received any orders, which was a source of frustration. They were fighting blindly, not knowing the overall situation in Warsaw and what their objectives and priorities were to be.[48] An AK situation report for 2 August received at 21.00 hours revealed that the Germans were not going to give up Warsaw so easily. The report began by stating that generally the situation was difficult, but at the time the Poles were holding all the areas they had captured in the first two days of fighting. A reconnaissance patrol operating in the direction of Three Crosses Square was met with heavy enemy fire; an hour later, at 18.00 there was a report from 3rd Region that parts of Jerusalem Avenue, from the direction of the Telecommunications building and the central railway station, had been captured by the AK. Weak enemy fire was reported from around the Telecommunications building's offices but the AK was holding their newly captured positions. However, determined to recapture the building, the Germans were bringing up tanks to support their counter-offensive.

The AK met with tank fire from the corner of Hoza Street in the area of the Telecommunications building's offices on Poznań Street. Apart from the tank fire the enemy response was weak, but there was a new danger to be faced: snipers, as enemy sharpshooters fired down from the rooftops into the streets below. The Germans defended the offices at the Telecommunications building using not only regular infantry but also air force personnel deployed as infantry. This suited the AK, as they only had ninety poorly armed fighters in the area. As a consequence of the Germans also being short of infantry, the Poles were able to give a good account of themselves without receiving any casualties. It was also noted, almost as a footnote, that civilians under the direction of Polish sappers were building more barricades.[49] This was not only a practical measure as it released fighters, but also by involving civilians as much as possible they were kept from thinking about their present living standards – or the possible consequences if the uprising were to fail, as it

---

47 *Powstanie 1*, Document 277, Report from Central Warsaw, 3 August 1944, pp.320-2.
48 Ibid. Document 280, Warsaw-Mokotów, 2 August 1944, pp.324-5.
49 Ibid. Document 282, 2 August 1944, pp.324-7.

was clear that the enemy was slowly yet methodically destroying Warsaw. The Warsaw AK leadership had to keep civilian morale up as well as that of their soldiers.

As it does not suit the general historiography of the Warsaw Uprising another aspect, not often discussed, was the involvement of the 1st Polish Army, the "Berling Army". This body was later to become the Polish Peoples' Army, the military wing of the communist system in Poland between 1944 and 1989. However in late July these troops had arrived at Warsaw alongside the Red Army. It was yet another example of Poles fighting as part of a foreign army which might not necessarily having Polish interests foremost in their objectives. This sad tradition had everything to do with the loss of nationhood, and reached back to the Napoleonic Wars. The Second World War saw stateless Poles fight as part of the British armed forces from the summer of 1940, spread across the army, navy and air force. The question in the summer of 1944 was just how communist was the 1st Polish Army ?

The 1st Polish Army was nicknamed the "Berling Army" in recognition of its commander, General Zygmunt Berling and just how Communist he was is another question. Berling's career in the interwar Polish Army and his captivity would suggest that owing to professional failings he was more of an opportunist than an ideologue. Both British and Polish archival papers point towards the 1st Polish Army being "Polish patriots" rather than Communists.[50] General Wojciech Jaruzelski, the last military dictator of Poland, said in a BBC interview regarding his service in the 1st Polish Army that at first it was a matter of survival, as by joining it he was able to leave the mines where he was being used as slave labour by the Soviets after deporting him as a sixteen-year-old boy in 1939. His father had already died in the mines, so after the war Jaruzelski stayed in the Polish Army, serving as an officer, as it meant that he could provide for his widowed mother and his younger sister.[51] Even if in later years Jaruzelski was connected with doing the Soviet government's bidding in Poland (as Polish workers' revolts were frequently broke up with the use of the Polish Peoples' Army) it is interesting to find that his original cooperation with the Soviet Union was based on avoiding a premature death as a slave worker. He cannot be blamed for this, and it does raise the question of just how politically motivated the Berling Army was in 1944. However by July 1944 this army found itself on the eastern shores of the River Vistula; willing and waiting to aid their compatriots on the other side of the river, irrespective of their political loyalties and beliefs.

Operational Report no. 78 sent to the 1st Polish Army Staff at 01:00 hours 3 August reflected the situation before Warsaw from the eastern banks of the Vistula. The Poles reported that they had been under intense fire all day from artillery, mortars, and automatic weapons as well as from rifle fire. Infantry attacks, supported by mobile artillery units as well as air raids, were also reported. Quite simply there was nothing quiet about the eastern front on the Vistula at that time. Nevertheless, at 10.00 on 2 August, the soldiers of 1st Polish Army were in a position to try to cross the river, perhaps to try to aid their countrymen fighting in Warsaw.

One of the formations used to try to effect a crossing of the Vistula was a so-called "punishment company", made up of those whose lives were already forfeit, which was deployed with II/2 Infantry Regiment. Using a punishment company to undertake such a dangerous mission changes the entire way many might view this part of the Warsaw Uprising because knowing that Soviet commanders had at their disposal men whose lives could be thrown away without any question or consequence calls into question the whole nature of patriotic motivation. Corrigan notes that Soviet "penal" or "punishment" military formations were essentially suicide squads. They were

---

50   NA: FO 371/39426 C/7397/61/55, Roberts, 8 June 1944; PISM, A.XII, Papers of the Ministry of National Defence (Poland) A.XII 1/101, 'Armia Berlinga' undated.

51   'The Cold War' BBC 2, Broadcast, 26 September 1999.

often sent out as human mine detectors, simply ordered into a suspected minefield rather than having it swept, or sent out on hopeless frontal attacks.[52] After two hours of fighting both II/2 Infantry Regiment and the punishment company no longer existed: they had both been destroyed.

There were further attempts by the 1st Polish Army to establish a bridgehead on the western side of the Vistula, using elements of 4th, 5th and 6th Infantry Regiments, but the casualty rate was horrendous: 300 dead and 145 wounded.[53] But, brutally, such an operation was not in the interests of the Soviet government or the Red Army: the latter sought to avoid fighting in cities, as this was generally costly in casualties and could not be easily supported with armoured units. The Red Army might have found a way over the Vistula, but it would have been quite willing to bypass Warsaw and leave it with its German garrison stranded in the midst of its relentless westward advance, to be mopped up later. The Soviet general staff also saw the natural barrier of the River Vistula as an opportunity to rest their troops and regroup, while the Germans set about slaughtering the AK in Warsaw, saving the Soviets a task later.

Meanwhile during the first week of the uprising the AK was still reporting successes, despite the appalling circumstances they endured in their struggle against the Germans and their allies. A report from the AK Chief of Staff to the Commander of Polish Armed Forces in London observed that heavy fighting continued in Warsaw, with enemy infantry getting stronger and being supported by tanks and artillery. It was further reported that the AK had captured several strategic buildings as well as the Wola district, the Old Town and other parts of Central Warsaw: Polish flags were flown from the captured buildings. The same report observed that wrecked German vehicles and tanks, as well as enemy corpses, lay uncollected in the streets, while the AK had taken a large number of enemy prisoners. The relationship between Polish soldiers and civilians was reported as "good", with civilians aiding the military as much as they could in the fighting. A twelve-year-old boy was reported to have destroyed an enemy tank. Information was plentiful in Warsaw, as news was relayed by megaphone, with women taking a leading role in communications. However, there was a sinister sting in the overall tone of this communiqué, as it was reported that from the beginning of the uprising the main German method of striking back was to destroy both houses and the local population.[54]

In the Praga area the AK was holding down districts they had previous captured, in addition to the Eastern and Wileński railway stations, while on the Kierbędzia and Poniatowski bridges and at the Central Railway Station there had been hand-to-hand fighting. It was noted that every objective taken or attempted meant heavy and bloody losses for the Poles. Once again the AK launched an attack on the PAST building, this time via Zielna Street. Every attempt by the AK to try to clear the enemy and open communication arteries along Marszałkowska and Leszno-Wolska Streets was in vain. During the evening there was further fighting in the area the Poles were trying to clear in order to try to coordinate units and offensives. This time the fighting was against Ukrainian units, supported by tanks, in the area of 129 Marszałkowska Street. Many Ukrainians were killed in this fighting, while the Luftwaffe carried out air raids on AK positions in the north of Warsaw. In the same report there was a discussion about what was happening outside Warsaw, with a mention of fighting in south-east Poland which had met with success.[55] However what the AK Command in Warsaw was probably not aware of was that despite the successes in south-east Poland, the Soviets were disbanding any AK units they met, and murdering AK officers.

---

52   Corrigan, op.cit. p.246. The training of the Polish Army in the Soviet Union by the Red Army was at best patchy with disastrous consequences later on the battlefields of Europe. See Kochanski, op.cit. pp.380-3; p.520.
53   *Powstanie 1*, Document 288, 3 August 1944, p.332.
54   Ibid. Document 292, 3 August 1944, pp.335-6.
55   Ibid. Document 297, 3 August 1944, pp.339-40.

A further report for 3 August, sent at 0.300 hours, illustrated the problems the AK faced in their titanic struggle for Warsaw. It was not only that the Soviet government wanted to see the Warsaw Uprising fail which conspired against the Polish revolt, but also the manner in which the Germans were waging war during this operation. They were willing to stoop to some of the most disgraceful methods, calculated to cause terror and mayhem amongst the defenceless civilian population in Warsaw. Once again a report had reached the AK: twelve German tanks were moving towards the Poniatowski Bridge herding 300 Polish civilians in front of them, again being used as human shields. When the Germans had reached the bridge, their hostages were released.[56]

Towards early evening of 3 August it was becoming clear that the Germans were being forced from Praga. An observer on a roof on Szara Street reported that German infantry was withdrawing from Praga back into Warsaw itself via the Poniatowski Bridge, accompanied by a single tank and an armoured train. The infantry retreating over the bridge took full advantage of a smokescreen laid down for the purpose of covering the German withdrawal. It was also observed that a Red Cross hospital in Praga was ablaze, and that German civilians were also crossing the Poniatowski Bridge into the capital. Every two or three minutes, barges disembarked people, having just ferried them over from Praga.[57] By the third day of the uprising how to destroy it was becoming quite clear to the Germans: it was beginning to look as if the revolt was badly coordinated and seemed to be a number of small separate offensives within the city, with little chance of outside support or reinforcement.

The first German orders for a counter-offensive were given to 4th and 9th Panzer Divisions, who were ordered into battle in the Wola area. Their task was to attack the railway line there as the 74th Panzer Grenadier Regiment had previously been forced to withdraw from the district. The earliest that this German counter-offensive could begin was the following morning, 4 August.[58] The War Diary of German Army Group *Mitte* gives an insight into the German attitude towards Warsaw in the early days of the fighting. Various units, not necessarily German but loyal to the Nazi cause, were ordered into the Polish capital. As already indicated, German Army units did not always have to be deployed in large numbers in order to defeat the revolt. Instead SS-Police and SS units were used. The loss of Warsaw would have been humiliation for Germany, putting aside the issues of racism and Nazi ideology; it was a capital city and its loss a major embarrassment given events elsewhere, not only the advance of the Red Army but the western allies having already landed in France.

A telephone call at 16.15 hours on 3 August, showed the interest that Himmler had in the uprising as his personal assistant Gruppenführer Herman Fegelein (and brother-in-law to Hitler's mistress and eventual wife, Eva Braun) rang the chief of staff of Army Group *Mitte* to request information about the uprising and how best to bring in reinforcements for the German garrison in Warsaw. It was then revealed that the biggest load of rogues and murderers were on their way to the city: 2,000 men from the Dirlewanger Brigade under the command of SS Obersturmbahnführer Oskar Dirlewanger were coming from East Prussia, as well as 2,000 men from the Kamiński Brigade from Częstochowa, southern Poland. Further police personnel were also on their way to Warsaw.[59] These were not ordinary policemen but thugs who gave a whole new meaning to the concept of criminal police – they did not investigate crimes; they committed them, wholesale. Kochanski observes that the Dirlewanger Brigade were mainly recently released

56   Ibid. Document 319, 3 August 1944, p.358.
57   Ibid. Document 328, 3 August 1944, p.367.
58   Ibid. Document 334, 17:30 hours, 3 August 1944, p.371.
59   Ibid. Document 337, 3 August 1944, p.376.

criminals sent to the Wola suburb of Warsaw with the order "kill anybody you want, according to your desire".[60] And so they did.

The fighting in Warsaw grew increasingly bitter, as a Polish report for the previous day's action, dated 4 August, made clear. In contrast with the German information that their air force was limited in its operations owing to poor weather, the Poles asserted that they had been bombed all day (3 August) and into the evening by German aircraft, which had also harried Polish attacks between Jerusalem Avenue, Senator Street, Towarowa Street and Nowy Świat Street by strafing houses. During the afternoon of 4 August, the Germans were setting alight areas in Warsaw they occupied. Blazing buildings could be seen along Jerusalem Avenue and ran quite a distance from the Poniatowski Bridge to Żalazna Street, while many other fires were seen in the direction of Wiejska Street and Żelazna Brama. The fires had been started deliberately as part of the German plan to destroy the revolt. Tank and artillery fire also played their part by destroying buildings and incendiary bombs also set fire to property. The sound of detonations proved that the Germans were also using explosives to destroy buildings along Jerusalem Avenue systematically.

At 07.30 hours on 4 August, a report was received giving the very alarming news that the enemy was murdering Polish civilians. The report stated that dozens of inhabitants of a block of flats close to Aleja Marszałkowa had been seized by German gendarmes, who had broken into the flats, taken them outside and shot them in full view of their own homes. The AK decided to respond to this outrage by deploying a "Storm Section" at the flats and see what was going on in the area of the massacre. After several hours of fighting in the block, four Germans were killed and two were taken prisoner by the Storm Section. However, there was confusion as to who was actually responsible for the murders of the Polish civilians. Witnesses said that the orders were issued in German but they claimed that Ukrainians or Russians had carried out the murders.[61] The question of Ukrainians and Russians being used by the Germans in a difficult one, as Davies – for example – observes that despite a popular retelling of the Warsaw uprising which asserts that both the 14th Waffen-SS Galizien Division (the Ukrainian SS) and the Vlassovites were present in Warsaw during the uprising, neither statement is true.[62] Part of the problem is that there is confusion about the identity of Russian anti-Soviet formations such as the RONA Brigade and the Kamiński Brigade, often indentified as one and the same and at times in part deployed as such.[63] A further problem was that many Poles, when referring to anti-Soviet but Soviet citizens fighting alongside the Germans, usually referred to such people as "Ukrainians" unless they were clearly of Asiatic appearance.[64] However it is quite clear that members of the SS and their allies, whether RONA or the Kamiński Brigade, fell on hospital staff and their patients, raping the women and girls and murdering all that fell into their hands during at least the first ten days of August 1944.[65] In Ralph Smorczewski's reminiscences there is a mention of Tina Donimirski's ordeal during the Warsaw Uprising "at the hands of the thugs from the Kamiński Brigade"; there is no detail but given their reputation one can surmise what happened to a woman in their hands and only wonder how she was not murdered as well.[66] Even if the identification of the non-German personnel is not clear,

60   Kochanski, op.cit. p.406.
61   *Powstanie 1*, Document 362, 17:00 hours, 4 August 1944, pp.395-6.
62   Norman Davies, *Rising*, pp.284-6.
63   Ibid. Kochanski, op.cit. p.406.
64   Warsaw interviews with author, 16 July 2012. See also *German Crimes in Poland, Central Commission for Investigation of German Crimes in Poland*, New York, Howard Fertig, 1982 (2 Volumes bound as a single volume) pp.187-8.
65   Bożena Urbanek, *Pielęgniarki i Sanitariuszki w powstaniu Warszawskim 1944r.* Warsaw, PWN, 1988, p.158, pp.177-8.
66   IWM, 12787 03/41/1 Smorczewski, op.cit.

what is certain is that the Germans and their allies made no attempt to respect human rights at this point of the uprising. They did not even kill their victims "cleanly" but instead degraded and tormented them before finally killing them: these people should have been taken away from the battlefield at the earliest opportunity and not used as playthings for their captors to indulge their warped lack of humanity. There was the occasional break when at St. Stanisław's Hospital at 37 Wolska Street an "energetic intervention" in German by a Polish doctor, Dr. Paweł Kubic and a German, Dr. Hartlieb, prevented Reinefarth's men from killing everybody at the hospital.[67]

During the evening of 4 August a situation report was received regarding yet another AK attack on the PAST building. The offensive began early in the morning at 05.45 when a Polish pioneer section exploded a mine under the gates of the building, wrecking them in the process. The attacking AK units were then able to get to the front of the building and during the ensuing fighting the building caught fire. The Germans replied to the Polish offensive with mortars (more often referred to as mine throwers) which forced the lightly armed Poles, despite fighting well, to withdraw to safety. The Polish casualties were slight: two dead, one missing, four officers and ten fighters wounded. The PAST building remained in German hands but under Polish observation as they began to besiege it, firing the occasional harassing shots at the German defenders.

At 06.00 hours another report was received which said that Germans in 2nd Region were using human shields to cover their withdrawal. Ten minutes later the commander of 3rd Region reported that an attack on a German position at the hospital on Śniadecki Street had failed, but the AK had captured Warsaw Polytechnic and the Noakowski Hospital. However other areas of fighting such as on the junction of Sucha and Walewski Streets were proving more difficult; Poles attacking German positions there came under artillery fire from 88mm flak guns, which had caused huge casualties. In the Aleja Szucha region enormous fires were blazing, while the sound of heavy artillery could be heard clearly. At this time a more promising report came from the commander of 4th Region who was able to report the capture of the Phillips building. There was also a report that on Zydowska Street in a series of small and rolling skirmishes with the enemy, the Poles had captured an enemy ammunition dump.[68]

It has been noted that the German response to the Warsaw Uprising, especially at the beginning, was racist and ideologically based but ultimately militarily illiterate. In Warsaw unorthodox units were deployed against the AK. These units were not accustomed to having the quarry fighting back. Forczyk observes that despite intelligence gleaned in Warsaw by the Gestapo, Himmler refused to believe that there would be an uprising in the city (no doubt owing to his blinkered notion that the Germans ruled all, despite evidence to the contrary). He therefore removed several "capable" SS units stationed in Warsaw to participate in anti-partisan operations in other areas.[69] This was a curious thing to do but realistically they hunted down defenceless Jews hiding in the countryside and murdered them. They were not soldiers in any shape or form.

Earlier Hitler had issued an order altering Warsaw's status from a city to a "fortress" or *Festung*, thus *Festung Warschau*, with orders to hold the "Warsaw communications centre with all means and weapons available". However no real defensive lines were established while plans to defend the city from both AK and Soviet attacks were hampered by the lack of a unified communications system.[70] This had a profound military effect in the initial stages of the uprising. The Poles, given their extremely limited numbers and resources, were able to outperform the defending Germans, but at a horrific cost in human lives: civilians caught between the two warring sides were sacri-

---

67   Ibid. p.177.
68   *Powstanie 1*, Document 365, 18:00, 4 August 1944, pp.404-5.
69   Forczyk, op.cit. pp.35-7.
70   Ibid.

ficed in the fighting or simply murdered by the Germans and their allies. What is curious, if not surprising, was the extent that the Germans tried to use armour in the streets of Warsaw. Most tank commanders, then and now, avoid urban or built up areas if they can, as narrow streets and tanks are a lethal combination. However the use of armour in the streets of Warsaw does go some way towards explaining why the Germans burnt down entire districts of Warsaw. It not only terrorized the local population but also provided space for German armour to move over in relative safety.

During the morning of 5 August the fantastically named Herman Goering Parachute Panzer Division arrived in Warsaw to reinforce 19th Armoured Brigade.[71] Captured German documents reveal that the Hermann Goering Division was already in Warsaw by the end of July.[72] During June this division had been busy murdering Italians in reprisal for an attack against them by Italian partisans; the division was responsible for the slaughter of over 200 men as it retreated up the Val di Chiana in Tuscany.[73] It was only recently that Italian courts were able to sentence to life imprisonment nine elderly Germans, who as young men and members of the Hermann Goering Division had murdered Italians during the summer of 1944.[74]

However on 5 August the Poles were still fighting hard; capturing territory as well as taking desperately needed weapons from wherever they found them. As usual the Poles were up against Germans and Ukrainians who were "barbarically" burning down homes. As usual, they were supported by tanks.[75] A further AK report of the same day noted a strong German attack on Wolska Street, resulting in heavy fighting and causing the Poles to withdraw from their position on Działdowska Street, where the Germans had murdered sixty civilians. It was widely reported that the tanks were accompanied by Panzer Grenadiers: specialist infantry support for armour.[76]

There were further reports that in the very centre of Warsaw in broad daylight at 11.05 hours on 5 August, the Germans had taken the entire population of those still living towards the Bristol Hotel down to the Staszica Palace along Krakowskie Przedmiescie, a major thoroughfare of Warsaw, hostage. These captives were divided into two groups and placed in front of tanks. The tanks, now with their human shields, were then divided into two groups, ready to take part in operations.

A summary of the first five days of fighting was a series of failures on both sides because the Germans had not really taken the uprising seriously at first, while the biggest failure of the AK was its inability to capture any of the bridges over the Vistula.[77] The Germans, frustrated with Polish attacks, continued to vent their rage on the civilian population, mainly using the SS as their chosen tool. Goebbels ordered the execution of all 600 Polish prisoners held by the Gestapo in Warsaw. SS Polizei units, using hand grenades, murdered dozens of civilians at a Jesuit seminary. However, by the third day of the uprising Polish attacks began to peter out, owing to a lack of ammunition. Small groups of AL and the NSZ joined the uprising.

Colonel Antoni Chruściel, or "Monter", the AK commander of AK troops in Warsaw during the uprising (promoted to general, 21 September) estimated that by 3 August he had 30,000 troops available in the city but very little in the way of weapons and ammunition. On 3 August, the only Polish successes were the capture of the *Nordwache* police station in central Warsaw by Chroby I

---

71 *Powstanie 1*, Document 380, 4 August 1944, 02:30, p.419.
72 NA, HW 1/3116 – Hermann Goering Division, 27 July 1944.
73 R.J.B. Bosworth, *Mussolini*, London, Bloomsbury, 2010, p.25.
74 *The Daily Telegraph*, 10 July 2010.
75 *Powstanie Warszawskie 1944, Wybór Dokumentów*, Volume 2 Part 1, (5-7 August 1944) ed. Piotr Matusak, Warsaw, Egros, 2001, Document 11, Communiqué – Commander AK in Warsaw, nr. 24 Warsaw, 5 August 1944, p.15. Hereafter referred to as *Powstanie 2/1*.
76 Ibid. Document 17, 5 August 1944. p.23.
77 Forczyk, op.cit. p.43.

Battalion and the occupation of the abandoned Polish National Bank. On the part of the Germans there were a few tanks from 19th Division along Jerusalem Avenue, coming from the direction of the Poniatowski Bridge, but their advance was hindered by barricades and frequent ambushes. The barricades were many and served their purpose well by blocking German armoured advances. This was the main reason why the Poles devoted much of 3 August to improving these brilliant and easily defended obstacles.[78]

It was around this time that SS Police General Heinz Reinefarth arrived in Warsaw. He was sent by Himmler from Poznań, and made Chief of Operations to Erich von dem Bach-Zelewski, the German commander for the battle for Warsaw. Reinefarth brought a force of about 8,000 men, including a militarized police battalion. Some of these men had worked at the Chełmno death camp and with other of Reinefarth's retinue were to go on the rampage in Warsaw. According to Polish estimates, in their opening days in Warsaw, Reinefarth's men massacred between 30,000 and 40,000 civilians in the Wola and Ochota regions of Warsaw.[79] Reinefarth and his men, skilled in the hunting down and murder of unarmed civilians, were cruelly exposed as military incompetents once they came up against armed and determined fighters. Reinefarth sent unsupported armour into Warsaw and promptly the AK, using a *panzerfaust* – a hand-held German anti-tank weapon similar to the rocket propelled grenade launcher of today – destroyed two Tiger Mark I tanks. The Poles had found the panzerfaust abandoned by German troops.

However, the Germans were beginning to use Stuka dive-bombers (JU 87), to which the Poles had no answer. Monter, realising that the Germans were about to mount a counter-offensive; ordered the Warsaw AK to go onto the defensive. They needed to conserve ammunition in order to fight off German attacks. At this the AK had begun to demand that the allies make aerial drops of much-needed supplies.[80] On 5 August Reinefarth using 5,000 troops in the suburbs adjacent to Wola and Ochota, punched a hole in the Polish defences in an attempt to clear a route there to link up with Stahel's trapped force still at the Brulit Palace.

A consequence of Reinefarth's action was the massacre of Polish civilians already mentioned. However Reinefarth idiotically made the rookie mistake of splitting his "hunting forces" into four uncoordinated groups on a broad front moving west to east, with limited air support (which was of no consequence as the AK had no defence against aerial attacks) and some assault guns borrowed from other German units. Overall his units, now deployed as infantry, were a mish-mash of cadet officers, Luftwaffe personnel, SS-Polizei, renegade Azerbaijanis and Russians, as well as German criminals. The most important group for the Germans was the so-called *Volksdeutscher*, Germans who lived in Poland. Most of them were Polish citizens, but during the German occupation of Poland they scandalously betrayed their neighbours by claiming German identity as a benefit against local Poles. *Volksdeutscher* living in the Wola area collaborated with the Germans during the uprising and often provided them with local knowledge and worked against the AK.

Despite being numbered in thousands in nearby Wola, the AK was unable, owing to a badly deployed and feeble communications system, to intervene and prevent the massacre of Polish civilians. These massacres were also carried out by the Dirlewanger Brigade under the command of Oskar Dirlewanger (1895-1945). In spite of his apparent importance, his rank was that of a mere Oberstrurmführer (Lieutenant). He was later allegedly killed by his Polish captors at some point during June 1945, following torture and general beatings. However in Warsaw during August 1944 he was the devil incarnate. Dirlewanger and his men had been ordered to Warsaw by Himmler

---

78   Ibid.
79   Catherine Epstein, *Model Nazi: Arthur Greiser and the Occupation of Western Poland*, New York, Oxford, 2010, p.295.
80   Forczyk, op.cit. p.47.

in person in an attempt to break the morale of the insurgents by using their horrific methods of waging war. At first the Germans shot their victims on the spot but as the resulting corpses lying in the streets slowed down their military operations the captives were later removed to the rear to be murdered: thousands of people were massacred in the yard at the Ursus tractor factory just outside Warsaw. To underline the indifference of some Germans towards the Poles, it was recorded that Reinefarth, while watching columns of civilians being led away to their deaths, remarked: "this is our biggest problem. Those refugees! I don't have enough ammunition to kill them all!"[81]

Dirlewanger's Brigade rampaged through Warsaw killing hospital staff: at Wola 500 medical staff and their patients were slaughtered, followed by another 600 victims at the St. Lazarus Hospital. The horror continued as renegade Russian troops, fighting alongside the Germans, later advanced into Warsaw and joined in the mass slaughter and rape of Poles. Once more this included hospital staff and patients, this time at the Marie Curie-Skłodowska Radium Institute. An eyewitness, an AK fighter from a platoon of the "Parasol Battalion" which was defending the Wawelska redoubt, saw people in the park of the institute doused in petrol and set alight. The brutality of the Germans and their allies made the AK understand that this was to be a fight to the bitter end. At that time there was no question of surrender: there was no doubt Poles would have been murdered in a similar fashion by men who were not soldiers but thugs.

To be fair, it should be noted that regular Wehrmacht troops, consigned to support another group of criminals, the Kamiński Brigade (sometimes known as SS Sturmbrigade RONA, part of a renegade anti-Soviet group again consisting of Soviet citizens fighting alongside the Germans), were disgusted by the atrocities committed by the brigade and many Wehrmacht members refused to cooperate with them. However this is subject to revision as since the 1990s it has been found that the Wehrmacht committed many atrocities in the east. Alexander Werth, writing in 1964, observed that, because many hangings occurred in occupied territory on the first day of a German occupation prior to the arrival of police battalions, it would appear that from the outset of war on the eastern front the Wehrmacht, as well as the SS and other groups, committed atrocities.[82] There is no reason to believe that they behaved in any other way in Warsaw during the uprising. No matter who committed the war crimes in Warsaw during the 1944 uprising, they were carried out with the explicit knowledge of the German command and involved all members of the German armed forces.[83]

The Kamiński Brigade was named after a traitor Soviet general, Bronislav Kaminsky (1899-1944), who having turned against his homeland, commanded it in Warsaw. Eventually even the German authorities considered the Kamiński Brigade to be beyond the pale as they were undisciplined and unreliable. They were removed from Warsaw by late August 1944. Kaminsky himself died in mysterious circumstances. He was ordered to attend a conference in Łódź, a Polish city about an hour's drive north-west of Warsaw. He appears never to have arrived, and it is variously claimed that he was killed by Polish partisans, executed by the Germans after a trial (possibly for looting in Warsaw), or just shot out of hand by the Gestapo. Clearly he was in bad odour with everybody and his demise passed without mourning.

The massacre of Polish civilians by Reinefarth's men in Wola – 30,000–40,000 people murdered between 5-6 August – was the worst battlefield atrocity committed in Europe during the course of the Second World War. The consequence of German atrocities was to drive Polish civilians to support the AK and the fight for Warsaw. They might have done so reluctantly but they had nothing to lose and possible everything to gain. Reinefarth was never to pay for his crimes. He was

---

81   Ibid. pp.52-5.
82   Werth, op.cit. p.376.
83   *German Crimes in Poland*, pp.187-8.

always able to evade justice, despite numerous attempts to have him extradited to Poland to face a criminal investigation into his wartime activities. Instead after the war Reinefarth was to enjoy life in West Germany and have a reasonably successful political career there. As early as 1951 he was elected Mayor of Westerland on the island of Sylt. In 1962 he was elected to the Schleswig-Holstein state parliament. He died at home in 1979.[84] Clearly he was a man of no conscience, and the world allowed him to move on. Warsaw was not London or Paris and certainly not New York, it was not even Dresden. Some cities simply fail to make an impact on humanity's collective conscience.

Bach-Zelewski, the German commander in Warsaw, realised that the very public atrocities being committed there were creating a problem for the German offensive as the Poles were resisting in spite of German actions. As a result he changed his tactics regarding civilian prisoners. Instead of very public mass murders, Polish women and children were not routinely slaughtered but sent to a concentration camp recently established at Pruszków just outside Warsaw. Men were still being murdered in the capital. The AK leadership in Warsaw was slow to keep pace with events in the city and very quickly began to lose territory they had captured during the first six days of fighting. No doubt as a result of Reinefarth's murderous onslaught, between 6 and 11 August the districts of Wola and Ochota were lost to the Poles, while during the period of 8-19 August after very heavy fighting the Germans were able to recapture the Old Town district.[85]

Overground movement was becoming extremely hazardous for the AK once the Germans began to regain the initiative in Warsaw. It was during this period, on 6 August, that they began to explore using the Warsaw sewage system as a method of moving around the city. At the same time new tactics were beginning to evolve, brought about by the difficulties of fighting in such a limited area of operations. The Poles ran a telephone line through the sewers in order to connect Monter's HQ in the city centre to that of Bór-Komorowski, located in the Old Town. The Germans in turn had learnt hard lessons, such as that frontal attacks on Polish barricades made from paving stones were futile and costly in casualties. To deal with such obstructions, the Germans developed the "Goliath" remote-controlled miniature tank. Each tank was about three feet long and about a foot high and a foot wide. It was packed with high explosives, directed at the barricades and exploded remotely with the intention of destroying the barricades. The AK swiftly learnt that the way to deal with the Goliaths was to attack the remote control cables with hand grenades and so immobilize them.[86] Davies notes the actions of a child fighter, aged twelve and fighting illegally for the AK, who died on the barricades of Warsaw. His specialization was to crawl through rubble whilst under fire in order to cut the control cables of Goliaths.[87]

An incident at this point of the history of the Warsaw Uprising point to the Germans' wealth of combat experience, compared with that of the AK. The Germans appeared to have abandoned a light tank and the AK assumed that they had captured it. Members of the "Gustav" Battalion drove their trophy back to Bór-Komorowski's HQ on Kiliński Street. Once there, hundreds of soldiers and civilians swarmed around it. Then a 500 kg charge inside of exploded and killed 100 soldiers of the "Konrad" Battalion, twenty from the "Wigry" Battalion and about 200 civilians.[88] This tragedy could have been prevented if the Poles had had a little more experience of warfare instead of plotting. Furthermore the AK commanders in Warsaw underestimated the Germans on the Russian front (of which by then Warsaw was a part,) booby-trapped items were a feature everywhere, but the Poles were yet to learn this lesson.

---

84   Epstein, op.cit. p.338.
85   Forczyk, pp.52-5.
86   Ibid.
87   Norman Davies, *Europe at War, 1939-1945: No Simple Victory*, London, Pan, 2007, p.373.
88   Forczyk, op.cit. pp.60-1.

It was not only the AK who had to learn the harsh lessons of war. Reinefarth and his thugs were also learning some of the reality of fighting in an urban space, and of fighting an enemy who shoots back. Reinefarth and his men were more used to murdering unarmed civilians. After attacking the Old Town for a week Reinefarth had little to show for his efforts as German armour could not operate in the narrow streets. Whenever they engaged in street fighting against the AK; the German casualty rate was in the region of 25-30%. The German decision to burn down the Old Town using Stuka and artillery attacks achieved nothing while the AK drove off every German infantry attack in additional to the aerial and artillery attacks as mentioned. Each failed German attack meant new weapons for the AK, as whenever the Germans withdrew from a position they had been holding, they had a tendency to abandon their equipment (which suggests that they were unlikely have been regular German troops). This was then taken by the AK, however they still remained extremely vulnerable in open fighting, as they were still outnumbered and under-armed.[89] The inability of Reinefarth to make any immediate military impact in Warsaw was confirmed, perhaps prematurely, in the War Diary of 9th German Army, dated 4 August (which also confirms his presence in the city).[90]

To illustrate how well-armed the enemy was can be illustrated in an undated report from the Ochota region. This relates that a Polish patrol had observed that a group of German infantrymen were all armed with automatic weapons, while elsewhere it was noted that regular German troops were supported by Ukrainian and other auxiliary troops. Later the same evening, an armoured column consisting of dozens of Panther tanks and large numbers of armoured cars were seen moving towards the fighting in Warsaw. Once in position these tanks began to shell the Post Office railway station and destroyed barricades there. The AK damaged several tanks, but eventually the enemy captured the railway line though not the station itself. A further dozen or so tanks moved from Jerusalem Avenue to Starynskiewicz Square then to Nowogradski Street.

In contrast an AK patrol located towards the Poniatowski Bridge noted that there was no activity in that area and that the Praga area was very quiet. There were not even fires. It was obvious that the Red Army and the Germans were not fighting and that the AK would not get any help from the Soviets. Away from Praga Polish patrols in the Mokotów area, moving in the direction of Jerusalem Avenue, noted the presence of Tiger tanks while large areas of this district were on fire as the Germans systematically torched buildings in order to deny Poles cover and shelter. One patrol had failed to return, and it was considered that its members had all been killed, as there had been heavy enemy fire at the time the patrol had started out.[91] Polish intelligence reports also pointed to the huge numbers of infantry the Germans were deploying, as well as the large quantities of armour available to them. A report of 4 August concerning the Fort Bem area discussed the fact that 1,800 enemy infantrymen, supported by thirty Tigers, were being deployed against the AK in the direction of the former Jewish ghetto. There were also air raids for which there was no defence.[92]

An hourly Polish intelligence service report from the city centre and Powisła on 5 August could only confirm a litany of destruction by the Germans and their allies. The Poles could only look on in disbelief.

At 08.00 on 5 August locals reported that the Germans were building a pontoon bridge over the Vistula to move units from the eastern side to the western shores and into Warsaw ready to fight. The Germans remained confident that even if there were some artillery fire from the Soviet side

---

89   Ibid. p.61.
90   *Powstanie 1*, Document 384, pp.425-7.
91   *Powstanie 2/1*, Document 18, pp.23-4.
92   Ibid. Document 26, pp.31-2.

of the river or as the Polish report had it the "Bolshevik side" they could still complete complex exercises such as bridge building relatively unhindered.[93] This was obviously bad news for the AK as quite clearly the Germans were able to complete relatively complicated military manoeuvres, which could have been totally disrupted by accurate and determined Soviet artillery fire from their positions across the river at Praga. At this stage it was not in the interests of the Soviet government to destroy the Germans, as the Germans were destroying the AK, which – as already discussed – was needed to make sure of a Soviet annexation of Poland. Davies observes that if the AK had remained intact they might have well have had the power to have brought the Soviets to the negotiation table regarding the post-war situation in Poland.[94]

---

93   Ibid. Document 28, Hourly Situation Reports, 5 August 1944, pp.83-4.
94   Davies, *Rising*. p.458.

4

A Declining Situation

Even if the Warsaw Uprising seemed upbeat at the outset it is evident that it was badly prepared, badly executed and from the very first day was obviously going to end in catastrophe for the Poles and for Poland. However there was more at stake for some of the AK leadership than mere Polish independence: there was also post-war power for them if the uprising was successful.[1] Alan Clark observed as long ago as 1965 that the various underground movements began fighting each other during the first week of August.[2] It is not surprising that the Warsaw Uprising failed when even in the face of national destruction the Polish political-military circles still took time out to fight each other for power – the curse of a politically underdeveloped country.

After a week of fighting it was blatantly obvious that the uprising was going nowhere, even if the Germans had initially been caught off guard. Within a few hours the Germans had recovered and began to retaliate in the most brutal ways imaginable; however they were yet to commit themselves to an all-out offensive on Warsaw. The Germans did not really consider their counter-offensive as an orthodox military measure but more of an anti-partisan operation, illustrated by the calibre of troops brought into the city at the beginning of the uprising. The German response only became more military once it became clear that their brutal methods were actually working against them as they sought to put down the revolt swiftly and efficient. However the worst mistake was made by the Poles, who expected that the Red Army and the Soviet government would come to their aid.[3] Indeed it was noted by the Poles in Warsaw that just before midnight on 7 August, there was a deadly silence on the Soviet Front.[4]

A Red Army intelligence officer, Konstantin Kalugin, who had been sent by the Soviet authorities to establish contact with the AK in Warsaw, described the Poles as putting up a heroic fight. After familiarizing himself with the general situation in the Polish capital, he was able to provide the Soviet authorities with an urgent list of needs required by the beleaguered Polish garrison. Kalugin made the case for the AK to be supplied with automatic weapons, ammunition, grenades and anti-tank weapons. He even gave his reasoned views of how and where the Soviets could drop by air the weapons necessary for the continuation of the Polish uprising.[5]

Kalugin's report was reinforced by messages from a British airman, Sergeant (later Lieutenant) John Ward, who had been shot down earlier in the war, escaped from a POW camp and had been a member of the AK since 1941. During the uprising Ward was able to make reports to the outside world from Warsaw. These accounts reached the British War Cabinet; some were also published in *The Times*. Even if Ward was optimistic in his evaluation of the fighting in Warsaw he correctly reported on 7 August the events of 6 August inasmuch as the "greatest part of the

---

1   Anne Applebaum, *Iron Curtain. The Crushing of Eastern Europe, 1944-1956*, London, Allen Lane, 2012, p.119.
2   Clark, op.cit. p.391.
3   Applebaum reflects that the Poles were not alone in their naivety and considers that the East Europeans were all guilty of assumption about allied motivations as the war drew to an end. Applebaum, op.cit. p.23.
4   *Powstanie 2/1*, Document 122, 23:00, 7 August 1944, p.129.
5   Ibid. Document 62, 6 August 1944, pp.67-8.

City is in Polish hands" and that Warsaw had "excellent chances"; he also made a request for the urgent dispatch of weapons and ammunition. The opening sentence of his report laid bare the brutality of the Germans. Ward wrote that at 5 pm yesterday German tanks of 'Tiger' type came through the streets of Warsaw with captured Polish female civilians tied on to the tanks to prevent attacks from Polish troops. One German tank was destroyed with a petrol bomb owing to the lack of anti-tank guns.[6] Zagorski records that there was a whole plethora of nationalities and beliefs fighting alongside the AK including other "Englishmen"; he also noted the beginning of famine in southern Warsaw.[7]

Ward's reports should be treated with an element of caution as in his debriefing with M.I.9 (British Military Section 9) which dealt with Allied prisoners of war and escapees he made it quite clear that his movements as he tried to monitor the situation in and around Warsaw were hampered. This was due to the ebb and flow of the fighting but overall his reports, transmitted in code, give a vivid picture of the situation, as did his broadcasts in English from Warsaw.[8] SOE reports reinforced Ward's words as a report on the first week of fighting in Warsaw noted on 5 August that the character of the battle was changing owing to the lack of arms: this had caused a lessening of AK attacks unless an objective was considered to be achievable. It was further noted that from the very beginning of the uprising the Germans had driven civilians in front of their tanks.[9] Via Ward, the Poles did indeed have a voice which mattered coming out of Warsaw during the uprising.

Finally the penny began to drop: the British government understood why the Soviet government was not helping the AK in Warsaw. It was not in their interests to do so. The British Foreign Secretary, Anthony Eden, wrote to Winston Churchill: "It occurred to us, and of course to the Poles themselves, that the Russians may be delaying the occupation of Warsaw in order that the Germans should liquidate a large number of patriots during the present uprising in that city who might later on be troublesome to the Russians. I have enquired of the War Office whether there is any military reason for the Russian delay in the capture of Warsaw and am told that the Germans are making great efforts to hold this nodal point in their communications and that they have surrounded and annihilated a Russian armoured force which was advancing on that city. This, if true, does put Stalin in a slightly better light, although it is odd that he did not say so in his message to you!"[10]

It is obvious from the above exchange and others before and after that the British government believed little, if anything, that the Soviet government said. It certainly did not trust Stalin at all but was forced by the circumstances of the war against Germany to try and maintain publicly a united front with the Soviet Union: this was frequently at the expense of the exiled Poles. Churchill was also to receive a letter from the Polish President in exile, Władysław Raczkiewicz, who cited a message from the Polish commander in Warsaw, General Bór-Komorowski. He gave a detailed assessment of the situation in Warsaw, including that of the Soviets, and it is worth quoting:

> The character of the fight in Warsaw is changing owing to a shortage of ammunition so we
> must limit the action of our detachments to the securing of points needed for the improve-
> ment of our position and the maintenance of initiative in our hands. Barricades in the streets

---

6   Warsawuprising.com/.../dispatches_pri... accessed 30 March 2011.
7   Zagorski, op.cit. pp.43, 151.
8   Royal Air Force Museum Archives, Colindale, London NW9, File X002-9271/002 appendix C. M.I.9/S/
    P.G. (P) 2930. Escaper's name – 542939 Sgt. Ward, John George, 226 Sqn. Bomber Command R.A.F. Date
    of Interview, 22 March 1945.
9   NA: HS (SOE) HS4/159, 5 August 1944.
10 NA: PREM 3, Prime Minister's Papers, PREM 3/352/12, P.M./44/580, Eden to Churchill, 8 August 1944.

are numerous and elaborate. There is mass production of incendiary bottles (petrol bombs) for use against armour. Our detachments which have evacuated from Zoliborz have returned to action. There is a great dearth of commanders as many were killed in the first phase of the fight and also a lack of arms. On August 3 we partly extended our hold in the southern part of the city and in the centre, the western part is almost entirely in our hands. The bridges over the Vistula and the main railway station changed hands several times at the cost of big losses on both sides. They are now in German hands. The "eastern" and the Wilenski railway stations remain in our hands. The attempt by the enemy to gain mastery over the arterial communications, Leszno and Wolska Streets and Marszalkowska Street failed. The enemy has with great effort secured freedom of movement along the Jerusalem Avenue and Grojecka Street. The enemy is increasingly basing his operations on heavy tanks driving the civilian population in front of them and on both sides of the tanks by way of protection (i.e. humans shields). The Germans are burning down all the houses in Jerusalem Avenue from Nowy Swiat to Marszalkowska Street. The inhabitants of the burnt houses are rounded up by the Germans and marched off in an unknown direction. On the evening of August 3 big fires spread in the city. The Germans are using bombing planes. The BBC in London gave incorrect information regarding the alleged co-operation of the Red Army and the Home Army in the fight for Warsaw. No Contact could be so far established (with the Red Army) and to date we have received no help from the Red Army in our fight.[11]

A few days later Bór-Komorowski wrote to General Tabor, nom-de-guerre of Stanisław Tatar (1896-1980), who had been an AK commander and had been involved in the planning of "Operation Tempest". Just before the uprising had begun Tabor was brought to London to assume the post of Deputy Commander-in-Chief for Home Affairs and he made this assessment of the situation in Warsaw:

We begin the sixth day of the battle of Warsaw. The Germans are introducing into the fight technical means we do not possess – armour, artillery, flame-throwers. That is their advantage – we dominate them by the morale of our troops. I state solemnly that Warsaw in fighting does not receive assistance from the Allies, as Poland did not receive it in 1939. Our alliance with Great Britain has resulted only in bringing her assistance in 1940 in repelling the German attacks against the British Isles, in fighting in Norway, in Africa, in Italy and on the Western Front. We request that you state this fact before the British is an official démarche; it should remain a document. We do not ask for equipment – we demand its immediate dispatch.[12]

This was probably one of the more foolish statements of the Polish wartime canon of hyperbole as it clearly ignored the reality of the situation in 1944. It also exaggerates and misrepresents the Polish role in the Second World War. The roles mentioned were minor ones in much larger campaigns, including the Battle of Britain. This was a British Empire victory, largely due to the sacrifice of young British, British Empire and Dominion pilots, some hardly out of their teens, defending their homeland or mother country. It should be noted that the magnificent stand of the First Polish Armoured Division at Mount Ormel, which decided the Normandy campaign, was yet to take place. Tabor, instead of trying to castigate the British should have considered just how Poland had arrived at such a situation. This would have meant having to consider twenty years of interwar neglect of the Polish Army after 1921, a military coup in 1926 followed by a

---

11   NA: PREM 3/352/12, Raczkiewicz to Churchill, 5 August 1944.
12   NA: CAB 80 Chiefs of Staff Memorandum, CAB 80/86, C.O.S. (44) 704 (0) 7 August 1944.

military dictatorship and then after 1935 a quasi-fascist dictatorship. This was also accompanied by a foreign policy which was too close to Nazi Germany, and which rebounded adversely against Poland after March 1939, when Hitler began to make territorial demands on Poland regarding the Free City of Danzig and West Prussia. Furthermore, during the autumn of 1938 Poland, with Germany and Hungary, had participated in the dismemberment of Czechoslovakia. It was just as well that Tabor's words were kept as a document and not widely broadcast. They would have caused the exiled Poles further hurt and difficulties as they continued to lose their political battle against the massive influence of the Soviet government on British affairs.

Prior to the outbreak of war the Poles had acquired very few friends, while the Warsaw Uprising appeared to be yet another case of Polish folly. However, the Allies (not including the Soviet Union), were still willing to aid Poland in spite of unfair and untrue comments such as Tabor's. The main point was that even though the Germans were putting down the rising with every available modern weapon and deploying the most brutal of troops, the Poles had very little room for argument. They had been foolish enough to listen to Soviet entreaties to rise up broadcast by radio, while previously (and quite correctly) had disbelieved anything that the Soviets had ever said. Not only was it a case of folly but also extremely curious. Why did the AK leadership in Warsaw choose to listen to, and believe the Soviets at that particular time? Even if everything seemed to have been in favour of the Poles: the Germans only "appeared" to be leaving Warsaw; equally the Red Army "appeared" to be on the eastern side of the Vistula at Praga. Perhaps the Warsaw AK should have stayed its hand to see if the Germans were indeed going, which was the popular perception amongst Poles in the capital.

And so the Poles continued to defend themselves, using ancient or stolen hand weapons and attacking enemy tanks with petrol bombs. As the AK headed towards a second week of fighting, the situation was not brilliant. A Polish message of 7 August noted that things were getting worse and that the Germans were continuously on the offensive; firing from the ground and air without let or hindrance from the "Bolsheviks".[13] Another report of the same day was received at 09.20 on 7 August. It concerned a German offensive, which had begun at 23.00 on 6 August, and stated that there was a determined attack on 1st Group's barricades on Miodów Street. According to journal entries this was the fifty-second attack on this group: once more it was able to hold its position successfully and cause the enemy, though supported by armoured cars, to withdraw. Throughout the same night there was continuous tank action "as usual" in the direction of the Kierbedz Bridge, while around six to eight Tiger tanks moved towards the bridge. Throughout the day Poles had been patrolling this area while patrols passing through warehouses in the grounds of Leszno Street Hospital had had several gun battles with marauding Ukrainians. However the story for the AK remained the same: lack of ammunition for weapons, especially automatic weapons, and the loss of fighters including two entire companies: "*Genowefa*" and "*Gertrude*". They were personnel that the AK could ill afford to lose.

The Warsaw AK saw some relief on 6 August. It was reported that at 06.00 from the southwest of Warsaw about twenty transport planes, probably American, had dropped equipment in the direction of Zoliborz. Three hours later, from the south, a further twenty-two planes dropped equipment. However this was the only good news for the day, as heavy fighting continued on the ground. The AK also discovered from a German military doctor that Wehrmacht units were withdrawing from Warsaw, but their withdrawal was being covered by a division of anti-Soviet Cossacks, about 10,000 in number and complete with artillery, who had also been given the task of erasing Warsaw from the face of the earth. Further information came from a Polish woman whose brother worked for the Gestapo. The woman managed to phone a warning to the AK that

---

13   *Powstanie 2/1*, Document 122, 7 August 1944, p.129.

during the night of 6-7 August or on the morning of 7 August Warsaw was to be bombarded – a clear indication of a coming offensive against the city.[14]

The relationship between the Gestapo brother and the Polish patriot sister must have been an interesting one and should be noted. Loyalties were clearly divided here as the brother was a traitor but still loyal to his sister, who was obviously devoted to her country as she shared her information with the Polish Underground. If the Germans had discovered her, she would have been without doubt been tortured and later murdered by the Gestapo. One can only assume that her brother was unaware of her AK links or was perhaps having a crisis of conscience. The same message noted that on 4 August, during fighting around the *Sejm* (the Polish parliament building), the enemy withdrew from the area but left the building in flames. It was also clear that the Sejm Hotel was a central ammunition magazine from which tanks were being supplied, and as a consequence was defended furiously by the Germans, consisting of about 200 SS and German military police. During the evening of that day the AK sent out patrols to try to find out what was happening in the area; German tanks were discovered nearby while the enemy was busily engaged in murdering Polish civilians. A further group of about 300 Polish civilians were being held under armed guard; their fates yet to be determined.[15]

At 06.00 on 7 August, the Germans attacked to the north of the city centre. This attack lasted until 14.00. Once again it was an infantry offensive supported by armour; the infantry were mainly units of German gendarmes and not regular Wehrmacht. At that time the Germans still regarded the uprising as an insurgency and not the full-blown military offensive which in fact it was, because the AK lacked the heavy weaponry and aircraft normally associated with a conventional military campaign. The German gendarmes were deployed in small groups of twelve to eighteen men, supported by Ukrainians. The attacks were mainly in the Hal Mirowski region but were later repelled and confined to a single area, where there was fierce fighting. It appeared that the main German objective of this local offensive was to open up an artillery communication line between the Kierbedz Bridge and Wola. The result was that the Germans did not try to attack the crossing at Chłodna Street and only attempted to occupy Chłodna, Ogrodowa and Krochmalan Streets. The Poles, using three "Storm Units", unceasingly continued to attack the Germans, who were trying to withdraw from the area; at 02.30 there was a further attack by the Poles. The Polish casualty rate was surprisingly light – one dead and four wounded. The enemy suffered thirty-seven dead.

An AK patrol consisting entirely of officers under the command of Lieutenant "Konrad" with an independent unit, whose operational purpose was to set out to reconnaissance territory ahead and were more or less allowed to operate independently of the main AK formations, set out to discover the situation in central Warsaw. They found there were a number of German units contained in an area running along Jerusalem Avenue, Marszalkowska Street to Plac Unii, Lubelski Street and along Aleja Niepodległości (Independence Avenue). They noted that a municipal building, Dom Pracy (Labour House) was in enemy hands while the main fire station was in Ukrainian possession. Along Aleja Szucha there were seven tanks, 300 Ukrainians and 200 SS and gendarmes. Everywhere it was evident that the area was dominated by heavily armed troops supported by armour. By this point it was noted that AK patrolling was reconstructed, not only because of the perennial shortage of weapons but also by the fact that the enemy was recovering territory. This was beginning to contain the Poles in ever-tightening areas that were getting smaller by the day. Even so, some of the Polish patrolling was quite daring: one patrol from 1118 Company AK,

---

14   Ibid. Document 187, 7 August 1944, pp.185-7.
15   Ibid.

while operating in these difficult circumstances, was able to work at the rear of Wehrmacht units. Increasingly, though, many parts of Warsaw were rapidly becoming no-go areas for the AK.[16]

Reports of German movements from Praga gave quite a disturbing picture. It seemed that the Germans were able to move quite freely over the River Vistula, without attracting much attention from the Red Army supposed to be holding Praga. Over a two-day period (7-8 August) the following were noted: 07.00 – coal barges moving from Praga; 11.00–12.00 – twelve armoured cars and three tanks moved; 15.00 – a car and tank; 15.30 – one locomotive, an armoured train wagon and three lorries; 8 August, 07.30 – twenty-four empty railway wagons; 11.35 – five Pullman coaches, while via the Średnicowy and Poniatowski Bridges, six railway wagons crossed the Vistula at separate times from Praga.[17]

One can only wonder just why the Red Army allowed this volume of traffic across the Vistula? The Polish report makes no suggestion that the Red Army tried in any way to interfere with these movements. It was just another example of how the Soviet government saw fit to ignore events in Warsaw, and allow the Germans a freedom of mobility that ensured their attacks on the AK continued. An example was an attack during the night of 7-8 August, which began at 22.00 with an enemy infantry attack supported by an armoured car; the AK was able to destroy the vehicle and broke up the offensive. At 03.00 on 8 August the "Radosław" group attacked a German armoured train, with the intention of destroying it. This offensive was a failure and left the Poles with six dead, two wounded and two light machine guns lost. It was obvious that the section of railway track along which the armoured train ran was much more heavily defended than the AK had anticipated.

Throughout the night German tank movements were noted across the Kierbedz Bridge area. It was thought that there were probably between six to eight Tiger tanks operating in that area. At 06.00 the enemy attacked the "Radosław" group's barricade at the junction of Żytnia and Karolkowska Streets. In total there were four attacks against this position, which left the enemy with fourteen dead. They withdrew quickly after their final sortie failed. Later the offensive continued, with artillery support from the west.

At 11.30 the "Radosław" group beat off an attack from the direction of Karolkowska Street and fifteen minutes later further assaults were being launched from the direction of the Evangelical Cemetery. Observations from along the Wolska-Chłodna route were impossible owing to the dense smoke obscuring the area. Further heavy fighting continued throughout Warsaw with the usual consequences: the Germans shelling and burning properties and their use of human shields to protect armour, while the AK were fighting desperately and making small gains; capturing a few weapons but in the main outmanned, outgunned and running out of options.

Despite this the morale of AK units remained high, even if they complained bitterly about the lack of ammunition and that the expected aerial drops for the night had failed to arrive. However, civilians were becoming more agitated. Many had been burnt out by the Germans while others had to share the little they had with the victims of German atrocities, who were left with nothing.[18] The decision to revolt in Warsaw during 1944 was a total and utter disaster for the Polish civil population. They had to endure the worst, without the necessary means to defend themselves. They had no say in the decisions being made by the AK commanders, which were wrecking their lives unnecessarily. As ever in war, the rights of civilians had been suspended.

---

16   *Powstanie Warszawskie 1944 Wybór Dokumentów Okres Przejściowy, 8 – 10 VIII 1944r*. Volume 2 Part 2, ed. Piotr Matusak, Warsaw, Egros, 2002, hereafter referred to as *Powstanie 2/2*, Document 230, 8 August 1944, pp.57-8.
17   Ibid. Document 236, 8 August 1944, pp.62-3.
18   Ibid. Document 246, Old Town, Warsaw, 8 August 1944, pp.70-1.

The ammunition shortage became more acute as a report from Żoliborz for 8 August made quite clear. On the slopes of the Citadel an AK reconnaissance patrol saw that in one enemy position on Krajewski Street there were between thirteen and fifteen heavy machine guns, as well as seven 88mm anti-tank guns on the railway bridge. At the Gdansk railway station about forty enemy soldiers were seen, as well as an armoured train and a railway wagon complete with artillery pieces fitted out as a mobile artillery platform. At the Institute of Chemistry there were about 200 Ukrainian troops armed with anti-tank guns and heavy machine guns as well as five 88mm artillery pieces. Further heavy machine guns were seen at Burakowa Street. It was considered by AK commanders that to try to capture the Gdansk Station was extremely dangerous, owing to its strong defences. The author of the report was quite clear in his opinion that any such offensive against such German positions was more or less impossible owing to the AK's lack of ammunition.[19]

However despite the shortage of ammunition the AK maintained their campaign as a message from the Old Town, originating at 09.30 on 9 August 1, stated that an AK position, with twenty-three fighters, had come under an armoured attack. Very quickly the defenders managed to destroy one of the attacking tanks, probably with a petrol bomb.[20] On 8 August at 16.00 hours it was reported that Polish outposts at the Royal Castle had managed to capture two armoured cars. However, reconnoitering during the night established that, because of the perennial lack of ammunition, the AK lacked the resources for an offensive against the enemy even using the captured armoured cars. In consequence the AK destroyed both vehicles.

Throughout the night there were further enemy offensives throughout Warsaw, including an armoured attack at 22.00 against barricades at Miodówa and Senator Streets. In this assault the Germans used Tiger tanks, accompanied by heavy mortar fire. At 03.00 hours there was a heavy artillery barrage and an air raid, both against the Old Town. While this was taking place, a group of SS and Kalmyk soldiers, thirty to forty in number, advanced through the ruins of houses on Senator and Miodówa Streets and attacked the Polish barricades on Miodówa from the rear. Cadet Officer Firlej with four soldiers beat this attack off: it left the enemy with one dead and one wounded. Throughout the same night the State paper factory was shelled from enemy positions still located in the Praga area: about twenty shells landed. In the morning at 10.00 the armoured train located at Gdansk Station also began to shell the factory. It was around this time that messages to the effect that AK positions in besieged areas were out of ammunition began to arrive once more. These reports were from people almost begging for more ammunition.[21]

A report to the commander of the German Ninth Army to the Army Group *Mitte* on 9 August reveals how the Germans saw the situation in Warsaw. The conclusion of the report was that the uprising was actually intensifying.[22] It was probably not clear to the Germans at this stage just how desperate the AK was for ammunition supplies. What was clear though was that they were enduring very high losses in men and armour, which surprised them. The Germans remarked on Polish improvisation, and their own inability to "round up" the so-called insurgents. This report expressed the fear that the rising might spread further, which suggested that the Germans might have considered that their tactics of terror and murder were not working. However they were not privy to the fact that within a week there were two aspects of the Warsaw Uprising working against each other: the unrealistic jingoism of the AK, especially its High Command in Warsaw, and the

19   Ibid. Document 250, Warsaw, 8 August 1944, pp.74-5.
20   Ibid. Document 331, p.159.
21   Ibid. Document 332, Old Town, Warsaw, 9 August 1944, p.159.
22   Ibid. Document 354, Report from Commander of 9th German Army to Commander Army Group *Mitte* on the Situation in Warsaw, 9 August 1944, p.182.

agitation of the civilian population, who had to endure the madness and mass murder which the uprising had produced.

In order to fight back, the Germans had been forced to fight in the streets of a large city, thus causing their very high casualty rate. The Germans more or less admitted that their strength at the beginning of the uprising was not enough to defeat the AK.[23] One can only wonder whether if the AK had received outside aid, especially from the Soviets, it might have been possible for them to have driven the Germans from Warsaw during the first week of the uprising? This possibility was reinforced by the messages sent to London by John Ward, as noted earlier. However history has no business with "ifs" and "buts": it is a brutal subject and can only comment on what actually happens.

It was not only the acute lack of ammunition that worried AK commanders. The growing shortage of suitable fighters was beginning to try them as well. At the same time the Germans were reinforcing their positions. From the late morning of 10 August and for several hours to follow, a seemingly unending motorized column came from the west – in stark contrast to the single company of infantry, which came from the Saxon Gardens. The Poles at a position at Wolska Street came under heavy fire from the direction of Młynarski Street and Bem Street. Every entrance to the AK position at Chłodna Street also came under heavy fire, but this did not deter the continuing construction of barricades at the junction of Wrona Street with Łuck and Prosta Streets. AK authorities noted that a lack of commanders and ammunition whilst under rocket fire was a constant worry. A further problem was that of civilians, burnt out by the enemy and with nowhere to live, started to take up residence around barricades and AK positions. Meanwhile the enemy, using local people as forced labour, reinforced their positions on Krochmalan Street at the junction with Wrona Street, and on Grzybowski Street at the Towarowski Street turning. A Polish report about the same area claimed that from19.00 on 8 August until 14.00 on 10 August, the noise of battle and bombardment could be clearly heard. Ciepła Street was under very heavy fire from a nearby fire brigade tower, which was being used as a firing position. From his position at 28 Grzybowski Street Lieutenant "Janusz", in a section of Krochmalan Street still in Polish hands (though this position was under artillery fire), noted that the sector between Chłodna and Krochmalan Streets was basically "no-man's-land".

A Polish report of 10 August from the Old Town made the position there very clear. It opened with an account of the fighting around Gdansk Station and Okopowa Street. Overall the situation had not changed; orders for attacks on the station were received. In preparation for this offensive the station and railway line was reconnoitred. Also, there was an abortive attempt to set the station on fire. At the same time, the enemy launched a heavy attack supported by armour along Okopowa and Spokojna Streets. The AK managed to disrupt this attack after setting fire to an armoured car and destroying a German tank as well as managing to capture weapons.

Artillery fire from an armoured train had started in the early hours of the same morning and shells had rained down on the Old Town from north to south and into parts of the former Jewish ghetto, burnt out since the previous year following the unsuccessful Jewish revolt. The AK was able to establish from prisoners that there were two armoured trains in Warsaw. Both were armed with a huge artillery piece as well as other guns and were crewed by about 150 personnel. Ward described the horrors of 11 August: "Despite all efforts of the AK the Germans were continuing their ruthless terror methods." He described how the Germans had burnt down whole streets of houses and shot all of the men who lived in them while turning the women and children into the streets. Ward recorded that in one house in Krolewska Street where elderly retired professors from a number of Polish universities lived, SS troops forced their way in and killed several of them – but

---

23   Ibid.

not before some of them were able to escape through cellars into other houses. Ward claimed that at this point of writing the morale of the AK and of the civilian population was of the "highest standard" and the watchword was "death to the Germans".

Ward related that during the night of 10-11 August German tanks made a "determined effort" to aid some of their strong points around Warsaw. He spoke well of the Polish barricades, which were built on every street corner and made mainly of concrete paving slabs ripped up from the streets. On the whole the German offensives failed, and often tank crews vented their frustration by setting fire to houses while shelling others from a distance. He also noted that the Germans, in obvious acts of desecration, set fire to Polish corpses lying in the streets, but were beginning to have respect for the Polish barricades " ... for they knew that behind each one wait determined troops of the AK with petrol bottles (bombs). The same petrol bottles that have caused the destruction of many of their comrades." Ward also asked for various types of weapons to be sent to Warsaw: anti-tank weapons, grenades, rifles, machine guns, pistols and ammunition. He made the case that anti-tank weapons were of extreme importance to the AK because without them the Polish fighters could not engage tanks at a range greater than fifteen yards. He also advised where weapons would be of the most use: Jerusalem Avenue, Emilia Plater Street, Noakowski Street, 6th August Street, Mokowska Street, Three Crosses Square and Bracka Street.[24]

An AK report from the direction of Wola received during the early evening of 11 August stated that the route from Zielona and Pańska Streets to Towarowski Street was under heavy enemy fire. Furthermore an armoured train was causing mayhem as it shelled Wrona Street, the railway line leading from Towarowski Street and the corner of Pańska and Wrona Streets, Towarowski Street, Kazimierz Square and the corner of Sienna and Towarowski Streets. An armoured train was more or less impregnable if the enemy could be kept at a distance, rather like a Norman keep of medieval times. Krochmalan Street was completely in the hands of the enemy: it was there that AK outposts were involved in a number of skirmishes with the enemy from the direction of Wrona Street. Enemy soldiers, about thirty to forty in number, armed with automatic weapons and supported by machine guns attacked an AK position on the corner of Wrona and Grzybowski Streets. This was defended by only seven soldiers, who could hardly hold the post owing to the perennial shortage of ammunition. In another enemy attack about fifteen soldiers, supported by two heavy machine guns, attacked Srebna and Towarowa Streets. Again this AK redoubt was defended by Lieutenant Żuk and thirty soldiers, lightly armed with rifles and precious ammunition.

During the night of 10-11 August, German tanks and armoured cars were seen coming westward from the direction of Praga. By this time Żelazna Street from Chłodna to Grzybowski Street was ablaze, while Grzybowski Square, the corner of Żelazna street as well as Brama and Rynkowa Streets were under fire from Tiger and Panther tanks and heavy mortars. Despite this the AK continued to fight back, but had little ammunition to do so. The civilian population was becoming jittery as a result of the terrifying tactics being used against them by the Germans. The AK needed to rethink its campaign.

Soldiers under the command of Lieutenant "Janusz" moved to the sewers under the Old Town, in order to guard sewer outlets ready to be used as communication tunnels by the AK. If the sewage system was to be used for moving around Warsaw, it has been suggested that there was a need for gas masks because of noxious fumes: also, that a renewed attempt to enter the city's sewer system should be attempted at night. There was a real need to use the sewer system as a means of getting around the city, illustrated by an account for the early evening of 11 August. This claimed that the top of Smolna Street, Smulikowski Street, Elektrownia and Dobra Streets up to Lipowa Street was under constant mortar fire all day until 16.00 hours, while Smulikowski Street had also been under artillery fire from the Poniatowski Bridge area. Throughout the region the picture was dismal with fighting and with homes set on fire, while the streets were littered with dead and wounded. The situation was getting worse, as lookouts saw that the Germans, using the railways, were bringing further military equipment from Praga to be deployed against the AK. It was estimated that 150 wagonloads of equipment passed into Warsaw that way, without any hint of interference from the Red Army. Further reports asserted that fighting continued throughout the city, accompanied by the destruction by fire of many buildings. Slowly but surely the enemy recaptured buildings and flew the swastika flag of Nazi Germany from them. As usual the defenceless civilian population bore the brunt of the fighting and were later seen waving white handkerchiefs as they surrendered to the enemy in Koszykowa Street.[25] What else could they do?

A report from the Polish Scout Movement serving at a "help point" on Noakowski Street sent at 07.00 on 11 August bore testimony again to the ruthlessness of the enemy. The scouts' report to the AK Chief of Staff stated that Ukrainian units had mercilessly attacked an AK position at the regional administrative officers on the corner of Filterów and Szucha Streets. The AK fighters there had fought hard against the Ukrainians but ran out of ammunition and after two days had to withdraw to AK positions nearby. The Ukrainians then vented their frustration on the local population, raping and murdering as they passed through. At one address alone they shot twenty people dead. Eventually the Ukrainians withdrew and were replaced by regular Wehrmacht troops. The report concluded with routine reporting of continued fighting, the burning by the enemy of Polish homes and gave the whereabouts of entire streets that were ablaze.[26]

Some of the heaviest fighting in Warsaw was on 12 August. At 18.00 on 12 August it was reported from 35 Królewska Street that this position had been shelled from the Saxon Gardens by enemy tanks throughout the night of 11-12 August. The tank shelling was accompanied by mortar fire and by attacks of infantry, which the AK had been able to repel. During this bout of fighting the Poles had been able to capture fifty shells and a single Schmeisser machine pistol (probably a MP 40 and ideal for fighting amongst the ruins of Warsaw). Further afield the AK continued its offensive against the PAST building as the Germans tried to withdraw from it. From their post at 35 Królewska Street the Poles were able to kill eighty enemy soldiers while their own casualties were light: one dead and one wounded. In the Krakow Przedmiscie area the AK was taking the fight to the Germans and it was further speculated that the Germans were without food there, because the AK had been besieging the German positions. During the early evening of 12 August, a message came in about an enemy offensive against AK positions at 3/5 Miedzian Street from the direction of Srebna: Pańska and Łuck Street. The Poles requested reinforcements: they were being attacked by about 100 Ukrainians.[27]

From 13 August it was becoming increasingly obvious that the Germans were beginning to get the upper hand in Warsaw. Even though the AK had increased its holdings in Żoliborz, this was only because the enemy was concentrating on taking the Old Town. Żoliborz would be picked off when it was ready to do so. The enemy attacked the Old Town with heavy artillery and armour, capturing Stawka Street and setting it alight. The AK fought back and returned to the offensive in areas they still held. However the Germans had already learnt how to deal with the stout street barricades, which had defied German armour for nearly a fortnight. They now deployed multi-barrelled *nebelwerfer* mortars as well as Goliaths to destroy them. After a "heavy rain of fire" the enemy began to attack AK positions in the Old Town. The Poles recorded that they were suffering

---

25   *Powstanie Warszawskie 1944 Wybór Dokumentów Tom 3, Okres Przejściowy 11-14 VIII 1944* ed. Piotr Matusak, Warsaw, Egros, 2003, hereafter referred to as *Powstanie 3*, Document 35, 11 August 1944, pp.43-5.

26   Ibid. Document 37, 11 August 1944. p.46.

27   Ibid. Document 112, 12 August 1944, pp.118-20.

large numbers of wounded, especially in the Old Town. However the enemy was also suffering large losses, not only in manpower but also in equipment, such as tanks and artillery. In their offensive against the Old Town the German even attacked from the River Vistula. They brought up a gunboat to the banks of the river and shelled the Old Town and the embankment (*Powiśla*).[28] Even if the Vistula was not at its widest at Warsaw, the size of the rivers in Eastern Europe , made the deployment of gunboats worthwhile. Both the Germans and the Soviets made use of these vessels.[29]

Ward also recorded the events of 13 August. The first thing he reported was the mass murder of wounded and sick men at the St. Lazarus Hospital on Wolska Street and at the Karol & Maria Hospital on Przejazd Street by German armed forces. He also reported further German use of human shields, as enemy armour advanced through Warsaw. Ward was able to confirm that despite the lack of arms and ammunition the AK was still able to hold the initiative, and in places had managed to break into German strongholds and capture replacements. On 12 August the AK captured 11,600 rounds of rifle ammunition, five machine guns, and 8,500 rounds of small arms ammunition, twenty pistols, thirty anti-tank mines and an assortment of non-armoured vehicles. On Jerusalem Avenue the AK set fire to a building the Germans had pressed into use as a fortress. Two Germans soldiers from the fortress tried to surrender to the AK, but were seen by a SS officer who shot them dead. At 01.00 hours during the night of 12-13 August, the AK received weapons dropped from Allied aircraft.

Ward was also able to report on the fighting for the electricity power station that provided much of the city with electric current. The fight for the power station had begun at precisely 17.10 on 1 August, at the beginning of the uprising. Twenty-three AK soldiers were already positioned at the station, as they worked there, and were waiting for the uprising to begin and take control of the power station. On the previous day the Germans had strengthened their garrison at the power station by increasing the number of military police deployed there to 150. They were housed at the works in concrete pillboxes and blockhouses.

The signal for action was the detonation of a mine under one of the buildings. By noon on 2 August, after nineteen hours of fighting, the electricity station was totally in the hands of the AK. Polish losses for this operation were seventeen dead and twenty-seven wounded; German losses were twenty dead, twenty-two wounded and fifty-six taken prisoner. The Polish detachment that captured the power station consisted solely of manual workers and others employed on the site. Although under fire daily with 75mm shells the Poles managed to maintain the electricity supply to the civilian population of Warsaw without interruption, at least until the date of Ward's message.[30]

The following day the Polish commander at Warsaw ordered AK units outside Warsaw to come to the city and help their comrades as they fought for liberty.[31] Bór-Komorowski's order to the provincial AK was to prove the Soviet resolution not to allow the Warsaw Uprising to succeed. AK units moving towards the capital were routinely disarmed by Soviet security services; the officers were frequently murdered and their men conscripted into the Berling Army. If they refused to comply they were also killed. However this had the effect of diluting any ideological resolve the force might have ever had, and therefore made the communisation of Poland extremely suspect.[32]

28   Pomian, *Warsaw Uprising*, op.cit. p.9.
29   Nik Cornish, *Armageddon Ost. The German Defeat on the Eastern Front, 1944-5*, Hersham, Surrey, Ian Allen, 2006, p.27.
30   www.warsawuprising.com
31   Pomian, *Warsaw Uprising*, op.cit. p.9.
32   McGilvray, *A Military Government,* op.cit. pp.149-56.

According to Ward the following day, 14 August, was one of mixed feelings as he reported that the British dropped supplies during the night of 13-14 August, These had been greeted "enthusiastically" by Poles who ran into the streets, despite the shrapnel raining down from German anti-aircraft artillery, crying "they are ours; they are British". Ward commented that because of the aerial drops, morale amongst Poles in Warsaw rose by 10% compared with the previous day. One of the aircraft dropped a wreath with an inscription: "from British soldiers to our fighting comrades of the Polish Army". One is not too sure just how Ward arrived at the figure of 10% when he measured the increase in Polish morale at this time.

However the fighting in Warsaw continued to be bitter, very bitter, as the Germans fought for every inch of ground. In some places reports said entire districts had been burnt to the ground and the inhabitants either shot or deported to Germany, probably as slave labour. Soldiers of the AK continued to repeat the mantra "when we get weapons from England we will pay them (the Germans) back". Ward noted the unshakeable faith in Britain as their liberator amongst the Polish population. At the same time he reported a new menace for the AK – enemy snipers on rooftops. These sharpshooters – mainly Ukrainians, if prisoner returns are taken as evidence – took a heavy toll amongst Poles as the rooftop snipers used "hand machine guns" and had plenty of ammunition.[33]

There were others reports of fighting in Warsaw especially in the Old Town. On 16 August Captain J. Posdoski informed his British counterpart, Major M. J. T. Pickles, of a message dated 14 August which had been sent from Warsaw. The message ran as follows:

> The enemy stubbornly continues his efforts to liquidate the Old Town area. Today his main effort was against this sector. After strong artillery and mortar shelling, several assaults took place at 10.00 hours, heavy fighting continues. Our barricade on TLOMACKIE STREET had to be abandoned as a result of the burning buildings on both sides of the street, and heavy artillery barrage. Our counter-attacks enabled us to maintain our positions. During the last two days nine German defences were destroyed in this sector. In the centre of town anti-aircraft (what or from who is unclear) aimed at cutting the enemy communications but were unsuccessful. Enemy attacks were repulsed but the Tourists Hotel was lost. Enemy weapons captured. German bombers inactive. Enemy continues artillery fire. Large-scale destruction in the old part of town.[34]

A further report from Posdoski to Pickles pointed to the successes of the AK, which continued to fight on with very little if any support from the Allies, as he wrote "Intensity of the fighting in the most difficult sector of the north is decreasing. The enemy had heavy losses yesterday. We are in full control of Tlomackie Street, Krasinskich Park, Bonifraterska Street, tram sheds, Konwiktorski Street and the government paper mills. All enemy attacks repulsed. Our hold over the Town Hall prevents the enemy using the highway across Theatre Square. Artillery and mortar fire not as heavy as before."[35]

It has already been stated that the Soviet government had no intention of allowing the Warsaw Uprising to succeed, and the reasons have been discussed. To prove the thesis of annexation in the guise of liberation, with the aid of Soviet puppets such as General Michał Rola-Żymierski, his Order of the Day for 13 August read: "the whole world is waiting for the liberation of Warsaw, for

33   www.warsawuprising.com
34   NA: HS4/157, SOE Poland 30, Warsaw Uprising – Reports from Poland on Situation, FO Correspondence re: Operations to Warsaw, 2 August 1944 – 21 August 1944, HS4/157, Captain J. Posdoski to Major M.J.T. Pickles, 16 August 1944.
35   Ibid.

your victories. Marching side by side with the best army in the world, the brotherly Red Army, you must cover with glory the red and white flags of the reborn Polish Army."[36]

This was an interesting statement of intent given that it was the Red Army which had collaborated with the German Army in the destruction of Poland in 1939. Furthermore it totally ignored the role of the Polish Army in the west. It was still relevant, even if it did generally inflate its own importance. By the end of the Warsaw Uprising, the First Polish Armoured Division had covered itself in glory, as it had fought during August 1944 from a "death or glory" position in Normandy, totally disrupting the German retreat from Northern France at a deadly cost to the Poles. In other theatres Polish 2nd Corps continued in its support of the western Allied campaign through Italy. Polish airman and sailors provided valuable help to the Allies, especially the British, as they had done since 1940.

Ward continued to give testimony about the uprising: he wrote on 16 August that the Germans were causing a "great deal of damage with mine throwers" (a type of heavy mortar). He explained that the Germans were using a 50-50 mixture of explosive and incendiary compounds. The result was that the explosive made huge holes in the walls of buildings while the incendiary material set fire to houses. He commented that some of the finest houses in Warsaw had been destroyed in this manner. He also commented on the high civilian death rate. He said that practically every house in Warsaw that had not been burnt down had been given its allocation of refugees; thousands of people had not only lost their homes but also everything they possessed. Often they arrived at a house, but a few hours later they had to go and look for a new house, as the original refuge had also been set alight or bombed out.[37]

It was around this time that the Germans literally brought up a "big gun": the 600mm self-propelled siege mortar "Karl, sometimes referred to as "Thor". This beast of a weapon arrived at Warsaw's West Station at 07.00 hours on 17 August. Its ammunition arrived the next day. "Karl" could destroy entire buildings with its concrete busting 4,800lb shells. By the end of the uprising, it is thought that four such pieces had been deployed against Warsaw. A Polish reconnaissance report from the Old Town estimating the German strength in Warsaw recorded the presence of "Karl" (60 cm mortar) on 18 August.[38] The War Diary of the 9th German Army Staff noted that on 15 August a new piece of equipment was to come to Warsaw: the 60 cm mortar "Karl".[39] A Polish message brought the news that the Adrii building was completely destroyed by shells from "Karl" and that there was little that the AK could do about it. It was asserted that the shelling came from a great distance.[40] "Karl" had a maximum range of 4,320 metres. It is interesting to note that as Warsaw is rebuilt for the 21st century, munitions from the Warsaw Uprising still cause problems when they are uncovered, halting building work until they are dealt with. Recently a 1.5 tonne shell from "Karl" disrupted work on the Warsaw metro.[41] The misfortunes of the Warsaw Uprising linger on seventy years later.

Ward wrote of 18 August that the main situation in Warsaw remained the same. The rate of fighting continued, while the enemy continued its destruction of the city using every means at

---

36 NA: FO 371, Foreign Office Correspondence, FO 371/39492, General Rola's Order of the Day to Polish Army on Concentrated Assault on Warsaw, 13 August 1944.

37 www.warsaw.com

38 *Powstanie Warszawskie. Wybór Dokumentów*, Volume 4, 15 August 1944 – 18 August 1944, Piotr Matusak (ed), Warsaw, Egros, 2003, hereafter referred to as *Powstanie 4*, Document 266, Old Town, Warsaw, 18 August 1944, pp.232-5.

39 *Powstanie 4*, Document 85, War Diary Staff 9th German Army, Warsaw, 15 August 1944, p.77.

40 *Powstanie Warszawskie. Wybór Dokumentów*, Volume 5, 19 August 1944 – 21 August 1944, Piotr Matusak (ed) Warsaw, Egros, 2003, hereafter referred to as *Powstanie 5*, Document 33, Sitrep 21, Warsaw, 07:00 hours, 19 August 1944, p.35.

41 www.deon.pl/druk/ZJGj3qVnZtGYdGqpag.html accessed 29 July 2012.

its disposal. He reported that 40% of the city was already completely destroyed, with a further 20% reported as being badly damaged. Reports from the suburbs also spoke of the same "terrific destruction". It was all too clear that the Germans were carrying out their threat to destroy Warsaw while loss of life amongst Poles was horrific.[42] During the afternoon of 18 August German envoys, under the protection of a white flag, approached Polish positions near the Saxon Gardens: they bore a letter from General von dem Bach-Zelewski for General Bór-Komorowski with a proposal that the AK in Warsaw should surrender. Bór-Komorowski ordered that the letter should remain unanswered.[43]

Information from Warsaw on 17 August concerning the fighting in the Old Town discussed the fact that the action was on a smaller scale than before, but with a successful localized AK night offensive. The enemy had turned its main effort against the city in the Chłodna Street area towards Grzybowski and Kazimierz Squares and Hal Mirowski. The thrust of the German offensives were against AK strong points and barricades: this involved hand-to-hand fighting as it was the only way the enemy could engage the AK in the reduced spaces left by the Polish defences. With fires burning around them from incendiary, mortar and artillery fire, the AK maintained its previous hold everywhere. It was reported that the German 494th Infantry Regiment had suffered 50% casualties since they had began fighting the AK on 3 August. One platoon of East Prussian infantry surrendered as a body, while several armoured cars were also destroyed in the same area.[44] An entry from Bach-Zelewski's diary mentions the very heavy fighting in Warsaw and the resulting high German casualties. He also mentioned that he had been promised the Knight's Cross if he conquered Warsaw and that he was in charge of every aspect of the German operation, both civil and military.[45] Truly in charge of life and death.

The War Diary of the 9th German Army Staff gives further indications of German frustration regarding operations in Warsaw. A report from General von Vormann, Commanding Officer German 9th Army to the CO of Army Group *Mitte* stated that the Hungarian regiments in the Warsaw area could not be trusted to fight the Poles. There was a long tradition of Polish-Hungarian friendship, so these regiments should be sent to the rear and away from the fighting.[46] Hungarian sympathy towards the Poles is confirmed in the reminiscences of AK veteran Ralph Smorczewski. He recounted how his mother was able to enlist the aid of a Hungarian colonel, Colonel Kovacs, to convince the German political police, the SD, that they were mistaken in their identification of the young Ralph as an AK fighter. Kovacs told Mrs Smorczewska that it was not the first time during the uprising that he and fellow Hungarians had helped Poles in various ways.[47] Kochanski notes that benign attitude of the Hungarians towards Poles, even in the areas of Poland where they were the occupants.[48] Davies observes that the 2nd Hungarian Corps seriously considered joining the Polish insurgents but were told by the Hungarian government "not to join the Poles, but … not to fight them".[49] A very interesting state of affairs with an enemy considering helping the Polish uprising while an ally was determined to see it destroyed! If the Hungarian government had given the 2nd Hungarian Corps permission to aid the Poles; the alliance system in central Europe would have collapsed. The Germans would have had to

---

42   www.warsawuprising.com
43   Ibid.
44   Pomian, *Warsaw Uprising*, op.cit. pp.9-10.
45   *Powstanie 4*, Document 86, Diary of Erich von dem Bach-Zelewski, 15 August 1944, p.77.
46   *Powstanie 5*, Document 71, Report by 9th Army Group to CO Army Group *Mitte* 19 August 1944, pp.68-9.
47   IWM 12787 03/41/1. Smorczewski Reminiscences, op.cit. See also Lesław M. Bartelski, *Mokotów 1944*, Warsaw, MON, 1971, p.374.
48   Kochanski, op.cit. p.263.
49   Davies, *Rising*, p.284.

occupy Hungary and relocate troops there, otherwise needed for the eastern and western fronts. The SD were, of course, correct in their assumptions: Ralph Smorczewski was a brave and gallant member of the AK.

The ongoing Polish-Hungarian friendship was a subject of discussion in the War Diary of the 9th German Army staff. It was eventually decided that the Hungarian 1st Cavalry Division, along with 5th, 12th and 23rd Reserve Hungarian Divisions should be removed from the fighting as the Germans could no longer trust the Hungarians. The diary also laments that despite heavy German attacks in the northern sectors of Warsaw, supported completely with artillery and armour, very little impact had been made on the defending AK positions as they held out stubbornly. The Germans considered the Poles to be senseless and suicidal.[50] However the Germans overlooked the fact that they were slaughtering civilians. How was an AK fighter supposed to surrender to members of the SS or SS police units deployed around Warsaw – let alone to the renegade foreign units fighting alongside the Germans, causing mayhem and committing mass murder on their behalf?

On 20 August the Kiliński Battalion captured the PAST building. This had been the scene of some of the worst fighting since the beginning of the uprising. Kurt Heller, one of the German defenders of the building, kept a diary with an interesting account of how the isolated German garrison struggled against the AK as their supplies slowly dwindled. Equally the AK have a valuable eyewitness to the attacks on the PAST building. Mrs Barbara Matys, still alive at the age of 89 in 2012, was a 21-year-old sapper in 1944. She had previously trained as a nurse, and had been part of the Polish Underground since 1940. Mrs Matys recalled that the first major attack against the PAST building was very early in the uprising between 4-5 August. During the attack, sappers under covering fire had been able to force the main entrance of the PAST building, but little else.[51] However this did allow the AK to besiege the building.

The second major attack against the PAST building was altogether more elaborate. Mrs Matys says that the operation began at 02.00 hours on 20 August. Some publications say that it was between 02.30 and 03.00, but Mrs Matys is clear that it was 02.00. The attack saw woman sappers playing a major role, deploying Wanda Maciejowska ("Iza"), Irena Grabowska ("Hanka"), and Barbara Matys with sapper officers; their patrol commander was Captain Jerzy Skupieński ("Jotes"). Just before midnight on 20 August this small group met at an operational position on Zielna Street where they collected equipment, including plastic explosive necessary for the coming operation. Everybody had their own equipment to carry: Matys said that she had plastic explosives, which looked like a round loaf of Polish bread, as well as percussion caps and fuses. Once equipped and armed Matys' patrol moved out and took up positions with other AK units adjacent to the PAST building. Her patrol went to the northern side of the building. Matys says that when they got to the building, they could see that there were homes on the second and third floors. On entering the cellars they also discovered a large number of people and everybody there was willing to fight for the AK. There were many old people in the cellars, who had taken refuge there as a result of the fighting. Matys said that there were no children, but the number of toys showed that there certainly had been some living there recently. Negotiations were carried out to convince the people to leave the building. They were very scared and left without a word. They knew that they were never coming back to this place. It was a difficult moment for the AK fighters when they saw the levels to which their people had been reduced because of the fighting. One can only guess at the level of reconnaissance the AK had been able to carry out: in spite of besieging the building for over two weeks they had no idea that vulnerable civilians were living in the building. Also, as

50 *Powstanie 5*, Document 76, War Diary 9th Army Staff, p.69.
51 Matys.

Matys observes, they had no idea just how thick the walls of the building were. As a result, twenty-five kilos of plastic explosive were used, which caused more destruction than had been anticipated and actually confused the AK in their assault on the PAST building.

A sapper patrol under the command of Captain Paroński, "Chevrolet", was due to detonate a mine at 03.00 hours in the PAST building as the signal for attack (this is probably why there is a discrepancy in the timings). For reasons unknown this did not happen, so Matys' patrol took the initiative and made their way to where the first mine was supposed to have gone off. They fitted a mine to a wall there before retreating, paying out the fuse as they withdrew to a relatively safe position and waited with their eyes closed. Just after 03.00 there was a terrible explosion as the mine did its work, but within seconds there was also a fire.

After the explosion of the mine, the first AK unit to attack was "Koszta" under the command of Stefan Micha "Kmita", an artillery officer, a qualified paratrooper and a fine man according to Matys. Matys and the sappers were to withdraw to the cellars at the PAST building after the detonation of their mine. Only "Kmita", "Jotes" and AK fighters were left above. Most of the sappers were already down and trying to get away. The stairs to the exit were still intact, but upwards from the third floor just about everything had been knocked down by the explosion and was rubble. Assault ladders were used to effect a getaway from the wrecked building. AK fighters who had been on the third floor were also leaving rapidly; not only as a result of the explosion, the damage and the fire but also because the Germans had already recovered themselves and were returning fire.

The German counter-attack produced the first AK casualties, as "Iza" fell from the ladder as they escaped the building, shot in the heel; Hania carried her to safety while Matys with her CO, "Jotes" also ran to cover. They dropped into a room which Matys described in July 2012 as being like "hell" owing to the fire created by the mine her team had exploded. On the other side was a darkened opening with a breach caused by the AK mine. Outside this breach the Germans had machine guns and fired at the Poles as they tried to withdraw from the cellars. Matys said, looking back, it was a difficult moment but Captain Kmita had a brainwave and shouted, "who has grenades?" Matys handed him the last of her plastic explosive – about a kilo – and he blew a hole in a wall away from the enemy and the fiercely burning fire. Blowing the hole in the wall was a risky venture: as there was only a little fuse and a limited amount of explosive. Also, they were not sure just how thick the wall was. However, the wall was breached and the group began to drop into the darkness and, hopefully, safety. All was quiet. Matys said that most of the Poles were wearing German uniforms including the distinctive "coal-scuttle" helmets of the German army Only the red and white Polish national colours, mounted on brassards and displayed on the sleeves of their uniforms, distinguished them from their foe. As they were escaping the PAST building they must have been seen by a "Chevrolet" patrol, as there was a cry: "Don't shoot, don't shoot, they are Polish lasses!" This timely cry prevented a tragedy as the patrol was about to attack Matys and her comrades. She explained that although the German uniforms, made them indistinguishable from real Germans in the dark, one of the "Chevrolet" patrol had noticed her blond ponytail poking out from under her helmet, and so they were saved. Later that day Matys heard that the PAST building had fallen to the AK. As she said, it was "a beautiful moment".[52]

The testimony of Barbara Matys confirms that from early August the Poles were laying siege to the PAST building. As early as 4 August the German soldier-diarist, Heller, recorded that there were no adequate supplies of water or food at the PAST building. He noted the deaths of his comrades and the general air of desperation: however on 12 August the German outpost was resupplied. However, although the garrison was resupplied; the soldiers ran out quickly as the "police" (as he referred to them) had taken most of the soldiers' supplies for themselves. Heller

---

52 Matys.

recorded that the AK had captured tanks and were using them against the Germans. He wrote on 13 August that they were under heavy tank fire and the tanks were in the hands of "bandits".

The Polish shelling breached walls in the PAST building, but the Germans suffered no casualties. Between 14 and 16 August, Heller was at an all-time low. He complained about being very hungry, and that the outpost had been surrounded by the AK for ten days. On 19 August, he related how the AK continued to attack with petrol bombs, which caused a considerable loss of nerve amongst the German defenders; several of them committed suicide. Heller wrote of the terrible smell of unburied bodies, which were beginning to rot as the summer heat was so oppressive.[53] A German message of 20 August gave the temperature for the day as 29°C.[54]

In the Old Town the situation remained grim. It was shelled all day, while enduring infantry and armour attacks during the morning, especially from the direction of Leszno and Nalewski Streets. One section of German infantry was supported by four Tiger tanks: the AK destroyed three. The barricade on Nalewski Street was destroyed by three Goliaths, which also caused a huge fire. In the city centre the enemy was pressurizing Chopin and Koszykowa Streets with the Luftwaffe carrying out air raids. The Luftwaffe was in action during that morning, 20 August, from 08.00 to 11.00; each air raid lasted forty-five minutes.[55]

On 19 August, ,as the siege of the PAST building began to reach its climax ,the German diarist Kurt Heller reflected on his immediate future as the AK closed in. The AK had exploded mines inside the building during the night of 19–20 August which destroyed the first three floors and set the building on fire. Then the AK literally added fuel to the fire by using a fire engine to spray petrol into the inferno.[56] However the Germans still continued to defend their post quite defiantly, though some of them, members of the SS and the dreaded Gestapo, had a lot to fear. These men feared Polish retribution because of their organizations' mass murder of Polish civilians. However many Germans did surrender.[57] The AK took 115 prisoners as well, as capturing arms and ammunition. A Polish account for 21 August stated that after many hours of fighting the PAST building had been captured: the enemy suffering thirty-six dead, six wounded and the confirmation of 115 prisoners taken, plus the capture of arms.[58]

Ward continued to comment on the situation in Warsaw between 19 August and 24 August. He wrote that the people called German mine-throwers (mortars) "moving cupboards", as they sounded like heavy furniture being shifted, followed a few seconds later by a series of loud explosions. Ward recorded that the Prudential building on Napoleon Square, the tallest building in Warsaw, had been hit three times by mines or mortars and once by bombs – it was completely burnt out. Zagorski wrote on 20 August that since the AK had acquired some anti-tank weapons (anti-tank pistols – probably PIATs) the Germans "as it were out of sheer spite" changed their tactics. They no longer came up to the barricades, but remained out of range as they attacked Polish positions. The German tanks were used as mobile blockhouses and seemed to be able to shell Polish positions as long as they wished to. Zagorski claimed that nearly 500 shells had been fired at one Polish position alone. This seemingly endless shellfire was beginning to take its toll on Polish resistance.[59]

53 Adam Rozmysłowicz, *Gmach PAST-y w Powstanice Warszawskia 1944*, Warsaw, RTYM, 2008, pp.65-87.
54 *Powstanie 5*, Document 167, Daily Report 9th Army, 20 August 1944.
55 Pomian, *Warsaw Uprising*, op.cit. p.12.
56 Matys.
57 Rozmysłowicz, op.cit. pp.87-100. W. Zagorski ('Lech') *Seventy Days*, Maidstone, George Mann, 1974, Translated by John Welsh, pp.104-5.
58 *Powstanie 5*, Document 203, Sitrep nr. 23, Warsaw, 08:30, 21 August 1944, p.193.
59 Zagorski, (1957) op.cit. pp.102-3.

A gruesome detail was that as the paving slabs had been torn up to build anti-tank barricades, the pavements had been turned into graveyards. In many places it had become impossible to walk without treading on fresh graves. Ward commented on the conditions of the civilian population: he reported how they suffered, with thousands made homeless daily while hundreds were killed. Thousands of men, women and children had been wounded, as the Germans saw no difference between the AK and civilians. These wounds included burns, shrapnel and bullet wounds, however the German barbarism only encouraged the population to fight to the last man. Ward noted ominously that if the situation did not improve, the goodwill, such as it was, of the civilian population would soon be lost.

There was a shortage of everything, especially water. Ward wrote that, such was the seriousness of the water shortage; wells were being sunk in nearly every open space in Warsaw. He claimed that if the capital did not receive relief within ten days, everything would be lost. For the first time Ward mentioned a large concentration camp on the outskirts of the city, where women and children were dying in large numbers, while the men were routinely shot. Ward also admitted that the Germans had finally gone on to the offensive but he still had Polish successes to relate. He reported on 23 August that the Telephone Exchange on Pius Street had been taken by storm in an action that had lasted for twenty-six hours.

On the previous day the AK captured the Central Telephone Building on Sienna Street; 200 prisoners were taken during two operations, with minimal Polish losses. Ward described the efficiency of the German "mine throwers": in one incident twenty-two blocks of flats south of Jeroboams Avenue were destroyed. Each block contained between twenty and sixty flats. He also gave a bleak assessment of the fighting in general. He wrote that the fighting was total warfare and had been for twenty-four days. Normal life had been suspended owing to the destruction and savagery of the conflict, made worse by the German use of heavy artillery and their illegal and barbaric tactics that disproportionally affected the civilian population.

The civilian population had been more or less mobilized, with thousands being used to fight the fires raging throughout Warsaw; others were used to keep the streets, occupied by the AK clear of debris. There were also other duties for civilians, including couriers, field telephone workers and working for the Red Cross, which Ward described as "working excellently under the most difficult of conditions". He also gave an excellent first-hand description of the AK whose members he described as being a "queer mixture".

The ages of those fighting ranged from nineteen to over seventy. As ever there was a severe shortage of weapons, with only 1% of AK fighters being sufficiently armed. On the whole they had only pistols and rifles, with a few heavy machine guns which were only used in emergencies as they used up too much ammunition. It was also noted that few military formalities were observed in the AK, but as Ward reflected, it was impossible to enforce too much discipline in an army which was two-thirds untrained and had no uniforms. It was also noted that there were colonels fighting as "simple soldiers" under the command of youthful lieutenants.

The AK was also extremely resourceful in the manufacture of weapons. Ward described how hand grenades were made from old gas pipes filled with explosive and lit with normal household matches before being thrown. Flamethrowers were also manufactured in small workshops pressed into use given the dire straits imposed by the German occupation and the uprising. Ward was extremely impressed by a particular example of Polish resourcefulness, as he related how in an abandoned German weapon store over one hundred 80lb artillery shells, as Ward described them probably not being used to metric measurements were found. At first sight they seemed to be a useless find until a sapper, later killed in action, saw them and put two detonators inside some of the shells. He then attached a twenty-five second fuse to the detonators. When the time came to use the shells, they were thrown from a second storey window, as near as possible on to a German position. The AK fighters took cover as best they could, then launched an assault after the explosion, which proved to be very effective. No doubt the Germans did not expect shells to be dropped on them from a window. Ward also noted that weapons dropped by the RAF were of great value, but not enough in quantity.

Ward returned once more to the plight of the civilian population, especially the shortage of food. He had noted that the German occupying forces had starved the city for nearly five years: the quantity of food available had been inadequate since the beginning of the occupation. He also considered that the civilian population was extremely concerned about the expected Soviet occupation once the Red Army arrived in Warsaw. News from Polish territories already occupied by the Soviets was not encouraging. Large numbers of AK officers had been "put into Soviet concentration camps". It was believed that it was only a question of time before the Red Army entered Warsaw, and then what?[60] Not only was food running out but there was no water or electric light. Furthermore, people had been reduced to living at the most primitive level amongst the ruins of their city and constantly having to move from place to place as the enemy systematically destroyed Warsaw.[61]

A report for 24 August gave information about heavy fighting in the Old Town, beginning with a general observation that for several days there had been heavy and concentrated enemy attacks on Polish positions there. A more detailed account immediately admitted that after ten hours of fighting, during which the AK had made three counter-attacks, enemy forces had captured the western side of the John the Pius hospital building. Before the first attack there had been a ninety-minute artillery barrage using guns, mortars and grenade-throwers in an attempt to soften up Polish positions. Flame-thrower teams led the main assault.

In other directions enemy attacks had all been repulsed and the AK held their positions, basically without any change. In the Old Town on the previous day, 23 August the AK had suffered 100 dead and wounded. In the city centre the Poles had captured the police headquarters on Krakowskie Przedmiescie, the Holy Cross Church and the telephone exchange on Pius Street. The AK took about 160 prisoners, as well as capturing much-needed arms.[62] Ward wrote of the time on 25 August when during the previous twenty-four hours there had been no outstanding events in the "battle for Warsaw"; the fighting remained as bitter as ever, but without any result. He reported that the damage done by enemy mine throwers was "colossal". Streets he identified as "Wildcat", "Cruz", "Pius", "Mokotow", "TKOs" and "Jackdaws Avenue" had been badly damaged during the previous forty-eight hours, with high casualties. In the city centre, large fires burnt throughout the night. Meanwhile food supplies continued to dwindle, with no means of replenishing them; at night heavy artillery could be heard about twelve miles from the city.

On the same day, Ward reported the murderous German rampage through Warsaw. Three days earlier, two Poles who had been captured by the Germans brought a message to a local AK command post from Gestapo headquarters on Szucha Avenue. It was a request that German troops trapped in a position along Pius Street should be allowed to get to Gestapo headquarters. In exchange, the Germans said that they would release some Polish prisoners and bring medical supplies. The AK refused this request. The two Poles who had brought the message said that the Germans had constructed a crematorium, and were shooting, then burning, about 300 men daily. Up to the time the two men brought the message, 3,000 suits of civilian clothing had been received into the German store. This meant that at least 3,000 "Polish patriots" had already been "brutally murdered". It was known that there were another 2,500 prisoners held there, and more were arriving every day. Ward wrote that the AK was powerless to prevent this "brutal, wholesale

60   www.warsawuprising.com
61   Day-by-Day, 25 August 1944.
62   Pomian, op cit, p.13.

murder", as they did not have the types of heavy weapons needed to attack such a heavily fortified stronghold as the one on Szucha Avenue.[63]

The beginning of the end of the fight for the Old Town came on 25 August. During the night of 24–25 August AK commanders travelled through the sewers from the Old Town to the city centre. At the same time, under the new commander Colonel "Karol", the defence at Mokotów, was reorganized. He divided up the region into more manageable areas: the overall strength there was 3,500 fighters with 3,000 of whom served on the front line.[64] On 26 August the battle for the Old Town continued, especially the "bloody battle" for the State Manufactory of Securities. The Germans deployed artillery, mortars and tanks as well as aerial assaults, dropping 500-kilo bombs on Polish positions. The AK counter-attacked and recaptured the western side of the State Manufactory buildings. The German break-out between Kosciel, Bolese and Rybacki Streets was checked, but slowly but surely the AK was losing territory despite their "maximum efforts".

In an attack on the John the Pius hospital and the State Manufactory the Germans used tear gas, which incapacitated AK fighters defending these positions. The usual shortages were reported, including that of bread and water, while it was noted that the enemy were building barricades and strengthening their positions in the city centre. Furthermore, the German garrison at the National Museum was being supplied by an underground route, running from a railway tunnel. The enemy was also busily engaged in firing houses along the viaduct to the Poniatowski Bridge and May 3rd Avenue. The AK launched an attack on the cavalry barracks in Sadyba but was repulsed. The Germans were also able to extend their defensive network at the airport. While this happening, the entire city, especially the Old Town, was under bombardment from mortars, grenade-throwers, artillery and aerial attacks. A further report was received regarding Soviet intentions in Poland; this time from Lublin. AK units had set out to relieve Warsaw but had returned, fearing that the Red Army might intercept them, disarm them and then imprison them.[65]

Daily accounts gave the position in Warsaw on 26 August: The AK tried in vain to break the German encirclement in the vicinity of the Łazienki Park, in an attempt to link up with units in Upper Czerniaków. During the night two companies from the Baszta Regiment captured the Holy Family of Nazareth Convent on Czerniakowska Street; the nuns there were evacuated along with the wounded and civilians under their care. On 27 August units under the command of Captain "Boncza" foiled an attempt by the enemy to blow up St John's Cathedral. They captured about 100 kilos of explosives as well as taking prisoners from the Dirlewanger Brigade. However, the Germans were later able to capture the cathedral, and "Boncza" was severely wounded in the fighting. The following day, just before dawn, a German attack about 1,600 strong launched a final assault against the Poles holed up in the State Paper Manufactory Building. By 08.30 the building was entirely in German hands. In the basement of the building, the wounded, the field hospital staff and the civilians sheltering there were all murdered. At the same time the siege mortar "Karl" shelled the city centre. There was intense fighting for the Post Office railway station, Bormann's factory and its warehouses along Towarowa Street, but the AK was able to prevent a powerful enemy attack from the Saxon Gardens.[66]

During 29 August the Germans continued to reduce the area held by the AK in the Old Town, as the Poles moved away from the bridges and roads by the River Vistula. Heavy fighting continued in St. John's Cathedral: this sacred building changed hands several times during the day, but by evening it was firmly in enemy hands. Not only had the AK lost the cathedral and the

---

63   www.warsawuprisng.com
64   Day-by-day, 25 August 1944.
65   Pomian, op.cit. p.13.
66   Day-by-day.

State Manufactory building, but they had also lost other territories. The AK realised that there was no chance of launching counter-offensives at that time. The only good news to be had, which was mixed, was that a message suggested that about 300 men of the AL, the Soviet-backed Polish Army, had deserted from the Soviet side of Warsaw and were making for the Old Town.[67]

Every fifteen minutes there were air raids over the Old Town, while German artillery demolished AK positions in the FIAT works and the Blessed Virgin church, whose remains were fought over all day and changed hands several times. The enemy also captured a municipal shelter and murdered the old people and invalids who were taking refuge there.[68] The following day, the BBC reported that the British and American governments had granted combatant status to AK fighters, which meant that if the Germans or their allies captured AK members they had to treat them as prisoners of war, rather than executing them. The German authorities were warned darkly that there would be (undisclosed) consequences if they did not heed the newly defined status of AK fighters.[69]

Ward sent an illuminating report to London concerning the situation in Warsaw after a month's fighting. Having been resident in the city since 1941 as a member of the AK, he wrote that he could "be a witness to many acts of savagery" which would have beggared the belief of any civilized person. He reported the daily manhunts in the streets when SS troops blocked a road and took all men and women between the ages of 14 and 50 to "special concentration camps". Here the Germans sorted out people who showed "any signs of intelligence" and removed them to permanent concentration camps, where they were generally worked to death within a few months. The remainder was sent to Germany as slave labour; anybody trying to escape was shot dead in the street. Ward wrote that the situation was critical and that the only things that seemed to drive people on were a reaction to the "terrible bombardment and slaughter" being carried out by the enemy, and the legacy of five years of occupation. Ward observed that Warsaw had suffered incredible deprivations and heard "with hungry envy of the liberation of Paris after four days of fighting. They heard that the British Army rushed thousands of tons of food and fighting [supplies] and medical supplies to the French population." Ward noted that at the beginning of the uprising in Warsaw some supplies had been dropped by the western Allies but nothing further had been dropped for weeks.[70] The tone of the dispatch was very bitter.

The beginning of September saw some of the worst disappointment, as AK fighters began to evacuate through the sewers to the city centre. Hundreds of their number emerged from a manhole in Nowy Swiat after five hours of walking through the sewage system. The evacuation of the Old Town continued into 2 September: during that day German troops entered the ruins of the Old Town. About 7,000 of the civilian population and wounded AK fighters, including those in the Old Town hospitals, were killed by the Germans. Bach-Zelewski ordered the "cleansing" of further districts on the Vistula.[71] Ward wrote further of the fate of those who surrendered in the Old Town. Many women, children and old men seemed to have taken the enemy at their word: they had been told they would be well treated and that any private property they took with them would not be stolen from them. With no other choice, they left the city. The staff of the AK received messages that all valuables were taken from those who had surrendered and then, already

---

67   Pomian, op.cit. p.15.
68   Day-by-day.
69   Day-by-day. Ward in a despatch for 31 August 1944 reported that Polish military personnel captured by the German Army or their allies were routinely prior to the BBC announcement.
70   www.warsawuprising.com
71   Day-by-day.

weakened by hunger; they were marched nearly twenty miles in driving rain to an open compound and left under the guard of SS men.[72]

By the beginning of September it was reported from Warsaw that German aerial bombardment was being carried out without any breaks. Entire squadrons, working at low levels, were unhindered in their work as the Soviet Air Force remained inactive. This allowed the Germans to do as they wished.[73] A message received on 6 September makes the most distressing reading, as the Poles began to realise the truth of their situation:

> The situation is reaching its climax. The civilian population is living through a crisis, which may have a fundamental influence on the fighting forces. The causes of the crisis are: the increasingly and completely unhindered shelling and bombing of the city, the consciousness that the enemy is aiming at destroying the entire area of the city, the entire prolongation of the struggle, the continually smaller starvation rations for the fire victims and rapid exhaustion of food for others. The great mortality amongst infants, the agitation of hostile elements and finally the lack of water and electricity in all districts were all to add to the frustration of civilians. When to the above we add our ammunition is at exhaustion point, then we get a complete picture of the difficulty growing with every day and hour of carrying on our struggle. It is difficult to foresee the consequences of the main retreat of the people from areas within the terror of artillery fire and bombing and their concentration from which there is no exit. In accordance with previous promises I ask for a definite date to be given for the receipt of the promised help or else the notification that we shall not receive this help.This would be the conclusive factor in the decision we shall be called upon to make. Do you realise that operations on the Western Front may well bring the end of the war in the immediate future? We do not count on rapid mastering of the situation by the Soviets.[74]

This was a bleak, but for once a realistic, assessment of the situation in Warsaw and elsewhere in early September. Indeed a report of the fighting in Warsaw during August made a note of the fact that: "A characteristic feature is the almost total cessation of military operations (on the German-Soviet front in Warsaw) and soldiers, both German and Russian, have been observed sunbathing in the fighting line though the distance between the two positions is little more than three hundred yards."[75] The Germans, supported by artillery, continued their offensive in Warsaw; mainly in the Powisle and northern parts of the city centre. The AK forces in these areas were supported by units that had been evacuated from the Old Town. On 3 September, the city power plant at Powisle stopped, as it had been destroyed by artillery fire and air raids. At the same time, Captain "Krybar" was forced to order the evacuation of the civilian population from the endangered parts of Powisle to the northern city centre, while other AK units were redeployed at Upper Czerniakow. Powisle came under heavy fire, with the Germans attacking from three directions, while their infantry took up a position in an office block on Kopernik Street.

By 6 September all of Powisle was in German hands, and the AK was forced to withdraw to the city centre. The Germans dropped leaflets, signed by Bach-Zelewski, calling for the civilian population to leave Warsaw. The Germans claimed that they would cease firing during any such evacuation. On 7 September the Germans began an offensive against the northern sector of the city centre, attacking Nowy Swiat, Chmielna Street and Napoleon Square. They also tried to destroy

72   www.warsawuprising.com
73   Pomian, op.cit. p.16.
74   Ibid. pp.19-20.
75   Ibid. p.21.

the AK barricade on Jerusalem Avenue – the only link between the northern city centre and the southern areas of the city. The following day, between midday and 14.00 hours, German artillery fell silent as thousands of civilians fled Warsaw. After the ceasefire ended the enemy attempted a surprise attack on the city centre. The events of the previous two days made the AK commanders recognise the futility of the defence and agreed to negotiations with the Germans, via the Red Cross, regarding the evacuation of the civilian population. As a result there was another ceasefire and a further 8,000 people left Warsaw.[76]

On 10 September the Red Army made the first determined attempts to cross the River Vistula from the Praga side. The First Belarusian Front, which included the First Polish Army under the command of General Zygmunt Berling, started to advance towards German positions.[77] Berling gives further detail in his memoirs as he recounted that the offensive of 10 September began as being an attack on Otwocki by the 47th Soviet Army.[78] By 12 September the Soviet attack from Praga seemed to have been successful according to Polish accounts. These claimed the superiority of the Soviet Air Force with small aerial drops, and the sight of dogfights between the Luftwaffe and the Soviet Air Force, which bought German losses. Reportedly, these sights greatly improved the spirits of the AK and those civilians who remained in Warsaw. However the shortage of ammunition remained a huge problem for the AK. They sent a signal reading: "There is a danger that in front of our goal we may not be able to hold out. Immediate help in ammunition is indispensible."[79] However this was not the only problem for the AK. By the beginning of September the whole question of Warsaw was beginning to split the Allies.

The divisions over Warsaw were not necessarily public. They were often very private, occurring behind the scenes, once it became quite obvious that the Soviet government – or rather Stalin – would be very happy to see the AK destroyed by the Germans in Warsaw. Allied politicians began to question Soviet commitment to the alliance against Germany. A minute from Major Guy Lloyd, MP, to Anthony Eden, the British Foreign Secretary, illustrated what many people were beginning to realise:

> I feel that I must add my quota to the expressions of disgust and distress which you must be receiving just now about the manner in which our Russian allies appear to be deliberately allowing the Polish Underground Movement to be liquidated by the Germans, without the assistance which they must be in a position to supply from so close at hand. What a terrible indictment of this callous policy is our splendid and gallant effort to send supplies of arms and munitions from 1,700 miles non-stop to Warsaw, at great sacrifice of life. I shall always be glad and proud that we made this noble gesture to our Polish Allies in response to their frantic and pathetic S.O.S. and I am grateful for your response to this appeal. I have no doubt that you have done, and are doing, all you can to urge Moscow to give direct assistance but I have also no doubt it will be refused, accompanied by all kinds of excuses and "good reasons" and every effort will be made to fix the blame upon the Polish government and upon the Underground leaders in Warsaw, for lack of collaboration with Russia and for unilateral and premature action. Even if there is some truth in this, it is insufficient reason for refusing aid to those gallant men who are fighting the same enemy only 12-20 miles away, after five years of agony and self-sacrifice. The whole business is disgusting and contemptible. How can we work happily in the future with men who will do this kind of thing, and worse, without turning a

---

76 Day-by-day.
77 Ibid.
78 Z. Berling, *Wspomnienia: Wolność na przetarg* (Vol. 3) Warsaw, Polski Dom Wydawniczy, 1991, p.365.
79 Pomian, op.cit. p.23.

hair? The contrast between the BBC boosting of the Maquis in France and the comparative silence about our Polish allies in Warsaw, who have trusted us from the first, sticks out like a sore thumb. Can nothing be done to show sympathy for, and give more publicity to the gallant Poles in Warsaw? Is the fact that they obviously prefer to take orders from, and give allegiance to their legitimate government and not Moscow, sufficient reason for our attitude?[80]

This note reveals the extent of the concern felt by some within the British establishment about the cynicism of the Soviet government in relation to the Warsaw Uprising. A successful Polish revolt would have impeded the imperialist spread in Europe of a resurrected Russia, or Soviet Empire, as it pursued its policy under the guise of liberation. It also revealed that British attitude towards Poland, especially post-war Poland, was split. This arose because most of the British media had boosted Stalin and the Soviet Union, but had done so at the expense of the Polish government-in-exile. They were frequently portrayed as being anti-Semitic reactionaries, almost fascist in their outlook. Few people knew the truth about Stalin and the Soviet government – or chose not to, overlooking Nazi-Soviet cooperation between 1939 and 1941, which included the invasion of Poland in 1939. Instead many people were only aware of the fight of the Soviet people against Germany following the invasion of the Soviet Union in June 1941, after these two murderous regimes fell out like the criminals they were. Therefore even if people had heard anything negative about Stalin or Russia, they were prepared to give them the benefit of the doubt.

In turn, the British and American governments overlooked Soviet war crimes, as they needed the Soviet Union to remain in the war against Germany. This was the problem the London Poles failed to overcome as they were sacrificed on the altar of good Anglo-American-Soviet relations. The Soviet government got the best out of this relationship. Stafford wrote that the Warsaw Uprising ran contrary to British policy regarding SOE, as he considered Churchill's support for SOE and European resistance movements ran only so far as being " … a beacon of hope, not a mirror of self-delusion …"[81]

Once the Soviet offensive began, limited though it was, the Germans blew up all the bridges over the Vistula while on 13 September the AK general staff sent a message over the river to establish contact with Berling's army staff. On 14 September the Tadeusz Kosciusko First Division, a Polish military formation fighting alongside the Red Army, captured Praga. To aid this advance Lieutenant-Colonel "Radosław" concentrated his AK units closer to the shores of the Vistula to try to ensure that the Red Army could establish a bridgehead.[82]

The liberation of Praga caused the British Ambassador to the Soviet Union, Sir Archibald Clark-Kerr, to comment that liberation was "sincerely welcomed" by the locals with many enlisting in the Red Army or the Polish Army.[83] It is not clear whether these enlistments were voluntary or not; it is likely they were not. The British and American governments had negotiated POW status for AK soldiers captured by German armed forces: a further problem arose when the Soviets and Polish communists issued statements of intent to arrest and condemn officers responsible for the rising in Warsaw.[84] This certainly caused maximum embarrassment to the British and Americans. It was quite obvious that senior AK officers would be better off surrendering to the "barbaric Germans", rather than to their Soviet allies. They had already decided who was responsible for the uprising and its presumed failure, which they ascribed to an assumed premature launch.

---

80   NA: FO 371/39495/C11817, Major Guy Lloyd M.P.to Anthony Eden, 31 August 1944.
81   David Stafford, *Churchill & Secret Service*, London, Abacus, 1997, p.219.
82   Day-by-day.
83   NA: FO 371/39498/C12508, Sir A. Clark-Kerr to FO, 20 September 1944.
84   NA: FO 371/39498/C12570 HBP/PD/6287, Lieutenant-Colonel Perkins to G.W. Harrison (FO) 13 September 1944.

When the Soviet government realised in the middle of September that the AK might surrender to the Germans they cynically assumed a temporarily positive attitude towards events in Warsaw. Such a surrender would have been a disaster for Stalin's plan for European domination because large numbers of the AK would very likely survive the war, returning to Poland as a formidable force ready to oppose any Soviet attempt to annex Poland. Furthermore AK survivors would no doubt have nursed an understandable grudge against Stalin, given the inactivity of the Red Army at Warsaw during August and September. Therefore it suited the Soviet government and Stalin to give the AK the means to carry on fighting the Germans. This allowed the Germans to continue to destroy the AK and Warsaw: the ultimate Soviet plan.

On 13 September the Germans and Soviets began to shell each other from their respective positions along the shores of the River Vistula. This proved beyond doubt that the Red Army could always have aided the AK in Warsaw with artillery barrages onto German positions from across the river. As well as artillery duels there were also Polish Army reconnaissance patrols using amphibious vehicles and motorboats, but it remained unclear if any landings were made on the western shores of the Vistula.[85] It was certain that the Soviets were launching an offensive from Praga and they promised to drop supplies to the AK during the night of 14-15 September. Soviet artillery also shelled Gdansk station, which housed the armoured train that had so harried the AK during the early days of the uprising.

Despite the sudden resurgence of Soviet activity the Germans continued in their campaign to retake and totally destroy Warsaw and the uprising. The AK commander in the Mokotow area reported that during the night of 14-15 September there had been heavy artillery fire, as well two air raids by Stuka dive-bombers in the Sielce area. At 09.30 on 15 September enemy infantry attacked from the north (Podchoraczy Street) the east (Czerniakowska Street) and the south (Bernardynska Street). This offensive was supported by eight tanks and two armoured cars. An AK battalion continued fighting, shifting westward of Belwederska Street from the ruins of Sielce. However the overall situation was summed up as " ... enemy is deliberately clearing the area on the west bank of the Vistula in order to be able to withdraw freely to the west."[86]

There was further fighting as enemy infantry coming from the east, supported again by eight tanks as well as aerial support from Stukas, attacked AK positions on Belwederska, Dolna and Piaseczynska Streets. The AK battalion at Sielce was driven from the area and was pushed backwards; at the same time it had to be reorganised because of the loss of almost its entire command staff. However, the commander of this battalion noted the lack of Soviet activity on the shores of the Vistula.[87] The commander of the Zoliborz area made his report for 15 September. He began with a message concerning supplies dropped by the Soviet Air Force during the night of 14-15 September. The drop seemed quite niggardly with a report of a "few" automatic pistols and six mortars.

At 08.00 on 15 September, German aerial bombardment, accompanied by ground-based artillery fire as well as that from a German armoured train, began but no infantry attack. During the ensuing fighting two German tanks were damaged, and another set alight. From across the Vistula many fires could be seen while Brodno and Pelcowiczna Streets came under heavy artillery fire. At 11.00, after occupying Marymount, the Germans rounded up the civilian population and killed them.[88]

85   Pomian, op.cit. p.23.
86   Ibid. p.24.
87   Ibid.
88   Ibid.

Another message for 16 September discussed the Soviet supplies dropped each night over the city centre since the night of 13-14 September. These were considered to have been inadequate and were listed as: two heavy machine guns, fifty automatic pistols, 50,000 rounds of ammunition, eleven grenade guns and 500 shells, 3,000 cartridges for Russian rifles, 400 hand grenades, five boxes containing arms and ammunition (contents yet to be established). Food was also dropped, but in sacks and without parachutes. There were no reports from Czerniakow, Mokotow and Zoliborz, where supplies also fell. Part of the inadequacy of these drops was that no German ammunition was dropped. This was vital to the AK, who used captured German weapons. However the dropping of these supplies managed to stiffen Polish resolve and helped to improve morale.[89] One cannot help but think that the Soviets supplied just enough to allow the AK to fight on and destroy itself.

During the night of 15-16 September the commander of the Zoliborz area reported that the Soviets had dropped anti-tank weapons, which were useful to the AK. During that day, 15 September, Warsaw had suffered further Stuka attacks while the AK was driven out of the Dabrowski Legion Fort but they held the enemy west of Belwederska Street, with heavy losses on both sides.[90] Between 16 and 18 September much was happening. During 16 September AK units in Czerniakow Street were consolidated with troops from the Berling Army and were involved in fighting off enemy attacks. The following day, 17 September, a further group of about 1,200 Polish troops landed over a two-day period, assumed defensive positions in Czerniakow and were also able to launch counter-attacks against the Germans. However 18 September saw the most amazing sight as American Flying Fortresses of the 8th American Air Force flew over Warsaw and dropped 1,284 capsules containing weapons and ammunition. It was said that the AK was only able to gather 188 of these.[91]

A British report concerning the American operation to Warsaw was much more positive about the success of the operation. It claimed that 50% of the supplies had been received by Poles, whilst it was anticipated that more would be found by the AK during the coming night and taken in. The American aircrews reported fairly accurate anti-aircraft artillery (AAA) but no fighter opposition. Two Fortresses were missing while the remainder had landed at Soviet bases, and their fighter escorts (long-range Mustangs) were able to complete the operation without the need for landing.[92] An SOE report noted that one of the Flying Fortresses had been shot down over the Kampinos Forest, just outside Warsaw. One of the crew was able to bail out but was immediately captured by the Germans, who instead of giving him medical treatment for his wounds, began to beat him up most brutally.[93] The question of the physical, operational and political risks of supplying Warsaw by air is the subject of the next chapter.

---

89   Ibid. p.25.
90   Ibid.
91   Day-to-day.
92   NA: AIR 8/1169 – Warsaw –RAF Assistance – Results of Operations – AIR 8/1169, Air Ministry to Headquarters, BAF (Balkan Air Force) 19 September 1944.
93   NA: HS 4/159 SOE Poland 31, Warsaw Uprising Situation in Poland. Flights & Operations to Poland. Telegrams and General Reports, August 1944 – January 1945. HS 4/159 Polish Forces W/T Station, Warsaw, 18 September 1944.

An official photograph of General Tadeusz Bór-Komorowski, commander-in-chief of the Polish Home Army.

Lieutenant Stanislaw Jankowski "Agaton" from "Pięść" Battalion is pictured on patrol during "W Hour" (5:00 p.m.) at the start of the Warsaw Uprising, 1 August 1944.

Senior Sergeant Franciszek Jabłoński during the restoration of "Chwat". "Chwat" was a German *Jagdpanzer* 38(t) "Hetzer" tank destroyer which was captured by the Home Army soldiers during combat around the main post office. The vehicle was initially heavily damaged and had a barricade built around it, but was later fixed and kept operational until it was lost under the ruins of the postal building. 1 August 1944.

A group of insurgents from Company "Koszta" with flamethrowers in front of Ulrich's store on 11 Moniuszki Street (on the corner of 128 Marszałkowska Street), early August 1944.

A Polish barricade erected on Napoleon Square around the German *Jagdpanzer* 38(t) "Hetzer" tank destroyer (which was captured by the Home Army), 3 August 1944.

Jewish prisoners of Gesiówka – a Nazi concentration camp in Warsaw – were liberated on 5 August 1944 by Polish soldiers from the Home Army's "Zośka" Battalion.

The Kubuś – an armoured car used during the Second World War – was made by the Home Army during the Warsaw Uprising. A single copy was built by insurgents from "Krybar" Group on the chassis of a Chevrolet 157 van. It took part in the attack on Warsaw University.

A medical unit pictured at 9 Moniuszki Street on 5 August 1944. Pictured from the left: Elżbieta (Gabriela) Karska "Joasia" (wounded on 7 September on Nowy Świat Street), regional head of medical units Dr Zofia Lejmbach "Róża" (wounded on 7 September in hospital at Chmielna Street), Danuta Laskowska "Dorota", NN "Małgorzata", Halina Wojtczak-Fijałkowska "Halszka" (wounded on 24 August during an attack on the police station), Wanda Grochowska-Święcińska "Alicja" and Dr Danuta Staszewska "Marta" (died on 7 September on Nowy Świat Street). Walking alongside them is Melania Staniewicz–Wolska "Ewa–Samarytanka", 5 August 1944.

The civilian population fill sand bags in the courtyard of a townhouse on Moniuszki Street during the Warsaw Uprising, August 1944.

This German armoured fighting vehicle – an SdKfz 251 – was captured by Polish insurgents from the 8th "Krybar" Regiment from the German *SS* 5th '*Wiking*' Division. The capture took place on Na Skarpie Boulevard on 14 August 1944. In this photograph – taken on Tamka Street – is the vehicle's first insurgent commander, Adam "Grey Wolf" Dewicz, holding an MP40 sub-machine gun. From Dewicz's nickname, insurgents named the vehicle "Grey Wolf" and used it in an attack on Warsaw University.

A Home Army soldier defends a barricade in the Powiśle district during the Warsaw Uprising. The man is armed with a Błyskawica machine pistol, August 1944.

Home Army soldiers from "Zośka" Battalion in Gesiówka on 5 August 1944 during the Warsaw Uprising. The men are dressed in stolen German uniforms and armed with confiscated German weapons. Pictured from left: Wojciech Omyła "Wojtek", Juliusz Bogdan Deczkowski "Laudanski" and Tadeusz Milewski "Cwik". Milewski was killed the day this photograph was taken. Omyła was killed three days later on 8 August 1944.

A German Ju-87 Stuka bombing Warsaw's Śródmieście district, August 1944.

General Antoni Chruściel "Monter" (pictured in the middle), head of the Warsaw district of AK, alongside his Bureau of Information and propaganda officers at the main post office building on Napoleon Square, 10 August 1944. Pictured from left: Zygmunt Ziółek "Sawa" (in the background), with Jan Rzepecki "Wolski" in front of him and obscured by Lech Sadowski "Wasyl" (in front on the left); next is General Chruściel and to the right of him is Tadeusz Żenczykowski "Kania".

The kitchen in the Adria building on 10 Moniuszki Street, mid-August 1944.

German *SS-Gruppenführer* Heinz Reinefarth – nicknamed the "Butcher of Wola" (pictured first from left in Cossack headgear) alongside commander of the 3rd Regiment, Kuban Cossack Infantry Jakub Bondarenko during the Warsaw Uprising.

A German prisoner of war is captured at the Mała PAST building, 20 August 1944.

A German soldier killed by insurgents during the attack on the Mała PAST building,
23 August 1944.

The Polish barricade on Napoleon Square which was built around the *Jagdpanzer* 38(t) "Hetzer" tank following its capture by the Home Army.

The Prudential building was Warsaw's tallest building and was hit by approximately 1,000 artillery shells during the uprising. Nevertheless, it remained standing until the end. On 28 August 1944 AK cameraman Sylwester Braun "Kris" captured the moment of impact of a Karl-Gerät shell.

Insurgents from Company "Koszta" read a pamphlet from *SS-Obergrupenführer* Erich von dem Bach-Zelewski asking for their surrender on the corner of the Sienkiewicza and Marszałkowska streets. Pictured second from the left is Tadeusz Suliński "Radwan" (wearing glasses) and next to him (wearing the helmet) is Andrzej Główczewski "Marek", August 1944.

A moment of rest at the main post office on Napoleon Square, August 1944.

Soldiers from the "Radosław" Regiment after several hours of sewer marching from Krasiński Square to Warecka Street in the Śródmieście district. The boy in the helmet is Tadeusz Rajszczak "Maszynka" from "Miotła" Battalion, 2 September 1944.

Soldiers from Company "Maciek" of "Zośka" Battalion (part of the "Radosław" Regiment) after several hours of sewer marching from Placu Krasińskich to Warecka Street in the Śródmieście district, early morning on 2 September 1944.

Home Army soldiers on Stawki Street in the Wola district of Warsaw, September 1944.

Soldiers from "Zośka" Battalion – part of the "Radosław" Regiment – after their long march from Placu Krasińskich to Warecka Street, early morning on 2 September 1944.

Commanding officer Major Ivan Denisovich Frolov (pictured in the centre) with officers of the Russian National Liberation Army (RONA) during the Warsaw Uprising, August 1944. The officer to the right of Frolov is Lieutenant Michalczewski. The soldier first from the right is assumed to belong to the Russian Liberation Army (ROA – or POA in Cyrillic [see the arm patch]). Frolov, along with other ROA members, was charged with treason by the Military Board of the Supreme Court of the USSR and hanged in 1946.

A Don Cossack soldier fighting during the Warsaw Uprising. The patch on the soldier's arm has the "ВД" patch, which stands for "Войско Донское" – a Don Cossacks detachment from XV SS Cossack Cavalry Corps, September 1944.

Cossack and German soldiers fighting during the Warsaw Uprising, September 1944. The Cossack soldier probably belongs to the Russian National Liberation Army (RONA), Russian Liberation Army (ROA) or one of the several other formations.

A Polish flag on top of the Warsaw main train station in the last days of the uprising, September 1944.

Home Army soldiers Henry Ożarek "Henio" (pictured left – holding a Vis pistol) and Tadeusz Przybyszewski "Roma" (pictured right – firing a Błyskawica sub-machine gun) from "Anna" Company of the "Gustaw" Battalion fighting on Kredytowa-Królewska Street, 3 October 1944.

The ceremony of signing the Act of Surrender of the Warsaw Uprising. Pictured from left: Colonel Kazimierz Iranek-Osmecki "Heller", *SS-Obergrupenführer* Erich von dem Bach-Zelewski and Lieutenant Colonel Zygmunt Dobrowolski "Zyndram". This photograph was taken in von dem Bach-Zelewski's headquarters in Ożarów Mazowiecki, 3 October 1944.

Soldiers of the Home Army surrendering to the German *Wehrmacht* at the checkpoint in Warsaw, 5 October 1944.

After supressing the Warsaw Ghetto Uprising in 1943, the ghetto (pictured here circa 1950) was smashed into the ground by German forces in accordance with Adolf Hitler's order. The massive destruction of the city during the Second World War is still evident in this photograph, which has a northwest view of Krasińki Gardens and Świętojerska Street.

5

The Battle for Aerial Support

The Warsaw Uprising was always going to be dependent on outside support, as was any other rising against the Germans in occupied Europe. The Paris rising, also in August 1944, was proof that an uprising could be successful. As the Allies approached the French capital, the local French resistance groups rose against the German occupiers and in a popular move, set about liberating themselves. The difference between the Polish and the French uprisings was that the French had friendly allies close at hand. The French 2nd Armoured Division, supported by the 4th US Infantry Division, was rushed to Paris to support the insurgents. Furthermore, the German commander in Paris, General Dietrich von Choltitz, who had only arrived on 9 August, – perhaps with an eye to the future in the case of German defeat and the arraignment as war criminals of senior officers – did not behave as a thug. He appears to have ignored orders from Hitler to burn Paris to the ground. This is not to say that the French did not suffer under German occupation; the Gestapo, the SS and French collaborators behaved as appallingly in France as they did elsewhere in occupied Europe. However Paris got lucky during the summer of 1944. The Allies were genuine allies and were really liberating Western Europe, not annexing it: unlike the Soviets who were busy annexing everything they could seize as they marched westward towards Germany.

Many Poles, though, considered then and now that the Allies should have given greater aerial support to the AK in Warsaw. There are many reasons why the western allies failed to do so, despite their best efforts. The most obvious problem for the Allies was the distance, as a flight to Warsaw from either the UK or from Italy meant a flight of about 1,800 miles across occupied Europe and back. The round trip to Warsaw and back was just about at the end of the operational range of most Allied heavy bombers that would be necessary for the task.

Quite apart from the cost in human and material terms, the use of heavy bombers for Warsaw would have been a major distraction from the continuous bombing campaign against Germany and her allies. Support for the Paris uprising was much easier, as it was local to the Allied offensive in France and crucial to its advance across Western Europe. Poland was much further down the Allied list of priorities while the Soviet government was happy to see the Warsaw Uprising crushed. The British and American governments were reluctant to pick an argument with Stalin over this position. However Soviet intransigence in relation to the supplying of Warsaw placed the Western-Soviet relationship under great strain, especially as at first the Soviet government refused landing rights at Soviet bases to Allied aircraft operating over Warsaw. Quite simply, even if the Allies had suspended the bombing campaign against Germany, and the weather had been brilliant for such long distance flights, and every aircraft had been in perfect working order, the death rates from the operations which did go ahead suggest there would have been a hideous death toll.

Those sending aircraft out on missions to Warsaw would have to account to both their military and political masters for why there was such a high casualty rate for such little operational reward. They would had to justify every aircraft and man sent, for every death and every aircraft lost. The Poles in London were not interested in such considerations. Their view is evident in a Minute from Major-General Tabor of Polish VI Bureau (Intelligence) to his British counterpart, Major-General Gubbins, stated that he did not accept the argument that 50% losses were unacceptable; he considered that 100% loss rate could be justified and that if the British did not want to lose their crews, they should just give the aircraft to Poles to fly.[1] This was quite a reckless attitude, not untypical of some of the Polish senior officers of that time – especially as they were not sharing the risks.

Poland was not a democracy and had had little experience of that political system. This was a problem for the Allies when dealing with their Polish associates. As a result of this lack of experience, the Polish military and its civilian counterparts frequently hoisted the flag of Polish democracy but consistently failed to colour it in. This failure in democracy meant that the Poles never really understood what the British and American governments were really doing, or why they had to work within a framework of consensus, especially when unpleasant and unpopular decisions had to be made. A casualty rate of 100% would have caused resignations and unrest in Western democracies, even under the conditions of global war.

To look at the aerial supply of Warsaw one should consider the original need for any revolt against German rule in Poland, rather than the improvisation that became the hallmark of the Warsaw Uprising. One of the demands originally made for a successful uprising was the dispatch of Polish-piloted Mustang fighters to Warsaw but with the proviso that the AK should have captured airfields there. This was one demand that Tabor made of Gubbins. He made others, such as an increase in stores dropped over Warsaw; bombing the airfields around Warsaw; the dispatch of the Independent (Polish) Parachute Brigade; a declaration of "combatant rights" for the Polish Secret Army and the sending of an Allied Military Mission to the commanding officer of the AK.[2] The demand for the dispatch of long-range Mustang fighters, flown by Polish pilots, is interesting, as the original and more rational plans for an uprising called for the seizure of airfields around Warsaw. Indeed the main task of a rising was the seizure of airfields. This would further operations by providing much-needed bases for resupplying, as well as for Polish paratroopers. Any such rising would have to be part of a nationwide action, closely coordinated with the general offensive and direction of the Allies already in Europe.[3]

Within twelve months the situation in Poland had changed dramatically. Even though the Allies had landed in France during June 1944; the nearest ally, geographically, was the Soviet Union. By 1944 the Soviet Union had made it quite clear that Poland was to become a satellite state – or more honestly a colony of the Soviet Empire. Furthermore as far as the Soviet government was concerned the Polish government-in-exile, stuck in London, was an irrelevance. The Soviets already had a Soviet-backed Polish government, waiting in the wings to take power as the Red Army advanced across Poland. The rapid westward advance of the Red Army during 1944 had surprised everybody including the Allies, who were uncomfortable with it but could hardly complain. The Soviets were defeating the Germans in the east and so the Allies had to live with it.

The rapid advance of the Red Army into Poland created a sense of panic amongst Poles, especially those of the pre-war elites. They were determined to regain the privileged lifestyles they had enjoyed, frequently at the expense of the majority of their compatriots. This sense of panic manifested itself in the ill-considered judgments made at the end of July 1944 as the Warsaw Uprising was about to begin. These hasty decisions were not part of the original plans for a national uprising in Poland but were obvious compromises, and had repercussions. In particular, Warsaw could not be supplied as the uprising was not nationwide, while the Soviets refused to help until it was too late.

The result was that Warsaw was marooned: besieged by two vicious enemies who were determined to see the city and its inhabitants destroyed. One enemy, Germany, was active in this destruction;

1   PISM: LOT A.V. *Pomoc Lotnictwa Dla Kraju 1941-1946* (Aerial Support for the Homeland 1941-1946) LOT A.V. 11/2, Major-General S. Tabor (VI Bureau) to General Gubbins, 7 August 1944.
2   NA: HS 4/157, Major-General Tabor to Major-General C. McV. Gubbins, 3 August 1944.
3   PISM: LOT A.V. 11/1c, Meeting Between Polish General Staff and (British) Imperial General Staff, 5 August 1943.

the other, the Soviet Union, by doing nothing allowed it. The London Poles expected the Allies to operate in this morass of military-political intrigue, demanding that they drop supplies, send paratroopers and provide aerial support in general. Despite the operational difficulties as early as the night of 4-5 August the Allies did begin to drop supplies over Warsaw, when fourteen aircraft were dispatched between Krakow and Warsaw. Six of these drops were successful, while four British aircraft were lost.[4] The next day the Chief of the Air Staff, Marshal of the Royal Air Force, Charles Portal, wrote to Air Marshal John Slessor, C-in-C Mediterranean Allied Air Forces (MAAF), who was responsible for the provision of aircraft flying from Italy to Warsaw. Portal reported that the Chiefs of Staff had accepted the views of senior commanders in the Mediterranean that operations to supply Warsaw were not practical.

The Poles protested "violently" at the highest levels and the British Chiefs of Staff had to prepare a report to counter their arguments. The main points of the Polish argument were that the Germans had no anti-aircraft defences in Warsaw, and that on the same night aircraft flying from Italy had dropped supplies over another site in Poland at a greater distance than Warsaw. Portal observed to Slessor that there was no question of pushing him into providing aircraft for operations which he considered to have been costly and useless, but he emphasised that even a small operation – if it was considered practical – would be a "gesture" that might have "far reaching" results on future relations between the London Poles and the British government.[5] The claim that there were no anti-aircraft defences in Warsaw was untrue, as a Polish report later confirmed. It recommended that the anti-aircraft guns should be attacked with fighter planes.[6]

In trying to bully the Allies, particularly the British, into supplying Warsaw, the London Poles exposed the already broken relationship between themselves and the Soviet government. They made few, if any, appeals to Stalin to supply Warsaw and support the uprising militarily. The Red Army might have at least been able to help with long-range artillery and fighter and bomber support. Soviet aerial support would have been beneficial against the Stuka dive-bombers which were destroying at will large parts of Warsaw. Stukas as bombers had been largely redundant since 1940 when they were shot out of the skies at the beginning of the Battle of Britain, but they did retain a role on the eastern front. Whenever Stukas came under fire from Allied aircraft they had always come off worse but they were an ideal weapon for use against defenceless civilians.

As already discussed the Allies were also perplexed at the attitude of the Soviet government towards the Warsaw Uprising and the possibility of the Soviets supplying Warsaw by air which the Soviets could have easily done. A message from the Staff at the Headquarters of MAAF to 30 (British Military) Mission sent on 18 August 1944 reveals:

> I am of course not in position to judge why the Russians are not giving any assistance to underground army Warsaw. But understand you have instructions from Foreign Office about approach to Soviet government on this subject and following may be of use to you. With sole object of sustaining resistance in Warsaw and thus helping advance of Red Army the RAF in Italy have spent the past fortnight used every aircraft at our disposal with necessary range to drop supplies at Warsaw. We have very few which are capable of this job which involves a flight of nearly 1,800 miles at night through enemy fighter defences. Actually including the Polish flight, the establishment of the unit with the necessary capacity including night bombers diverted from strategic bombing amounts to only 62 aircraft, thought their actual strength at the beginning of the month was considerably less owing to heavy losses in July.

---

4   NA: AIR 8/1169, Warsaw – RAF Assistance – Result of Operations.
5   Ibid. C.A.S. to Slessor, 5 August 1944.
6   NA: HS 4/157, Lieutenant-Colonel Utnik to Perkins, 15 August 1944.

Of this force since the beginning of the fighting in Warsaw we have lost in operations in Poland 21 missing, 3 destroyed on landing owing to flak (AAA) damage, 9 seriously damaged including crews wounded and 6 less damaged. Quite simply within two weeks there will be no aircraft left. Russians arranging use of B.25 (aircraft) for shuttle service to Tito. (Yugoslav Communist partisan leader) These better suited for supplying Warsaw from Russia. West could supply Tito with planes that are useless for supply to Warsaw. The RAF have been helping Soviets – now they should help regarding Warsaw.'[7]

On the same day it was made clear that military operations under the command of General Dwight Eisenhower, the American Supreme Commander of Allied Operations in Western Europe, had priority. Italian operations came second for all sorties involving heavy aircraft. This included 148 Squadron RAF, which had been flying missions to Warsaw, as well as the Polish Flight, also operating from Italy.[8] Flights to Warsaw were to become a distraction, a luxury that could not be afforded on a regular basis.

Correspondence between General Sosnkowski and Sir Archibald Sinclair, the British Secretary for Air, illustrates that despite the tragedy unfolding in Warsaw; the Poles in London were still keeping faith with the British government. By the third week of the uprising it must have been obvious to many Poles that it was almost impossible to supply Warsaw from western airbases as the huge losses amongst British, South African and Polish aircrews clearly demonstrated. The Allies had tried to supply the Polish capital by air but continued losses amongst aircrews were unsustainable. Air Marshal Slessor had already ordered the suspension of all flights, both British and Polish. Even so, British flights were still maintained to points over south-west Poland. Slessor also underlined the fact that there was a need for experienced aircrews to fly to Warsaw but these crews could only be found amongst those who had already completed their set number of operational tours over enemy territory. It was against RAF regulations to insist that they should fly on operations over Warsaw.

By the third week of the uprising the London Poles were becoming anxious about the future of the revolt. Sosnkowski requested Sinclair's consent to a demand that crews who had done their required tours of operations should go on operations to Warsaw.[9] Sosnkowski's frustration could perhaps be understood, but it was yet another Polish failure to grasp democratic procedure. Sinclair was forced to tell Sosnkowski that he would like to help the Poles at Warsaw but geography, as well as the relationship between casualties and results, called into question how profitable such operations were. Sosnkowski gallantly replied that as a soldier he understood the situation.[10] This was extremely cordial given that Sosnkowski was being denied aid throughout the Anglo-American camp. It was made quite clear to him that operations in France and Italy were being prioritised over operations to Warsaw. This should have been clear to Sosnkowski after General Eisenhower refused his request to meet the commanding officer of the Polish Air Force, Major-General Izycki to discuss eventual operations over Warsaw.[11]

In a conversation the previous year with Air Marshal Harris, the commanding officer of British Bomber Command, Polish representatives stated that the AK needed 600 flights to supply an uprising. They were told that the Allies did not have the necessary aircraft for such operations,

7   NA: AIR 20/8414, Assistance to Warsaw, HQ MAAF SSO to 30 Mission, 18 August 1944.
8   NA: WO 204/4915, Transportation by Air by Military Aircraft, 18 August 1944.
9   PISM: LOT A.V. 11/2b, General Sosnkowski to Sir Archibald Sinclair, Secretary of State for Air, 19 August 1944.
10   Ibid. Sinclair to Sosnkowski, 20 August 1944; Sosnkowski to Sinclair, 22 August 1944.
11   PISM: LOT A.V. 11/2j, Sosnkowski to Eisenhower, 9 August 1944.

but the Poles persisted in trying to get the necessary aerial support.[12] Lieutenant-Colonel Leon Mitkiewicz, the Polish Military Representative in Washington DC, reported to Sosnkowski that Eisenhower had discussed with his air force generals, Carl Spaatz and Ira Eaker, the technical possibilities of supplying Warsaw but was still waiting for answers to their inquiries.[13]

Izycki also had written to the most senior British Air Force Officers as he was concerned about the morale of the PAF regarding Warsaw. He intended to visit PAF squadrons to explain the situation and tell them how it was going to affect the exiled Poles.[14] Meanwhile Anthony Eden told the Polish Prime Minister, Stanisław Mikołajczyk, that Churchill had personally asked Stalin to give assistance to Warsaw and that the Allies were trying to do all that they could do to supply the city. In a loose, undated Minute there was also a request for the transfer to Warsaw of the Independent Polish Parachute Brigade.[15] The request for Polish paratroopers was another sticking point in Anglo-Polish relations in the context of the Warsaw Uprising: predictably the British refused to allow their deployment to Warsaw, but later squandered them at Arnhem.

The relationship between the British government and the London Poles began to crumble, principally because of the confusion resulting from conflicting reports and the quantity and quality evidence supplied by various sources. Who chose to believe what – and whom – was very unclear. One example was the continued claim that Warsaw was open to Allied aircraft and had no aerial defences or anti-aircraft guns, but this was not true. It is therefore difficult to explain why John Ward, the RAF man in Warsaw, continued to claim the absence of air defences. One such report even ended up on the desk of the Chief of Imperial General Staff, Field Marshal Sir Alan Brooke.[16] In trying to obtain the Polish parachute brigade for Warsaw, Sosnkowski told Brooke that it had been raised to fight in Poland and while the city was still fighting and needed them it would therefore be difficult to tell its members that they were to fight on other fronts. However, in a spirit of compromise Sosnkowski suggested that perhaps it might be possible for only some of the brigade, maybe a company, to be sent to Warsaw, but with heavy weapons. In this way the Allies would not be deprived of the value of the entire brigade. Brooke refused this request also.[17] The question of the refusal to use Polish paratroopers is one that still festers amongst Poles. They might have a case if the Polish evidence is examined objectively, considering what was actually happening in Warsaw during the late summer of 1944.

There is evidence about just how the Polish paratroopers were to be deployed and how they were trained. It should always be remembered that the original reason for raising an independent Polish parachute brigade was to support an eventual uprising in Poland. This should be seen, though, in the context of a national rising in the countryside rather than a localised rising in a dense urban environment with hostile armies to the fore and the rear, making resupplying almost impossible except by air. There was no question of AK reinforcements from outside because of Soviet hostility. However there were other problems, about which the Polish High Command could do nothing.

The most obvious problem was that the Polish Army in the west was under British command. This meant that it was always at the disposal of the British Army and would only be used to further the Allied cause in the war rather than pursuing objectives important for the Polish government-in-exile. The Poles also owned nothing; the Dakota aircraft used for dropping paratroopers were

---

12 PISM: LOT A.V. 11/2l, Memorandum of Conversation with AC Harris, 10 October 1943.
13 PISM: LOT A.V. 11/2k, Mitkiewicz (Washington) to Sosnkowski, 16 August 1944.
14 PISM: LOT A.V. 11/2c (General Situation) Izycki to A.C.M. Sir Trafford C. Leigh Mallory and Sir Arthur T. Harris, 14 August 1944.
15 Ibid. Eden to Mikołajczyk, 17 August 1944, loose minute undated listed as number 5.
16 PISM: LOT A.V. 11/2 f, Sir Alan Brooke, 11 August 1944.
17 Ibid. Sosnkowski to Field Marshal Sir Alan Brooke, 13 August 1944; Sosnkowski to Brooke, 15 August 1944.

usually owned and controlled by the Americans.[18] The Poles had to apply to use these aircraft over Warsaw, and of course they were denied them. However the Polish paratroopers were well prepared for fighting in Poland. It was assumed they would capture German armoured fighting vehicles and so they were trained on such vehicles at the British infantry training depot at Catterick, North Yorkshire. Any problems regarding tactics had been anticipated, as it was anticipated that AK fighters would be at the drop zone after seizing and clearing it ready to receive paratroopers. The AK held on to the cemetery designated as the drop zone for a long time, despite its open position, in an attempt to keep it open and ready for the long-hoped-for landing of Polish paratroopers.[19] This highlights the fact that the Warsaw Uprising was doomed from the beginning. It was unable to fulfil the basic requirements necessary for a successful rising: one of the main tasks of which was the capture and holding of airfields ready for further operations, including paratroopers. All the same in 1943 it was recognised by both the British and Polish General Staffs that "action planned in Poland by the Secret Army cannot be deprived of the minimum air support. It is not only a moral necessity but also an operational" (necessity) and that considerable drops of arms were also necessary.[20]

However the problem remained that the Poles and Poland were no longer considered to be important to the Allies, who had more or less handed the country and its people over to the Soviet Union, in spite of its appalling reputation for human rights violations and aggressive foreign policy. Furthermore the concept of Britain going to war to defend Polish independence had largely been forgotten by this stage of the war, which was a defence against German, rather than Soviet aggression. An essential plank of the military-political situation in the war against Germany was the need to keep the Soviet Union on the side of the Allies. The question of aerial supply to Warsaw almost broke the alliance against Germany.

This was not lost on the German government, as a German Foreign Ministry official noted after the defeat of the uprising:

> The fruitless appeals for help which the Warsaw rebels made to the Allies, the paltry assistance afforded from the air, and the differences of opinion between the British and Soviet governments which all came to light, all combined to hinder the rebels in their fight to hold out and weakened their spirit of resistance. Of special importance was the fact that the Polish Émigré government in London could not bring in any aid from Britain, whilst the pro-Moscow Polish Committee of Liberation in Lublin not only refrained from assisting the movement but even, in later stages, fought in secret against it and its leaders.[21]

It is obvious that the Germans were clearly aware of the terrible difficulties Warsaw presented to Allied diplomacy. This quotation demonstrates that the Germans considered it an opportunity to try to split the Allies further and isolate the Soviet Union. Later, as Germany faced total defeat their government sought to wage a new campaign against the Soviet Union; a type of anti-Bolshevik crusade with the western Allies supporting Germany. This was a forlorn hope of a less than rational leadership. The Japanese Ambassador to Berlin noted the possibility of splits over the question of Poland within the alliance against Germany, and also German hopes of exploiting the

---

18   E-mail to author from Major-General John Drewienkiewicz (British Army – retired) 24 October 2011.
19   Ibid.
20   PISM: LOT A.V. 11/1c, Employment of Polish Air Force in View of Future Action in Poland, Meeting between the Polish General Staff and the Imperial General Staff, 5 August 1943.
21   NA: HW 1/3270, German Exploitation of Warsaw Rebellion for Propaganda Purposes, 17 October 1944, Ministry of Foreign Affairs, Berlin to all stations, written 12 October 1944 (Captured German Documents).

situation in an attempt to cause such a breach, with the Soviet Union the loser. He reported to his Foreign Ministry in Tokyo that:

> It was not doubted that the announcement by the Germans of a policy of magnanimity towards the Poles just as the moment when the Polish question was giving rise to complications between the British, the Americans and the Russians, was a very successful political move but the time and methods for implementing that policy had to be considered from the general standpoint of the handling of the whole eastern problem, and that it was therefore not possible to indicate at what point the question would be settled.

The ambassador was referring to the idea that Poland might get some measure of self-government, proposed by Hans Frank, the Nazi overlord in occupied Poland.[22]

The grim situation in Warsaw continued, and there was another flight to the city during the night of 8-9 August. Three Polish aircraft flew to the capital and dropped supplies. Slessor reported that many night fighters were seen over Warsaw, which was defended by anti-aircraft artillery. The Polish aircrews successfully completed their mission and Slessor described their action as a "gallant show". It was reported that the Poles were going to send a further five aircraft that night (9-10 August) and that they were also trying to persuade Slessor to send 148 Squadron. However, he declined as he wanted to maintain his numbers and not sent any more British Halifax heavy bombers until the last quarter of the moon which would be the night of 11-12 August. Slessor asserted that while a few aircraft might be successful; a large number would not be so.[23] Slessor was also critical of Sosnkowski, who was still trying to bully the British into continuing flights to Warsaw. Sosnkowski implied that Slessor was ignorant of the military and moral implications of not continuing the flights, and considered that he had been successful in his intervention as there had been a flight there. Sosnkowski made a big mistake in his actions. Slessor not only knew that Sosnkowski's demands had been ignored, but he further requested that in future the London Poles should be prevented from political interventions in operational concerns: basically they were a nuisance all round.[24] The London Poles were needlessly making enemies and powerful enemies at that.

By 15 August there had been further operations to Warsaw but with huge casualties. On the night of 14-15 August, twenty-six aircraft were sent out, of which eleven successfully completed their missions – but eight aircraft were missing. These were six Liberators from 205 Group, one from 148 Squadron and another from the Polish Squadron. Heavy AAA was reported, as well as night fighters. Over a period of only two nights the aircraft lost from 205 Squadron represented 25% of its strength. Clearly such a loss rate was unsustainable, and fully justified Slessor's misgivings about the entire operation to supply Warsaw. Slessor also reported that he had sent a message to the Polish President, Władysław Raczkiewicz, which had been reviewed by the British Deputy Prime Minister, Clement Attlee and the Foreign Secretary, Anthony Eden. Slessor noted that the final sentence of the original draft had been removed which had read: "I must warn you that we cannot maintain these arduous and expensive operations indefinitely on a large scale". An interesting omission. Furthermore Slessor asked whether the Soviets were doing anything to help

---

22   NA: HW1/3271, German Situation, Japanese Ambassador, Berlin, Reports Views of "Usual Contact" 18 October 1944, from Japanese Ambassador, BERLIN, to Minister for Foreign Affairs, TOKYO, 12 October 1944. (Captured Japanese Document).
23   NA: AIR 8/1169, Slessor to C.A.S. 9 August 1944.
24   Ibid.

because as he wrote, "We have now lost 16 heavy bombers trying to help Warsaw which I can imagine is about 1 for every ton of supplies that have reached the underground army."[25]

In a personal message to the Chief of Air Staff, Slessor severely criticized the Soviets. Slessor wrote that the "Frantic six" scheduled for that day (16 August) flying from the UK had been cancelled by the Soviets, apparently on the grounds that they did not agree with the target. Slessor wondered if the target was the supply of Warsaw.[26] Given that the "Frantic" operations were a series of shuttle-bombing operations using American aircraft operating between the UK and Italy, and using three Soviet bases in Ukraine, Slessor was probably correct about the Soviet decision to cancel the mission. He went further in the same communication as he stated that: 'You know we are continuing to extend full assistance to the Russians in their activities in Yugoslavia. 10 Dakota loads of medical personnel and stores are due to arrive from Russia tonight. We are also helping them with shuttle operations with B-25s which I feel would be better employed supplying Warsaw. Difficult to resist the Russian failure to supply Warsaw is deliberate policy.'[27] And there it was: the most senior British airman in the operational zone supplying Warsaw saw through the Soviet game, but had to keep his thoughts private. The Soviet government was fooling nobody; they did not have to as there was nothing that anybody on the side of the Allies could do about the Soviet policy, at least not in public.

The following day Slessor made another grim report to the CAS concerning operations to Warsaw for the night of 16-17 August. It was reported that eighteen aircraft had been sent out but six were now missing: four Liberators from 205 Group and two Polish aircraft from 1586 Flight. Slessor stated that this was the second time in three nights of operations in which around 30% of the force dispatched had failed to return. Polish losses over thirteen nights of operations to Poland during August had been twenty-one aircraft lost, with another three destroyed on landing as a result of AAA damage. Out of 113 aircraft sent out to Warsaw, most were damaged because of enemy action. Slessor concluded that he could not possible carry on with such a casualty rate and ordered the cessation of operations to Poland. Slessor noted that this rate of loss was not over Warsaw itself but over the forests just outside, which Slessor considered to have been of little value to the AK. Once more he made his feelings known, writing: "the fact must be faced that unless supplies can be sent by, say from the UK or by the Russians, the underground army is beyond our help." Slessor concluded that he considered that his decision to stop flights had been accepted, as Churchill had been informed with no repercussions.[28] It was at this time that Churchill had personally asked Stalin to give assistance to the AK in Warsaw.[29] Overall during August the British had sent 160 aircraft from Italy: eighty successful sorties and twenty-five aircraft lost.[30] The Poles were still willing to run the risk of flying on moonlit nights and requested the ban on flights during that period be lifted for Polish aircrews, as they considered that they might never get another chance of aiding Warsaw.[31]

By mid-September there had been further attempts to supply Warsaw from the air. The Balkan Air Force, Allied aircraft operating in the Balkans, in a report to the Headquarters of MAAF which was sent on to 334 Wing, noted that there was every intention to supply Warsaw, dropping supplies on to reception areas in the city and its surrounding areas. This was until further notice, subject to suitable weather every night. Supplies were to be dropped from 11,000 feet,

25   NA: AIR 8/1169, Slessor to C.A.S., 15 August 1944.
26   Ibid. Personal for C.A.S. from Slessor, 16 August 1944.
27   Ibid.
28   NA: AIR 8/1169, Slessor to C.A.S. 17 August 1944.
29   PISM: LOT A.V. 11/21, Eden to Mikołajczyk, 17 August 1944.
30   NA: AIR 8/1169, Dispatches from MAAF on Dropping Operations to Warsaw.
31   PISM: LOT A.V. 11/2g, 5 September 1944.

employing delayed parachute opening devices. The types of aircraft to be deployed were Halifaxes and Liberators but the numbers on each mission were quite modest, between two and twenty-five. The aircraft were to operate between 10,000 and 17,000 feet and the times over the target were to be between 2.00 and 02.00 hours local time.[32]

The greatest aerial supply success was the massive daylight American drop of 18 September, using 108 B-17 Flying Fortresses, whose presence lifted flagging Polish spirits. There are various reports on just how much aid the AK received from this single drop but a British account considered that 50% of the containers dropped into Polish hands, and it was anticipated that more would be collected by the AK during the coming night. The Americans reported fairly accurate yet moderate AAA, and no fighter opposition. Two Fortresses were missing but the remainder landed at Soviet air bases in Ukraine, while the American fighter escorts completed the round trip without the need to land. Overall on the ground there was no change, and the Poles said that no further drops were immediately required over Warsaw itself. Local SOE operatives provided fresh intelligence concerning new locations for further drops in the Warsaw area.[33] Two days later it was reported that the Poles had received 1,284 containers from the American drop.[34]

By the third week of September the AK began to take a more realistic look at what their resources actually consisted of, rather than relying on hope and wishful thinking. It was not a pretty picture. A message dated 21 September noted that Mokotow and Zoliborz were virtually cut off with the only military communication being wireless and the occasional courier. In the main part of the city there were 260,000 people, of whom about 50% were refugees from other parts of Warsaw. Just about everything, military and civilian, was in short supply, as there was only 100 tons of barley, fifty tons of wheat, enough fats for another two days and sugar for four days. It was thought that some people were hiding supplies but it was agreed that even this would not last for long. Furthermore there were no gas or electricity supplies, while water from a mains supply was a distant memory. However, ninety-two wells had been sunk. The medical services were doing their best but medical supplies and personnel were in extremely short supply.[35]

Within a week the situation had deteriorated further. Starvation was beginning to affect the civilian population, though not AK fighters who were given priority regarding food and treated separately. All of the wheat had been distributed and the remaining sixty tons of barley was being given out. There were no other reserves left to feed the people. Food supplies dropped by the Soviets without parachutes were destroyed on landing and played no part in the feeding of Warsaw. The civilian population was beginning to eat dogs. Once more the Poles were confronted with the fear of having to capitulate – or at least transfer the remaining civilian population into German custody – because of the threat of starvation. Without any large drops of food, it was calculated that the longest the AK could hold out was ten days. At the same time scarlet fever was beginning to break out.[36]

The Allies were clearly aware of the situation, as a report to the 30 Military Mission in Moscow described the general conditions in Warsaw. This report more or less confirmed what the Poles were saying: utilities were non-existent, the food situation critical, disease rife, and the wounded lacked medical attention while the Germans burnt down blocks of buildings in an effort to crush resistance. The strength of the AK in Warsaw was estimated to be between 25,000 and 30,000, but

---

32   NA: AIR 8/1169, Balkan Air Force to HQ MAAF, Repeated 334 Wing, 15 September 1944.
33   NA: AIR 8/1169, Air Ministry Whitehall, London, to Headquarters BAF (Balkan Air Force) 19 September 1944.
34   NA: AIR 20/7985, Williams to Slessor, 20 September 1944.
35   *History of the Second World War. British Foreign Policy in the Second World War. Volume III* (ed) Sir Llewellyn Woodward, London, HMSO, 1971, pp.70-1. Hereafter *BFP3*.
36   Ibid. p.71.

severely limited in operational ability owing to its lack of weapons. By mid-September the AK was only fighting in localized areas rather than throughout the city but morale was believed to be good.

The parts of Warsaw still held by the AK remained numerous but isolated from one another: a situation that might be described as a series of mini sieges. Weapons were still being asked for in aerial drops. The main requirements of the AK were portable anti-tank weapons, automatic weapons with ammunition and grenades. There was also a need for explosives, "engineer" material to be used for demolition and the construction of road traps, bombs and other such things. Medical supplies were also requested to fight disease, beginning to spread throughout the city, as well as dehydrated and concentrated foods including condensed milk and vitamins. It was noted that by 15 September the RAF had carried out ninety successful drops involving 145 tons of supplies. These consisted mainly of automatic and semi-automatic weapons (Bren and Sten guns), PIAT anti-tank weapons, explosives and ammunition. Of this tonnage 10% was made up of foodstuffs. The operations were flown by night from Italy. The US 8th Air Force planned a single day operation in order to drop 130 tons of equipment, which was to comprise 200 Bren guns, 100 PIATs, 2,700 Sten guns, 6.5 tons of explosives and engineers' stores, forty tons of food and 2 million rounds of ammunition. This was the celebrated drop of 18 September. Once more it was noted that the Soviets could help by dropping supplies as well as bombing airfields and other identified targets. It was recognised that the maximum benefit could be obtained if aerial operations took place at night, and the AK must be aware of pending operations, but this was not an essential criteria. The Allies recognised the fact that German weapons, equipment and especially ammunition were essential as the Poles had captured large quantities of German guns but little ammunition for these weapons. A number of targets to be bombed were identified, including some enemy strongholds such as the Gdansk railway station, an armoured train which caused havoc across the city was based, as well as two airfield and motorized columns coming in and out of Warsaw.[37]

The air campaign over Warsaw was a bone of contention between the London Poles and the western Allies, notably the British. Prior to the Moscow Mission report and the American daylight flight to assist Warsaw, Colonel Hancza, the Polish representative at Bari, Italy, considered that the aid being flown over hundreds of miles of enemy-occupied territory was merely "symbolic assistance". The British understandably asked about the thirty-five aircrews which they had "chucked away", as well as the many aircraft lost in this "symbolic assistance". Indeed, the British wanted Hancza removed ,as it would be better for all including the AK.[38] On the same day, 1 September 1944, Slessor bitterly complained about the high loss rate amongst air crews and aircraft. He noted that on the previous night there had been a 25% loss of both over Warsaw, with five out of twenty aircraft missing: while out of nine drops only four had actually fallen on the nominated places. This caused Slessor to conclude that every successful drop cost at least one airplane.[39]

Given this rate of loss, and the attitude of Hancza, it was not surprising that senior British air force officers became exasperated with the Poles. Indeed the first time that Field Marshal Brooke (CIGS) mentioned the uprising was on 9 August when he wrote in his diary that he had lunched with General Sosnkowski, who was "very upset that we are not providing more assistance to the Underground Army fighting the Germans in Warsaw".[40] The problem for the Poles was that the British War Cabinet and the Imperial General Staff were preoccupied with the fighting in

---

37   NA: AIR 20/2711, Assistance to Warsaw – Results Achieved 9/8/44 – 22/9/44 A.M.S.S.O. to 30 Military Mission, Moscow, 15 September 1944.
38   Ibid. HQ MAAR SSO to Air Ministry, Whitehall, 11 September 1944.
39   Ibid. Slessor to V.C.A.S., 11 September 1944.
40   *War Diaries 1939-1945. Field Marshal Lord Alanbrooke*, (eds) Alex Danchev & Daniel Todman, London, Weidenfeld & Nicolson, 2001, p.579.

Normandy and Italy, as well as dealing with German rocket attacks against London; a pitiful uprising a thousand miles away with no chance of success was of little or no relevance to them.

As hard as it sounds the Warsaw Uprising was a sideshow to the Allies and not part of the overall strategic plan to defeat Germany and Nazism. General Brooke had already observed that most of the Chiefs of Staff Meeting for 16 August was taken up with how the Warsaw Uprising might be supported as it was clear that the Soviets had no intention (at that stage) of doing anything. On 23 August, whilst in Italy, Brooke met General Anders, the Commander of Polish 2nd Corps. He remarked to Brooke that the Poles had two deadly enemies, the Germans and the Russians, but the Germans must be defeated first.[41] This in a nutshell presented to Brooke the problem faced by the Poles; enemies back and front, but they were also the only references made by the CIGS to the Warsaw Uprising. At the same time the Soviet government, hell bent on annexing Poland and as much territory westward as possible, successfully portrayed the London Poles and their supporters in Poland and elsewhere as being reactionary and of taking very little direct action against the Germans.[42]

During mid-September as world opinion had momentarily swung against them, the Soviet government finally began to allow the Allies to use their airbases. There was further good news as the Soviet Air Force was finally "strongly and successfully" attacking the Luftwaffe, while supplies received from the Soviets increased morale amongst the AK and civilians alike. The British Foreign Office determined that the Poles were likely to hold on for a "little longer", but as ever in Polish-Soviet relations there was a brickbat in the bouquet. The Soviet government demanded the dismissal of Sosnkowski, the Polish Commander-in-Chief.[43] The question of Sosnkowski's removal was one that more or less united the Soviet government with the British and American governments, as he was seen as a hindrance to smooth relations within the Allied camp, but little thought had been given to just who should replace him.[44]

In the absence of Soviet help, the Allies had worked out some plans for trying to help Warsaw. It was noted during mid-August that the American air commander, General Carl Spaatz, was "straining at the leash" to try to do something, but was waiting approval from the Soviet government to make drops. The original plans were quite grand: a proposal to dispatch seventy to ninety aircraft, each containing three tons of supplies in containers and after dropping their cargoes, heading for Soviet bases for any necessary refuelling, repairs or medical attention needed for wounded airmen.

It was considered necessary that all of the drop zones should be over Warsaw, as there was only light AAA cover but low-level drops were impossible, as few aircraft would reach their destinations. It was therefore decided that the optimal height to drop supplies was 10,000 feet, wind and weather permitting. Overall it was considered that using this method the success rate would be around 40%.[45] Unfortunately this was all dependent on Soviet cooperation, which was not immediately forthcoming.

British officials had already commented on the Soviet attitude towards the Warsaw Uprising. One senior British officer, in a dispatch to General Wilson which was for the attention of Air Marshal Slessor, wrote of the Soviet denial of landing facilities to American B-17s: "This is a grave matter and may have results beyond Warsaw."[46] Eden sent a Minute to Churchill saying that the Soviet government wanted to have nothing to do with the Warsaw Uprising, directly or

---

41   Ibid. pp.581, 584.
42   *BFP3*, p.203.
43   NA: PREM 3/352/12, Sargent to Eden, 15 September 1944.
44   NA: PREM 3/335/12, Eden to Churchill, 5 September 1944.
45   NA: PREM 3/352/12, Secretary of State for Air to Churchill, 19 August 1944.
46   Ibid. Colonel Kent to General Wilson for Air Marshal Slessor, 18 August 1944.

indirectly.[47] This was direct Soviet provocation towards Churchill and Eden, who had supported the Poles fighting in Warsaw even if – as Eden commented –the rising had "gone off at half cock". Eden agreed with Churchill in his assertion that the AK in Warsaw were fighting and killing Germans and that they should be supported for this. Churchill also demanded that Stalin permit aid to be send to support the uprising as the Poles, even they were non-communists, were helping the Soviet Union in its fight against Germany. Churchill made the point that the politics of the situation were not important as the British government took the view that anybody, whatever their background or loyalty, should be backed and encouraged if they were fighting the Germans. He noted that the Polish Prime Minister, Mikołajczyk, desperately needed Allied support over Warsaw politically and practically.[48]

Eden had condemned Soviet inaction at Warsaw from its opening days as it became clear during August that the Soviet government was quite resolute in forbidding the Allies use of Soviet air bases on Soviet territory. Eden wrote the following to Churchill: "Russian inaction is already giving rise to serious criticism here, which can be magnified if the suggestion gets afoot that Polish patriots in Warsaw have been deserted through the Russian failure to carry out supply operations which are well within their power." Eden also told Churchill that the Soviets claimed to have had a setback near Warsaw but he considered that the real Soviet failure was to continue their advance on Warsaw on which the AK "no doubt counted".[49]

Towards the end of the Warsaw Uprising Stalin admitted to the British Ambassador to the Soviet Union that the battle for Warsaw was not going well for the Red Army. Stalin claimed that the River Vistula was an impossible obstacle and that Soviet tanks could not cross it owing to German shellfire. He also reckoned that the Red Army could not get medium artillery across the river. Stalin then tried to blame the uprising for the failure of the Soviet offensive across the Vistula as the AK action had caused the Germans to become extra vigilant. In his explanations about the immediate Soviet failures at Warsaw he went further, claiming that it was not until the Red Army captured Praga that the Soviets finally understood what the insurgents in were up against, especially as the Poles were so badly armed; carrying only rifles and pistols.[50]

This, however, does not explain Soviet actions at Warsaw. They could have provided aerial and heavy artillery support, as well as furnishing bases for Allied aircraft to use for operations over Warsaw. Eden knew this and was well aware that Stalin's true aim was to see the AK destroyed, but there was little that the British government could do about it. The view that influential British officials considered that the Soviet government, in delaying support for the Warsaw Uprising would doom the entire rising, was reported in the *New York Times* as early as 6 August.[51]

By September both the British and American governments were getting decidedly testy with Soviet intransigence: so much that Churchill wrote to President Franklin Roosevelt, suggesting that perhaps American aircraft might just land at Soviet airbases to see what happened. Churchill even considered that "they (the Soviets) might even welcome it as getting them out of an awkward situation."[52] Churchill had recognised that the Soviet government, even though it was being extremely defiant regarding Poland was beginning to feel uncomfortable, especially in their relationship with the Americans. By this stage of the war the British government had very little input in the Anglo-American relationship with the Soviet government. Prior to the summer of 1944 the

---

47   Ibid. Eden to Churchill, 18 August 1944.
48   Ibid. Eden to Churchill, 16 August 1944.
49   Ibid. Eden to Churchill, 15 August 1944.
50   NA: FO 954 Lord Avon (Eden) Papers, FO 954/26, Sir Archibald Clark-Kerr to FO, 24 September 1944.
51   *New York Times*, 6 August 1944.
52   Brotherton Library, University of Leeds, Map Room Messages of President Roosevelt, Reel 5, Churchill to Roosevelt, 4 September 1944.

USA had played no military role in assisting the AK but by the middle of August had wrung out of the Soviet government the recognition of an independent American initiative for the Poles.[53]

It was politics that drove the Poles to revolt in order to try to remove the Germans and also to try and avoid a Soviet annexation. Equally it was politics that ultimately failed them, leading many Poles to this day to see this as their betrayal by the western powers. Politics was the Polish Achilles' heel and thus their downfall.

---

53   Richard C. Lukas, 'The Big Three and the Warsaw Uprising' *Military Affairs*, 39, 1975, 129-35.

6

The Polish Achilles' Heel

After the death of Władysław Sikorski, the Polish Prime Minister and Supreme Commander, at Gibraltar on 4 July 1943, the Polish government-in-exile was rudderless. From September 1939 until his untimely death Sikorski had just about kept his exiled government united and focused. He also maintained a working relationship with the British and American governments, as well as keeping a correct relationship with the Soviet government. Polish-Soviet diplomacy meant keeping Stalin and his Foreign Minister, Molotov, happy. As Prime Minister and Head of the Polish Armed Services Sikorski was able to dominate both Polish military and civilian politicians. This ensured that the Polish-Soviet Agreement, essentially a peace treaty between Poland and the Soviet Union, was signed at the behest of the British government (effectively Churchill) during the summer of 1941, following the German invasion of the Soviet Union.

The Polish-Soviet Agreement was controversial and caused three resignations from the Polish Cabinet. Basically the agreement set aside any grievances that the Poles had with the Soviet Union, especially in relation to the invasion and annexation by the Soviet Union of eastern Poland during September 1939. This included the deportation of the local populace as slave labour into the wastes of the Soviet interior. Once Sikorski was dead, Polish grievances were allowed to fester and became poisonous. There was no Polish figure, political or military, dominant enough to prevent Polish-Soviet relations reaching a total impasse. It is true there was a complete breakdown of Polish-Soviet relations during the final months of Sikorski's life following the revelation of the Katyń, massacre of leading Poles, especially military officers, but there was no opportunity to try to resume diplomacy with the Soviet government before he died.

Therefore after July 1943 there was not a single Polish politician or figure in the west with enough authority or influence to advance their case regarding Soviet intentions in Poland. Furthermore, given his political understanding and his military logic, it is unlikely that Sikorski would have sanctioned the Warsaw Uprising: he might even have seen it as a challenge against his authority, as so much of it verged on a coup d'état rather than a popular uprising. However returning to facts rather than speculation, Sikorski liked to keep his powder dry, and his powder was the AK. He would have never sacrificed this body so needlessly. He would instead have kept it intact for the moment when the Soviets tried to dominate the Polish forests and mountains. Even a reduced underground army made the Soviet army and Polish communists fight until at least 1948 before Poland was totally subdued by the Soviet Union. Applebaum notes that tiny groups of Polish partisans operated against communist rule into the 1950s with the final operator being captured as late as 1959.[1] That might therefore have been the case if the AK had not been wasted at Warsaw? How long would it have taken the Soviet Union to conquer Poland by conventional military means rather than hiding behind the fig leaf of "liberation"? Thus the Warsaw Uprising came down to politics and tactics.

Once Sikorski was dead the two wings, military and political, of the Polish government-in-exile were allowed to drift apart. Sikorski's successor, Stanisław Mikołajczyk, and the new

---

1   Applebaum, op.cit. 109-10.

Commander-in-Chief, General Kazimierz Sosnkowski, rarely spoke to each other and neither enjoyed the warm relationship with Churchill which Sikorski had had.[2] Leading British military and political figures were somewhat reluctant to accept Sikorski's successors. Sir Alexander Cadogan, Permanent Undersecretary at the Foreign Office, confided to his diary when he heard of Sikorski's death, "this is a great blow; there's *no-one* (sic) to take his place … "[3] The following day, on learning of Sikorski's replacements, he wrote that Mikołajczyk might "possibly be all right" but that he considered Sosnkowski as Polish C-in-C to be a problem.[4]

Equally Field Marshal Sir Alan Brooke recorded in his diary that with the death of Sikorski he had lost a real friend, but on meeting Sosnkowski noted that the new Polish C-in-C was quite second rate compared with Sikorski.[5] This was the problem which presented itself to the London Poles after Sikorski's death; nobody of any importance amongst the Allies believed in the exiled Poles. Critically, this was at a time when, following a conclusive victory at the battle of Kursk during the summer of 1943, the Red Army was going on the offensive and bringing the war back to Germany.

From the time of Sikorski's death until the Warsaw Uprising the Poles tried to make their case to the Allies against the Soviet Union and its aggression towards them. However Sosnkowski proved to be a stumbling block in Polish representations: a deeply unpopular figure with all of the Allies, especially the Soviet Union. They viewed him, unfairly as it happens, as a throwback to the pre-war Polish military regime or – as the Soviet government referred to him at every possible opportunity– a "Piłsudski-ite" after Marshal Piłsudski, the Polish interwar military dictator.[6] However Sosnkowski's time in office did nothing to refute his critics and eventually the British government demanded his resignation.[7]

Since the outbreak of war and after the fall of Poland during the autumn of 1939 it had always been assumed in the west that the Polish government-in-exile would be the body – perhaps in collaboration with political figures who had remained behind in occupied Poland – to restore the state, independence and democracy, absent in Poland since 1926. A rather tall order perhaps, but no consideration had been given to sharing power with Communists. Quite simply there had been little support for Communism in Poland between the wars; furthermore the Polish Communist Party had been all but wiped out under Stalin's orders just before the outbreak of war. Therefore it came as a rude shock to the London Poles and their supporters to realise that a post-war Poland might well be a Communist state. Using as its vehicle for this audacious move a resurrected Polish communist movement which was carefully controlled by the Soviet government, the Soviet Union would take control.

Once the Red Army went over to the offensive, the influence of the London Poles began to plummet as the Soviet Union held all the trump cards. As the Red Army advanced westward, it naturally began to reoccupy territory. At first it was driving the Germans from occupied Soviet territory, but on the night of 3-4 January 1944 the Red Army crossed into pre-war Polish territory: territory which the Soviet Union had annexed during the autumn of 1939 and was again retaking. Being once more physically inside pre-war Poland gave the Soviet Union a huge advantage in pressing the case for a Communist takeover of the country. From this position it was able to direct

---

2   Prażmowska, op.cit. p.50.
3   David Dilks, (ed) *The Diaries of Sir Alexander Cadogan, 1938-1945,* London, Cassell, 1971, diary entry, 5 July 1943, p.541.
4   Ibid. Diary entry, 6 July 1943, p.541.
5   Alanbrooke Diaries, diary entry, 22 July 1943, p.432.
6   NA: PREM 3/335/12, Eden to Churchill, 5 September 1944.
7   Ibid.

pro-Soviet propaganda attacking the Polish government-in-exile while praising the alleged virtues of the Soviet Union and the Red Army.

As the Germans retreated before the Red Army at the beginning of 1944, the Soviet Union was still perceived as a liberator. Having taken a considerable beating between 1941 and 1943, this force was perceived as being the only Allied army inflicting direct damage to the German war effort. The Soviet casualty rate was horrendous and made every other Allied offensive, whether in North Africa, Italy or, later, north-west Europe look puny, despite the huge numbers of men and vast amounts of equipment the Americans poured into Europe. If the Allied offensives, including the twenty-four-hour a day bombing of Germany, were of little value or of no interest to the Soviets; the Polish contribution to the war was therefore miniscule: a token only. That was the problem for the Polish government-in-exile by 1944.

The Polish government-in-exile was in grave danger of becoming an irrelevance in comparison with the Soviet Union and its support of the Polish communists. It could not counter the military and political arguments made by the Soviet government after the Soviet victory at Stalingrad at the beginning of February 1943. Furthermore, the London Poles were becoming increasingly estranged from those Poles who continued to endure German occupation but were unwilling to accept a communist takeover either by the Soviet Union or by Polish communists. The British government and the FO were well aware of Stalin, and his government's appetite for deceit, even if publicly they said very little because they needed to keep the Soviet Union in the war against Germany. The London Poles may have held the moral high ground regarding their relationship with the Soviet government, but war is amoral.

It was very clear that at a very senior level the London Poles did not trust the Soviet government, and especially its intentions for Poland, a single iota. Somehow the British government had to address this problem to prevent an open breach between the Soviets and other Allies. Such a breach would have given the Germans valuable ammunition as, in the wake of Red Army's advance they sought to whip up a crusade against the fear of Soviet tyranny spreading across Europe. The problem was that the British tended to ignore Soviet excesses at the expense of the Poles in the west, while the Soviet government, via its embassy in London, was able to win a propaganda war to win the hearts and minds of the British public, especially the working classes, against the London Poles.

The Soviet government's attitude towards Poland became more defined after the Allied conferences held during 1943 in Moscow and Tehran. During these conferences it was asserted by the Soviets that Poland and any subsequent governments; exiled or otherwise, were expected to accept the loss of lands to the east, with a promise of compensation of land to be taken from Germany in the west. But of course Germany had to be defeated first. Even though it was not spelt out as such, it was obvious that the Soviet Union had been given a free hand in east-central Europe; something that the Poles had long feared. In turn they got scant sympathy from the British government, which was single-minded in its prosecution of the war against Germany. Polish fears were dismissed, as Churchill considered that the Soviet Union should be compensated for its war against Germany. However, this was to ignore Soviet collaboration with Germany between 1939 and 1941 and Churchill said that the Poles were "silly" if they thought that Britain would start a new war over the Polish eastern frontier.[8] When Churchill heard from Sir Owen O'Malley, the British Ambassador to the Polish government-in-exile, that many Poles considered the Allied decisions taken during 1943 to be nothing less than "another Munich", Churchill replied that the

---

8   NA: PREM 3/335/7, Eden to Churchill, 6 January 1944.

taunt might be justified (to whom it is not clear) but not the Poles who " ... jumped on the back of Czechoslovakia in that moment of agony and helped rend her to pieces ... "[9]

Even if Churchill had overlooked Soviet collaboration with the Nazis he clearly had not forgotten or forgiven the pre-war Polish government's support for Nazi Germany, which lasted until Spring 1939 when Germany finally turned on Poland before finally invading on 1 September 1939. However not everybody of influence in Britain was happy with the manner in which Poland was being treated. Sir Alexander Cadogan wrote to Eden, voicing his apprehension of how the Soviet Union might treat Poland once the Red Army entered the country. He was concerned with the fate of the AK once they met with the Red Army, and what, realistically, could be done if the Soviets failed to behave correctly once in Poland. Cadogan made his reservations clear about any agreement with the Soviet government concerning Poland: he considered that the Soviet government, personified in the figure of Stalin, should be made to fulfill its commitments towards Poland and east-central Europe as a whole.[10] Despite Cadogan's criticisms, the fate of Poland had been decided in 1943 and the Soviet Union had been more or less guaranteed a free hand in east-central Europe. This is not to say that the British and American governments had totally given up on the Polish government-in-exile, as the political events of the Warsaw Uprising revealed, but political goodwill had to be tempered with military commonsense, which left the AK stranded in Warsaw.

Once Warsaw rose up, Mikołajczyk set out for Moscow to see Stalin. Davies considers that this was to try to strike a deal with Stalin for arms and perhaps reinforcements for the AK, as well as political and diplomatic support.[11] Mikołajczyk was wasting his time; Stalin was unmoved by the uprising. Furthermore Mikołajczyk had already been told by Clark-Kerr, the British Ambassador to the Soviet Union, that the London Poles needed to accept four points in order to come to anything near an agreement with Stalin. The four points were: the remodelling of the Polish government-in-exile so that there were no "reactionaries" (anti-Soviets), the acceptance of the revised Polish-Soviet frontier – the so-called Curzon Line – (basically the annexation of eastern Poland by the Soviet Union), a withdrawal of the suggestion that Katyń was a Soviet war crime and some kind of working arrangement with the pro-Soviet Polish Committee of National Liberation. Mikołajczyk was not prepared to accept this list of demands and was also somewhat disturbed to discover the pro-Soviet British line in Polish-Soviet relations.[12]

A further problem for the Poles, both Stalinists and those exiled in London, was that they were overawed by Stalin. Mikołajczyk and Adam Romer, a senior Polish politician and publicist, were both impressed by the Soviet dictator. Romer reported that he was impressed with Stalin's "quiet" and "wisdom", and his "apparent willingness" to reach a settlement with the Poles. Romer was deluded enough to believe that Stalin was impressed with Mikołajczyk.[13] It was all too reminiscent of Neville Chamberlain at Munich in 1938, haplessly negotiating with Hitler, who was out to start a war to suit his own ideology. Stalin was no different from Hitler and the British had not improved their hand either since then. It may have been a different dictator in 1943 but Stalin deployed the same gangster-style methodology.

The truth was that Stalin did not need to say anything, one way or the other. He was getting what he wanted: Poland. There was nothing that the London Poles or the AK could do about it if they were willing to waste the AK, their only asset in Warsaw. The London Poles and the AK had fallen into Stalin's trap; their political inexperience had found them out. A more experienced Anthony Eden told Mikołajczyk that it would be a mistake to be away from Moscow for too long

---

9   NA: PREM 3/335/8, Churchill to Eden, 15 February 1944.
10   Ibid. Cadogan to Eden, 13 February 1944.
11   Davies, *Rising.* p.226.
12   Jan M. Ciechanowski, *The Warsaw Uprising of 1944*, Cambridge, CUP, 1974, p.65.
13   *BFP3*, p.198.

as it would give the Polish Stalinists too free a hand in matters concerning the future of Poland.[14] Mikołajczyk may have demurred on this observation of Eden but he may have been cautious of being absent from London. It was not beyond the wit of the more reactionary Poles to remove him from office, as the military had removed August Zaleski in the summer of 1940, when he briefly replaced Sikorski. This caused Polish military officers to mount a coup in Central London, remove Zaleski and return Sikorski to office; all within a twenty-four-hour period.[15]

Churchill continued his support for the Poles in Warsaw, and very early in the uprising made approaches to Stalin requesting help for the Poles. On 4 August 1944 Churchill, at the "urgent request" of the AK, reported that subject to weather conditions sixty tons of equipment and ammunition required by the AK would be dropped over the south-western quarter of Warsaw. He also made another appeal for Soviet aid and told Stalin that one and a half divisions were attacking the AK in Warsaw.[16] Stalin was swift to reply, and predictably poured scorn on the AK. He claimed that they were exaggerating their numbers and had no chance of capturing Warsaw, which was defended by four German divisions.[17] Clearly there was no sympathy to be got from Stalin even with a personal appeal by Churchill himself. The Soviet attitude was resolute. Eden, in talks with his Soviet counterpart Molotov, got no further than Churchill had with Stalin.

Eden wrote that Molotov (and therefore Stalin), considered the Warsaw Uprising was a scheme for the reckless: just a huge adventure for its participants. Molotov asserted that the rising should have been arranged with the Soviet High Command, but Polish commanders and leaders did not want to do this. Molotov considered that the failure to do this was a crime and claimed that the AK had let down their people: the rising was failing and they were trying to shift the blame on to the Soviet High Command. Eden realised that Molotov had made up his mind and the reality was that the British and American governments were wasting their time (Eden's phrase was "beating the air") in trying to get Soviet cooperation over Warsaw.[18]

The Soviet assertion that nothing had been arranged with the Soviet High Command was a blatant lie. Soviet radio stations had for some considerable time been calling for the Polish population to drop all caution and start a general rising against the Germans. Eden had noted this and sent it to Churchill. It was too passed on to the American President, Franklin Roosevelt. As late as 29 July Moscow Radio broadcast an appeal from the Union of Polish Patriots (Communist-leaning) to the population of Warsaw, which after referring to the fact that the "guns of liberation were now within hearing", called on people to rise up against the Germans.[19] The Soviets played a completely dishonest game, because Mikołajczyk reported that when he saw Molotov on 2 August the Soviet Foreign Minister had made no criticism of the uprising.[20] Indeed not only had the Soviet broadcast urged Warsaw to rise up; the Soviets had also dropped leaflets signed by Molotov urging the Poles to arm themselves and revolt.[21]

In a short time a war of words had broken out over the timing and the responsibility for the beginning of the Warsaw Uprising. Some major figures lent themselves and their opinions to this major debate; others died on the barricades and in streets of Warsaw. In order to try to establish what was actually happening in Warsaw, the Polish government-in-exile despatched a senior political figure, Dr. Józef Retinger, to the capital. Despite his age – he was 56 – Retinger parachuted

---

14   Ibid. p.202.
15   McGilvray, *A Military Government in Exile*, pp.53-5.
16   NA: PREM 3/403/2, Churchill to Stalin, Personal Telegram, T.1547/4, 4 August 1944.
17   NA: PREM 3/352/12, Stalin to Churchill, 5 August 1944.
18   Ibid. Eden to Churchill, 18 August 1944.
19   Ibid. Churchill to Roosevelt, 19 August 1944.
20   Ibid. FO to Churchill, 22 August 1944.
21   Forczyk, op.cit. p.13.

into Warsaw to liaise with senior underground figures and to deliver money. He reported that during the night of 18-19 August the Soviets had dropped leaflets over Warsaw which described the uprising as "the work of an irresponsible clique in London", and encouraged people to cease fighting.[22]

The idea of placing blame was not restricted to the Soviet government, as a memorandum from Brendan Bracken, the British Minister of Information and personal friend of Churchill, reveals. He wrote to Churchill: "the main subject of discussion at the Foreign Press Conference was the question of guilt in the Warsaw Uprising. The *Wilhelmstrasse* spokesman (German) quoted a report from the London correspondent of *Morgontidningen* (Sweden) that in the opinion of the *Daily Worker* and *News Chronicle* (both British publications), 'The semi-fascist Polish government in London had prematurely given the order for the revolt to lead Moscow on to thin ice.' *Morgontidningen*'s comment on this view was that the 'Moscow transmission of the Red Poles' has 'continually bombarded Warsaw with the demand to take up arms' although, when the rising had taken place and the situation was 'desperate' the same station branded the insurgents as 'political snipers and military idiots'. The correspondent drew the conclusion that 'Moscow intends to pave the way for the future trial and liquidation of undesirable Poles'."[23]

Bracken's memorandum was inspired because it not only laid bare the infighting within the British press, in which Left-leaning publications saw one of the Allies as a "semi-fascist" government, but were also seen through, as were Soviet pretensions by a correspondent from a neutral state. The final analysis of Soviet propaganda was uncanny, as this was exactly what the Soviets did later when sixteen leading members of the AK were arrested and put on trial. Other AK leaders died in Warsaw, or fought the Soviets until 1948 and beyond or simply disappeared. However both the AK and the London Poles should have been alert to the Soviet attitude towards them, because on 31 July, just as the uprising was about to start, the Soviets invited thirty senior AK officers to a conference in Lwow. The Poles probably thought that it was to be some kind of liaison meeting with their Soviet counterparts but the Soviets immediately arrested them on arrival accusing them as being "criminals and Polish fascists".[24]

Churchill's response to Bracken was perhaps somewhat naïve, given that he was the British Prime Minister. He replied: "I see from the papers that the agony of Warsaw has been practically suppressed. There is no need to mention the Soviet behaviour but surely the facts should be given some publicity. Is there any stop on this matter! Is there any reason why the consequences of the strange and sinister behaviour should not be made public? It is not for us to cast reproaches on the Soviet government but surely the facts should be allowed to speak for themselves."[25]

Quite simply Churchill was bedeviled by the fact that Soviet propaganda was winning the war of words and that the Soviet authorities was able to put the Soviet point of view over quite persuasively. This was a time when many in British society considered that the war was one about equality in the future and the sweeping away of the old order. An example of Soviet propaganda in the UK was the publication in the English language of *Soviet War News* and *Soviet War News Weekly*, published daily and weekly respectively and distributed via the Soviet Embassy in London. In this way the Soviet Government was able to put forward its version of events in Warsaw; continuously glorifying the Soviet contribution while vilifying the AK in Warsaw, especially its commanders.[26]

---

22   NA: PREM 3/352/12, FO to Churchill, 20 August 1944.
23   Ibid. Minister of Information to Churchill, 22 August 1944.
24   Bellamy, op.cit. p.617.
25   NA: PREM 3/352/12 Churchill to Minister of Information, 23 August 1944.
26   *Soviet War News*, 14 August 1944; *Soviet War News Weekly*, 14 August 1944. These two editions are prime examples of Soviet propaganda in the UK during August 1944.

The British press was often against the Polish action in Warsaw. The British Communist paper, *The Daily Worker*, trumpeted the Soviet line that the AK had failed to consult the Soviet Government regarding the uprising in Warsaw.[27] Churchill's frustrations with dealing with the Soviet Government was as nothing, compared with that of the naivety of the Poles both in London and Warsaw, which was staggering and bordered on reckless. The Poles may have had a more realistic view of the Soviets compared with most people but they refused to accept their reduced status in the alliance against Germany.

Churchill was voted out of office in the British general election of July 1945: proof of a popular desire for change in British domestic politics and society. On the other hand, the Poles, with some justification, were portrayed as reactionaries. Many clung to their outmoded aristocratic titles, which reflected the eighteenth-century, and they seemed determined to revive the impoverished, corrupt and backward state which had been interwar Poland. It is equally true that many people did not know anything of the reality of Stalinist Russia. They considered that Stalin and the Soviet Union could change the world for the better, and that any criticism was merely reactionary propaganda. Even if Churchill could have laid bare the truth of the Soviet stance at Warsaw; the immediate consequence would have been dire, for the Soviet Union might well have removed itself from the alliance against Germany. Had this happened, the Germans could have diverted their forces from the east to the west and possibly pushed the Allies back into the sea in Normandy; the campaign that followed D-Day was still uncertain at that time. At home it was quite likely that many people would not have believed that the Soviets were behaving in such a treacherous manner in Warsaw.

Churchill obviously did not believe much that Stalin said and continued to badger him with messages coming from the Poles; either from Warsaw or London. However Stalin remained resolutely indifferent towards their plight. Churchill repeated a message from Warsaw, lamenting that not only were they not receiving any material aid but also complained that they were even denied moral support from the Allies. Churchill, almost in an aside to Stalin, requested that the Soviet Air Force should fly in equipment, especially machine guns and ammunition. The Allies were trying to do so, but over vast distances across enemy-occupied territory, while the Soviets could do the same, flying over Soviet-held territory and needing to fly only 100 miles to get to Warsaw.[28] Stalin in his reply to Churchill maintained the Soviet fictional account of events in Warsaw, as he wrote to the British Premier: "After the conversation with M. Mikołajczyk I have given orders that the Commander of the Red Army should drop arms intensively in the Warsaw sector. A parachutist officer was also dropped, who, according to the report of the Command, did not reach his objective as he was killed by the Germans. Further, having familiarised myself more closely with the Warsaw affair, I am convinced that the Warsaw action represents a reckless and terrible adventure which is costing the population large sacrifices. This would not have been if the Soviet Command had been informed before the beginning of the Warsaw action and if the Poles had maintained contact with it."[29]

Stalin's reply was largely a tissue of lies. As we have already seen the Soviet government called for the Poles to rise up in Warsaw, and therefore the Polish offensive was sanctioned by the Soviet authorities. However the AK were too successful, and the rising went on too long for Stalin's liking, and that was why he railed against the Warsaw Uprising in the middle of August. The AK was not dying quickly enough for him, and so posed a serious threat to Soviet imperialist ambitions. President Roosevelt and Churchill tried a joint approach to Stalin, trying to appeal

27   *The Daily Worker*, 14 August 1944.
28   NA: PREM 3/403/2 (Soviet Union Telegrams 1944) Churchill to Stalin, T. 1609/4, 12 August 1944.
29   Ibid. Stalin to Churchill, 17 August 1944.

to his sense of embarrassment as they wrote: "we are thinking of world opinion if the anti-Nazis in Warsaw are in effect abandoned". The two Western leaders expressed their most earnestly-held belief that they and Stalin should do their " … utmost to save as many patriots as possible". Again an appeal was made to supply Warsaw, either by the Soviets or allowing the Allies to do so. It was emphasized that time was of the essence and once more requested Stalin's approval.[30] In his reply, Stalin as ever condemned the rising in a single paragraph, which read: "Sooner or later the truth about the group of criminals who embarked on the Warsaw adventure in order to seize power will be known to everybody. These people have exploited the good faith of the inhabitants of Warsaw, throwing many unarmed people against German guns, tanks and aircraft. A situation has arisen in which each new day serves not the Poles for the liberation of Warsaw, but the Hitlerites who are inhumanely shooting down the inhabitants of Warsaw."[31]

As early as 9 August Stalin had promised to look into matters in Warsaw and give the necessary aid after conversations with Mikołajczyk, but went back on his word. Stalin's word was worth nothing anyway. Once back in London Mikołajczyk sent a telegram to Stalin; three days later on 16 August Stalin replied and bluntly refused to send aid to Warsaw. His reason was the false claim that the uprising in Warsaw had not been coordinated with the Soviet High Command. This was surely something he should have raised with Mikołajczyk when he was in Moscow, but of course Stalin knew that this allegation was a lie. On 18 August Mikołajczyk replied to Stalin, reminding him of the circumstances of the revolt and how the Soviet authorities had encouraged it. He also said that he had been told that the Red Army would be in Warsaw by 6 August, and repeated his appeal for Soviet support for Warsaw. Stalin ignored him.[32] The British government and the FO had no intention of allowing the Soviet government or Stalin to get away with their silences and a telegram was sent to Molotov. Once more the Soviet government was reminded that they were still Allies and remained obliged to support the Poles in Warsaw. The FO also observed that the AK were not operating in an underhand method but were helping the Allied cause in the war against Germany, and as such should be supported by the Soviet Union as it was the Ally geographically closest to Warsaw.[33]

There were further examples of Soviet skullduggery towards the Warsaw Uprising. The British had learnt from the Polish government-in-exile that the Soviet Air Force had dropped leaflets over Warsaw (not supplies or weapons) from the Soviet commander, General Rola: these stated that when Warsaw was liberated the leaders of the insurrection would be arrested and punished for their responsibility in provoking so many civilian deaths. At this Eden suggested that perhaps the problem was that Stalin saw the AK in Warsaw as being instruments of both Sosnkowski and Mikołajczyk. The Polish Prime Minister insisted that this could not have possibly been the case, as he had already explained to Stalin that the entire operation in Warsaw was part of an anti-German offensive and Stalin affected to understand what was going on. A further problem for Polish-Soviet relations was the question of the mass arrests of AK members and Polish civil administrators by the Red Army and the Soviet security police, the NKVD. When Mikołajczyk tried to raise this problem with Stalin he was brushed off. Eden asked Mikołajczyk what the British government could do to help. The answer remained the same: send arms and ammunition. Once more the question of how best this could be done would be raised, and so the circle continued.[34]

The British Ambassador to Moscow had already observed that the Soviets could not object to the British and American air forces dropping arms over Warsaw but did "decidedly object" to lending

---

30   Ibid. Roosevelt and Churchill to Stalin, 20 August 1944.
31   Ibid. Stalin to Roosevelt, 23 August 1944.
32   Ciechanowski, op.cit. pp.338-41.
33   NA: FO 371/39498, FO to Molotov, 18 August 1944.
34   Ibid. Eden to O'Malley, 23 August 1944.

air bases on Soviet territory as the Soviet government wanted to distance itself from the uprising.[35] The Foreign Office began a campaign against Soviet claims that the Warsaw Uprising was not coordinated with the Soviet General Staff, as a Minute from Frank Roberts revealed. Roberts noted that the Soviet newspaper, *Pravda*, had on the day of his Minute, published an editorial to the effect that Warsaw would be liberated by the Red Army but meanwhile lambasted the rising, which the Soviet government claimed to be "insignificant" and a fiasco. The Soviet editorial then went on launch a blistering attack on the "irresponsible London clique" as the Soviets termed what everybody else called it the Polish government-in-exile. It was this group whom it considered to be responsible for the rising and therefore for endangering civilian lives in the Polish capital.

Roberts made it quite clear that the Soviet claim that the British, American and Soviet governments had not been informed that the rising would take place was untrue and unfounded. To counter the Soviet lies, Roberts gave the news departments of the FO and PWE (Political Warfare Executive – British psychological warfare department) the necessary material to meet enquiries on this matter. He had to tread a careful line as he wrote that even though he (and the FO) did not wish to "engage in polemics" with the Soviet government, he still considered that the press and the BBC should be restrained from "accepting and repeating these Russian propaganda stories". Roberts also observed that during the night of 18-19 August the Soviets, instead of dropping supplies to the AK in Warsaw, dropped leaflets demanding that the Poles there should cease fighting or "resisting", as the rising was the "irresponsible act of a reactionary clique in London". Roberts finished by saying that Retinger, a member of the inner circle of the London Poles and currently in Warsaw on a secret mission, was quite mild in his response that the dropped messages would not help Polish-Soviet relations.[36] Roberts, of course, was aware that the Soviet government was getting away scot-free in its allegations against the Warsaw Uprising. They were simply lies, but even so diplomacy and the conduct of the war against Germany meant that Roberts had to stop short of calling Stalin and the Soviet government liars. The selling of Poland was the necessary sacrifice price to keep Stalin happy and ensure that the Soviet Union continued to fight Germany.

The question of Soviet ill intent regarding the fate of the AK whenever they identified themselves to the Red Army, and who was telling the truth, was to become heated. It also became part of the story of the Warsaw Uprising. A message from the exiled Poles, conveyed by the FO to both Churchill and Roosevelt, was quite clear. After the Red Army entered Polish territory, whenever members of the AK came into the open and declared themselves they were arrested, interned and even murdered. A further twist to this unhappy story was that by August the Red Army had captured the infamous Nazi extermination camp, Majdanek, near Lublin. The camp was more or less intact when it was captured and the Soviets began to use it as a prison camp for AK members. This illustrated perfectly what the Soviets felt about the AK. The Poles quite bluntly stated that they failed to understand why the West remained impassive in the face of such provocation.[37] Polish outrage was understandable and amazingly muted given how their compatriots were being treated by an ally yet Bór-Komorowski and Monter during the third week of September were still anticipating victory with Soviet aid.[38]

In the West people were moved by the plight of Warsaw, and were at best confused by the actions of the Soviet Union, which had received a favourable press in the UK and was now refused to help the uprising, despite having an army and air force on hand. Churchill, in an undated telegram seen by Roosevelt before being sent to Moscow, not only expressed the above sentiment but continued

35   NA: PREM 3/431/1 TOLSTOY, PREM 3/472, T. 1641/4, Churchill to Roosevelt, 20 August 1944.
36   NA FO 371/39494/C11440/1077/55, FO Minute by F.K. Roberts, 19 August 1944.
37   NA: FO 371/39494/C11445/G, Translation of Message from the Delegation of the Government and the Chairman of the National Unity's Council to be conveyed to Churchill and Roosevelt, 23 August 1944.
38   Zagorski, (1957) op.cit. p.199.

to press Stalin to help. Churchill told Stalin that he could not blame the ordinary people of Warsaw for the uprising, flawed or not. He simply could not understand why Stalin continued to deny American aircraft supplying Warsaw landing rights on Soviet airfields. Churchill concluded his missive by stating that if, as was feared, the Warsaw Uprising failed owing to Soviet inactivity, then it was obvious that the Soviet government was acting in variance to the spirit of Allied cooperation to which the British, American and Soviet governments attached so much importance for the present and for the future.[39] However Churchill had yet to recognise that Stalin did not see the western Allies as part of his programme. He was a dictator and did not have to answer to an elected body or to the people of the Soviet Union, as democratic leaders such as Churchill and Roosevelt had to. Stalin could do as he liked.

By 9 September the war of words about Warsaw drew a barbed response from the Soviet government, reported back to the FO by the British Embassy in Moscow. Molotov responded to Allied criticism by demanding that an "unprejudiced commission" (pro-Soviet) be organized, to ascertain who was actually responsible for ordering the Warsaw Uprising and therefore could be blamed for the manner in which it was being conducted. Basically the Soviet government was trying to distance itself from events in Warsaw. Molotov, lying as ever, claimed that the Soviet High Command had not been warned in advance of the uprising and furthermore claimed that no command, not even the British or American High Commands, would have tolerated an uprising in a large city opposite their front lines. The Soviet Command was no exception. Allied support for the Paris uprising laid that lie bare. Molotov claimed further that if the Soviet High Command had been consulted it would have advised against revolting as Soviet troops had recently advanced, fighting, over 500 kilometres and were exhausted. This meant that Soviet troops near Warsaw could not take it by storm, especially at a time when the Germans had just transferred their armoured reserves from the west to the Warsaw area. This was probably true, and it is more than likely that, given all of these circumstances, Sikorski himself would have forbidden the uprising if he had been alive. Molotov made further assertions claiming that the Soviet Air Force had been making supply drops over Warsaw. He also rejected British claims about Soviet inactivity, and began to hark back to how the Soviets had been vilified over the Katyń massacre. He also considered that public opinion in the West should be better informed about the Soviet Union.[40] If western opinion had been better informed about the Soviet Union; it would no doubt have turned against Stalin and his regime once it realised that there was little difference between Stalinism and Nazism, both were totalarian states.

Molotov's critique was riddled with lies. The uprising was virtually demanded by the Soviet government and appeared to have been underwritten by Molotov in the form of printed entreaties, signed by him, urging the city to rise up. His description of the Red Army once it arrived in the Warsaw area at the end of July was probably accurate, but still did not explain its lack of activity for much of the uprising. Furthermore, once the Red Army was on the shores of the River Vistula, directly opposite the German lines, reinforced and regrouped it still did not need to take Warsaw in a head-on assault. The usual Red Army tactic was to bypass a major city and leave it isolated, to be picked off at leisure later. Aerial and artillery support were always options for aiding the AK, as neither would have necessitated a river crossing. However the biggest lie told by Molotov had very little to do with military operations in Warsaw but had everything to do with Soviet credibility, and this was the matter of Katyń. This was a stain on Polish-Soviet relations that was to last until 1991, when the then Soviet government finally admitted that it was a Soviet war crime and not a Nazi crime. In 1991 archives were released by the Soviet authorities that clearly showed

---

39   NA: FO 371/39436/C11842/761/G, T.1741/4, Churchill to Roosevelt, text sent to Moscow, undated.
40   NA: FO 371/39496/C11965, Moscow to FO (From Molotov) 9 September 1944.

that both Stalin and Molotov had signed orders for the mass murder of Polish elites. However, since Vladimir Putin's accession to power in Russia there is a certain amount of backtracking concerning Soviet guilt in the Katyń killings.

Until 9 September the Soviets failed to respond positively to British and American demands for the Soviet Union to help the Poles at Warsaw. Suddenly there was what the British Ambassador to Moscow, Sir Archibald Clark-Kerr, described as a "climb-down", and the Soviets began to show signs of activity even if the government still continued to denounce the uprising.[41] The problem for the Allies and the Poles in London was that the Soviet Government held all the trump cards and would only cooperate with their Allies when it suited them to do so and not when Churchill and Roosevelt demanded that they should.

By the summer of 1944 the Soviet Union was capable of defeating Germany on its own. This meant that the Allies were more or less reduced to trying to liberate territory in western Europe in an attempt to prevent the Soviet Union from annexing most of Europe, especially Germany. It was clear by then that treaties and agreements meant nothing to either Stalin or Molotov, and were there to be broken. The Soviets considered that they were owed, as since 1941 they had fought a terrible war against Germany. They had conveniently forgotten that the Soviet Union was as responsible as its then ally, Nazi Germany for the outbreak of war in 1939, when it had participated in the invasion and annexing of Poland.

---

41   *BFP3*, p.218.

7

Civilians: The Ladies of the Warsaw Uprising

Throughout this narrative civilians have been mentioned here and there, but they were, of course, the main victims of the Warsaw Uprising. Between 150,000 and 200,000 civilians died, mostly murdered by the Germans and their allies. This number is comparable with the death rate of *both* Hiroshima and Nagasaki after the American nuclear attacks in August 1945. However the civilian casualties of the Warsaw Uprising is rarely discussed and is almost an embarrassment; even Poles do not want to think about it as it would tarnish the so-called glory of the uprising, because it immediately exposes the fact that the AK left its civilian population largely at the mercy of the occupying forces. During the Communist period in Poland the fact that the Soviet Union failed to aid the uprising was not mentioned, which meant that once more the fate of civilians was ignored. However much of the uprising depended on civilians, especially girls and women, and their story goes largely untold in the face of male daring-do, such is the macho world of Polish historiography. A consideration of the role of civilians, especially women, during the Warsaw Uprising reveals that if the uprising had been successful neither would have gained anything much post-war.

Basically no matter what sacrifices were made by the civilian population, the Polish military, a male institution, sought a return to power. It was only a question of which of the Polish military commanders – or warlords – would rise to the top. That was one of the main reasons for the uprising. The military not only sought to prevent a Soviet annexation of Poland, but having learnt nothing from the destruction of Poland and its people, also longed for a return to the shady and corrupt practices of the Polish Second Republic, an undemocratic fiefdom for senior Polish military commanders. The interwar military regime had been one of incompetence. It could not even defend Poland when war came, owing to the neglect of military doctrine and an inability to maintain a modern army.

During March 1944 the Cabinet of the Polish government-in-exile in London published an explanatory pamphlet *O Co Walczy Naród* (What the Nation is Fighting for). Point 4 of this project was that the Polish Army was to be apolitical.[1] This would have caused dismay amongst senior Polish officers, either in exile or in the AK. It produces another element to the Warsaw Uprising as it also had the air of a coup, taking advantage of the perceived weakness of the occupying German forces when they appeared to be withdrawing from the capital at the end of July 1944. At the same time, the AK in Warsaw could then establish themselves as the liberators of the capital before the Red Army could enter the city and re-establish military rule in Poland – but the uprising went off at half cock and the civil population suffered the consequences. The British government certainly did not trust that democracy would be re-established in Poland. This was because the Polish Army even in exile or underground remained politicized and fragmented, each group following its own leader rather than the legitimate Polish government in London.[2] From exile in 1967 Władysław

---

1   Hanson, op.cit. p.60.
2   McGilvray, *A Military Government*, passim.

Anders, the least trusted Polish General, condemned the Warsaw Uprising, especially its reckless-ness and lack of consideration for civilians. He had been against it at the time of the uprising, which he had condemned as senseless or "even a crime".[3]

Joanna Hanson's work also suggests that even if civilians initially supported the uprising, their support was quickly lost once it became obvious that it was going to fail. The most active supporters of the rising were trying in so many ways to restore a pre-war divided Poland made up of wealthy elites and everybody else. She points out that prior to the outbreak of war 67% of Warsaw inhab-itants lived in one- or two-bedroom flats, while just 16% lived in accommodation of more than four bedrooms.[4] Of the remaining 17% nothing is said but the overall thesis was that inequality was, like elsewhere, rife in Poland. The countryside was even worse. The actions of the inhabitants of the wealthier Warsaw suburb of Mokotów spoke volumes about the divisions in Polish society even in 1944. They thought that they could sit out the uprising and allow others to do the fighting. Once fighting began in Mokotów it was discovered that its citizens had no stomach for it, even for their own liberty. "Violent demands for capitulation" were made, and white flags put out.[5] No doubt fighting was for the small or little people!

It was this social attitude, and a more and more fractious relationship between civilians and the AK, which caused many ordinary civilians to begin to trust the left wing of politics, including the Communists. Newspaper sales after mid-August 1944 saw a decline in readership of AK journals, and a steady uptake of the *Armia Ludowa* which was considered to be the "only reliable paper". The AK papers were considered "trash, lies and fraud".[6] Of course the Communist press was as bogus as that of the AK but civilians, tired of war and afraid, were perhaps willing at least to give the Polish communists a chance. The pre-war military regime had failed them but was clearly trying to seize back power, so why not try a radical social change? Leading Poles, in exile and in Poland, gravely misread the situation and the peoples' desire for change. Hard as it might be to believe, the imposition of Communism did make many changes in Poland, and often for the better: such as free education, free health care and a measure of equality for the working classes which had never been enjoyed before. However, it was at a cost – political freedom – which many had not enjoyed anyway. The big losers were the pre-war elites who had lived the good life but at the expense of the majority of their countrymen. War often accelerates social change; Poland was not to prove to be any different.

Following the Soviet and German invasion during 1939, Poland was a country ripe for under-ground conspiracy. Many of the leading figures in 1944, both political and military, had been active in the various underground movements which had operated in Poland from the beginning of the twentieth century until independence came in November 1918. Another annexation of Poland was another chance to revolt, and so in the autumn of 1939 another Polish underground state was born as pre-war organisations continued their work but in secret once more. Many women and girls made major contributions to the struggle for freedom but are rarely credited in the pages of history of the world. In the case of the Warsaw Uprising the omission of the part which females played was largely due to a combination of male chauvinism and Communism.

A classic example of male attitudes towards the women who risked their lives for their country is found in Zbigniew Stypulkowski's account of his time in the Polish underground, during which he was imprisoned by the Soviets and the Germans. He considered that the women, or "little ladies", who served in the underground did so out of their love for certain men.[7] Stypulkowski

---

3   Ibid, p.146; Davies, *Rising*, p.348.
4   Hanson, op.cit. p.10.
5   Ibid. p.177.
6   Ibid. pp.171-2.
7   Z. Stypulkowski, *Invitation to Moscow*, London, Thames & Hudson, 1951, pp.83-5.

is a good case study of what was wrong with pre-war Poland because, as a lawyer and a parliamentarian, he was clearly out of touch with normal life even in Warsaw. He wrote: "... after an extremely good lunch at Krzeminski's in Warsaw, I queued up to enlist ..."[8] There in a nutshell is the case why Poles wanted change; many Poles in 1939 did not get a lunch, extremely good or otherwise, let alone queuing to enlist. Admittedly led by some quite good officers, most had been mobilised and pitched into battle with inferior weapons and equipment against an army that was well run, better equipped and determined to destroy Poland. Stypulkowski was a snob, as so much of his account illustrates, and totally at odds with most of his countrymen and women. His views make it easier to consider that the Warsaw Uprising was an attempted coup and a chance to return to the inadequacies of the old Poland.

Many of the rank and file who had joined the AK and the various other components of the Polish underground state did so from the desire to try and do something to help their country at a time of extreme peril. Poles in Poland were aware that their countrymen were fighting on various fronts as they struggled to get back to Poland, and so there was a genuine wish to fight as an army from within occupied Poland. Proving that Poland, in its many shapes and forms, was still alive was the very kernel of the underground movement.

This was the motivation of Wanda Lesniewska, who in July 2012 related to the author why she, and others, had joined the underground. Aged twenty, and serving as a nurse, she had done so to fight back. Lesniewska cited the joint crimes of the Germans and the Soviets; Katyń, Kraków (where priests and academics were murdered) the roundups, deportations, the continuous killings, especially of men, and the overall assault on and destruction of Polish culture. All the Poles were left with was honour and in 1944, unlike the victims of Katyń in 1940, they had a chance to fight back. They were going to avenge the murder of Poland.[9]

Unlike underground movements in much of occupied Europe, service in the Polish underground had a historical background because of the struggle for independence between 1795 and 1918. The concept of conspiring against an occupier was not outlandish to the Polish psyche, as firsthand accounts from family members or friends were well known to younger generations. Barbara Matys said that her father had been one of Piłsudski's Legionnaires and had fought in the Legions. This tradition of struggle, with reference to previous events, lasted into the 1980s, when in 1989 Poland retrieved its independence for the first time in fifty years.

Matys was sixteen when the Germans invaded Poland and immediately volunteered to work at a field hospital, where she encountered for the first time the horrors of war. She witnessed the influx of heavily wounded soldiers streaming in from the front. This was her first experience of serving Poland: it was followed in 1940 by training as a nurse in Warsaw, where she became more involved with the underground. Matys observes that there were social links in such groups as the Polish Scout Movement and those involved in nursing. The Polish Scout Movement was one of a number of Polish organisations trained for war in a non-military capacity; nursing was clearly another.[10] Polish history had dictated these necessities. In an undated interview Zofia Orlicka (1902-1983), a nurse who served in the Polish underground, observed that many of the medical orderlies during the Warsaw Uprising who served well were on the whole completely unprepared young girls who had previously worked with the Polish scouting movement.[11]

While she was receiving her nursing training Matys was inducted into the underground, and eventually came into contact with the AK sappers. She became part of a sappers' patrol under the

---

8   Ibid. p.9.
9   Lesniewska.
10   Applebaum, op.cit. pp.177-181.
11   Zofia Orlicka, undated interview, typescript (in Polish), *Głownego Archiwum Polskiego Towarzystwa Pielęgniarki* (Main Archive Polish Nurses' Association) Warsaw.

command of Dr. Zofia Franio. Unusually, Franio had received military and sapper training and was a commissioned officer in the Polish Army. She was responsible for the training of her young charges. There were nine members of the patrol, all girls or young women the same age as Matys. It was a difficult double life: she had to maintain an appearance of normality and continue to study, but at the same time she had to pursue her life as a member of the AK. This involved being trained as a sapper, becoming proficient with the handling of explosives and the construction of mines, and of course patrolling. Materials were either dropped from aircraft by the Allies or stolen by the women from enemy storage points. By the time of the Warsaw Uprising Dr. Franio had made the women available for action. They were assigned to guard a large printing press on Hospital Street. Very quickly the female sappers were in action as the Germans attacked them during the early hours of 2 August. The German attack was heavy and they were well equipped. The defending Poles were worried by this intensive attack as they had much to lose: there was a large store of military engineering equipment in the area as well as a weapons production line. At such an early stage of the uprising, the Poles did not have the knowledge or the equipment to destroy it, so the German attack made the fight very difficult.

The defending at the above Poles received information that there was a women's' sapper patrol (including Matys) across the street from their position, and requested their assistance in order to destroy a German tank which was by then menacing their position. The sappers knew that a conventional grenade thrown at a tank would merely be deflected, and even if it did explode it would do very little damage, if any, on the body of a tank. What was needed was a "sticky bomb" or *gamon*, as Matys refers to the device made from plastic explosive and applied directly to a tank. The sappers quickly made a sticky bomb and the tank, still pressing forward, was attacked and destroyed. The sticky bomb, to the surprise of Matys, totally destroyed the tank's heavy armour. The destruction of the tank greatly lifted the spirits of the woman sappers and resulted in their being accepted as equals by their male counterparts. It was at this time that three of the women received their nicknames; Matys was dubbed *Baśka Bomba* (Bomber Babs).

Sadly, on the same day that the women saw action for the first time the Commander of their patrol, Second Lieutenant Alina Bredel, was killed in an attack on the central Post Office in Napoleon Square. The Germans had a heavily defended bunker at the main gates of this position, mainly armed with automatic weapons and well positioned. Second Lieutenant Bredel was killed attacking the enemy bunker armed only with a pistol. Matys reflected sixty-eight years later that this day was one of mixed emotions. On one hand they had been accepted as regulars by the AK and were fighting alongside them, then several hours later Bredel was killed.[12] So much for "little ladies"! This was just the beginning of the involvement of the women sappers in the Warsaw Uprising as they were put at the disposition of Colonel Antoni Chruściel (*Monter*), who was one of the senior commanders of the uprising. Matys makes the point that her patrol, with regular sapper officers, were involved in every offensive in central Warsaw; most famously the assaults on the PAST building.

Many women and girls were nurses and medical orderlies during the Warsaw Uprising and were to suffer disproportionately the horrors of the revolt. Many nurses were raped and then murdered – the most unimaginable horror – by enemy troops as they rampaged through the capital, but even their work as they tried to help their fellow citizens was harrowing. In 2012 Wanda Lesniewska still found it difficult to speak of the Warsaw Uprising and its consequences. In 1944 Lesniewska was twenty years of age and worked as a nurse as part of a surgical ambulance team on Zlota Street before and during the uprising. She was to see the casualties as they came in, and was one of the first points of medical aid the wounded would receive.

---

12 Matys.

Lesniewska remembered the first day of the uprising. It was a beautiful day with lovely weather and the nurses were outside in their white overalls, prayers were being said in the courtyard and many people were praying. She said that at time the courtyard resembled a small chapel with the numbers praying. Then suddenly shrapnel began to rain down upon them; it was the first enemy attack and there were many to come. Large numbers of people were wounded by the shrapnel: not badly but still enough to make an impact. The wounded made their way down to cellars to be treated. At first they were a bit of a shock for the nurses as they were covered in dust and grime as a result of the explosions and the falling debris. The nurses were at a loss what to do as there appeared to be nothing wrong with these people, whose appearance made them look as if they were from another planet. However a young lad brought the situation to order when he said that there was nothing to stare at, and that the nurses should just get on with their work. In that second normality and duty returned and the wounded were treated. The wounds became obvious once blood began to flow through the dust, thus indicating where to investigate, clean and treat. The worse casualties come from the *Nebelwerfer* multi-barrelled short range mortars, known by the Poles either as *Krowa* or "Cow"; or, sometimes, as *Szafa* or "wardrobe" (owing to the bellowing noise or sound of furniture being dragged across a floor as rockets came toward their targets). They were terribly destructive as their rounds consisted of a mixture of incendiary and high explosive that blew up buildings and set them on fire. The next worse weapon deployed against Warsaw was the huge siege mortar, fired from what Lesniewska took to be an armoured train.[13] Indeed the crew and equipment needed to operate this beast was more or less an armoured train and crew. The devastation of its 680mm shells was total as they frequently smashed their way through the roof of a building, continuing through the entire structure into the basement, when its timed fuse would explode. Each shell was quite capable of destroying an entire block of flats. Lesniewska was not wrong to mention the used of armoured trains as artillery platforms, as Davies notes that German armoured trains "rolled round suburban railway lines, seeking out the best locations for their salvoes of high explosive."[14]

By the time of the Warsaw Uprising Polish responses to the experience of continued invasion, occupation and fighting in their territorial space was multifaceted, yet personal. Stefania Hoch, another nurse, explained that by that by the time of the Warsaw Uprising one of her brothers had already been murdered at Katyń, her father had been imprisoned by the Germans and was to die shortly afterwards, while another brother was to die during the uprising. Her mother had died before the war. The war had more or less wiped out her family, and the perpetrators were from both sides: the Germans and the Soviet Union. Her attitude towards life was that families, and therefore people, were more important than politics.[15] As a consequence Hoch was not too fussy about whom her liberators might be, so long as the war finished; quite an understandable motive.

However, the question of the timing and motivation of the Warsaw Uprising can be continuously questioned as these elderly ladies relate their experiences. Both Hoch and Lesniewska served as nurses, and despite their differing conclusions about the motivation of fighting in the uprising they both bear witness to the helpless situation in which civilians found themselves, and their fate after its failure. As medical professionals they could not help but be dismayed by the inadequate provision made for casualties and the sick during the revolt. Both women were critical of the fact that by the end of the uprising there was no food or water, which made basic hygiene – so important in medicine and especially surgery – impossible.[16] What can be established is that there was a

---

13   Lesniewska.
14   Davies, *Rising*. p.257.
15   Stefania Hoch, interview with author, Warsaw, 16 July 2012, hereafter referred to as 'Hoch'.
16   Lesniewska & Hoch.

dichotomy between those who had something to do, whether civilian or actively fighting with the AK, and those who were trying to live as they could. Those who were active had something to take their minds off what was happening around them; those who were inactive pondered and worried about their situation. Even if, as Lesniewska claims, morale was high until the very end of the uprising –whose morale was high? Hoch, decades later, maintained that the cost in civilian lives made the rising null and void.[17]

Barbara Gadomska, aged eighty-five in July 2012, was a young medical orderly in 1944. She had been trained by the Polish Scout Movement and was involved in working with the AK. She described the primitive conditions that she and other medical staff were expected to work under during the uprising. For her and others at their posts the uprising came as a bit of a surprise. She admits to having been disorientated when, though it was known that the uprising was to begin at 17.00 hours, she heard firing and learnt that in places fighting had began prematurely. Having discovered this Gadomska made her way to her gathering place for the beginning of the uprising, but found that the Germans were already in the area. With this piece of intelligence she made her way to Hoża Street and the Headquarters of the Women's Army Service, which was subordinate to the AK. She emphasized that the distances between the fighting Germans and Poles were only the width of a street. There were heavily barricaded obstacles made from street paving preventing the close approach of tanks towards Polish positions. Initially Gadomska was to be put on a barricade as a kitchen assistant peeling potatoes, but she protested and asked for more appropriate service. That was how she became a medical orderly at a medical clearing station in Mokotowska on Natolinski Street. This street was a small but a positive battlefield with the AK on one side and the Germans on the other. The Germans, having taken up positions in the building of the former Czech Embassy, were able to fire along the entire length of the street at the Polish positions.

There were inevitably casualties. Gadomska said that cellars were used as operating theatres; her position, though, was a very small post – more of a clearing station, which also had to deal with an influx of civilian refugees trying to get away from the fighting. This meant that no important operations could be managed here (but to be honest it was difficult to maintain any type of conventional medical service, owing to the conditions during the uprising) but many superficial head wounds were treated. Some amputations were carried out in the cellar's kitchen using a large kitchen table for the operations. The conditions were extremely primitive: everything was dirty as there was little or nothing to clean with. There was inadequate lighting at best using lanterns rather than the brilliant light usually associated with surgery. The first operation that Gadomska witnessed was a hand being amputated by candlelight; once the hand was taken off it was wrapped in newspaper and thrown away. Bandages were frequently made from paper in order to absorb blood. This experience had a profound effect on her. A further experience also caused Gadomska to wonder about the uprising as she witnessed mortar attacks on the position on Hoża Street, as half the building was used as homes. The destruction caused by the mortars when they hit the structure was terrifying, and half demolished it. There were many wounded; Gadomska had to take them to the hospital, such as it was, on Hoża Street. There were other casualties as well, such a young man in a nightshirt with a large heavy hammer with which he was striking the ruins, crying out: "my little daughter is there, my little daughter is there". It seemed that the man had been in one room and his daughter had been in the next when rockets struck the building and she disappeared as the room crumbled into rubble.

A further human and near tragic episode witnessed by Gadomska was the case of a wounded young man. This young AK fighter had been involved in heavy fighting with the Germans during 6 August in and around Plac Zbawiciel. During the fighting it seemed that the young man had

---

17 Ibid.

lost his harmonica. He was determined to retrieve it from German-occupied territory as without it he could not settle, and he moped for his precious instrument. This caused alarm amongst his comrades, who took it upon themselves to keep an eye on him, but Gadomska realised that this was unsustainable. Sooner or later he would give his guardians the slip and go and look for his harmonica. Gadomska had one at her home; a present from children who had been kidnapped from their home town of Zamość in Eastern Poland by the Germans and were entrained for Germany but who had been rescued by Poles in Warsaw just before the uprising. Gadomska had been helping to look after the children and also helped to establish a safe house for them away from Warsaw before fighting broke out in the capital. Zamość and the surrounding area had been selected by the Nazis to be a centre of German colonization. From 1940 onwards its inhabitants were expelled, often to be used as slave labour while children, if they met so-called Aryan standards, were adopted by German families. Gadomska makes no comment about these children but their presence in Warsaw is significant in the litany of German crimes against the Polish people.[18] Gadomska managed to get to her home, retrieved her harmonica and gave it to the young AK fighter. He then returned to his former self and no longer gave concern to his comrades or the nurses trying to look after him.

Gadomska was still critical of the Warsaw Uprising and believed that it was a terrible mistake. From her experience we know that in part it began prematurely, and as a result went off at half-cock as the Germans were alerted to the fact that something major was afoot. She believed that there had been no agreement as to the timing of the uprising. As a nurse Gadomska remained appalled at the situation in which civilians found themselves because of the destruction of Warsaw, about which they could do nothing. For her the worst was the plight of mothers with babies. Towards the end of the uprising these women had lost their milk, due to malnutrition, and could not feed their children; there was no water either. There was nothing to use to feed an infant. It was the civilian casualties that appalled Gadomska most of all, and that even if the "flower of Polish youth" died during the summer of 1944, nobody would discuss the extremely high civilian casualty rate. After the uprising even her own family was critical of it and often declared it to have been a mistake.[19]

In 2012 Dr Barbara Dobrowolska also discussed the hardships of the Warsaw Uprising, in which she served in as a seventeen-year-old medical orderly. She also testified to the horrors of the rising, especially the effect on civilians. She said that fighting began at 17.00 on 1 August and went on night and day. At the time of the outbreak Dobrowolska was not at her home but at a neighbour's apartment with her mother; about five minutes walk from their home but the start of the fighting marooned them with their neighbour. During the afternoon on the fourth day of being stranded in her neighbour's home, Dobrowolska went to the kitchen to make some tea and suddenly noticed that the Germans were systematically setting fire to the neighbouring homes. She quickly returned to the living room and told the men, who were mostly between twenty and thirty years of age. Dobrowolska observed that the Germans were being quite thorough in their action, as they went from one entrance to the next pouring petrol onto the stairs of each entrance, and then setting them ablaze. She stated the obvious – they could not possibly remain where they were and needed to escape, but how? It seemed an impossible task as they were on the first floor and there were Germans, including SS, everywhere outside. There was only one possible exit: out of a window. In order to get everybody out, which included an eighty-year-old; they began to lower each other down, youngest first, in effect forming a chain. They collected the older people so they evaded capture or a grisly death being burnt alive. They fled away from the burning buildings,

---

18   See Kochanski, op.cit. p.271.
19   Gadomska. Gadomska also gave the author a handwritten account of her memories of the Warsaw Uprising which is also referred to in this work.

expecting at any time to be shot in the back, but this was preferable to being burnt alive. The plan was to head towards Dobrowolska's family home, which normally would have only taken about five or six minutes to walk, but once the uprising had begun the geography of the city changed dramatically. Dobrowolska and her group had to travel via cellars in Poznański Street in order to get back to her home on Krucz Street. The journey took two days, owing to all streets being barricaded by the AK as they fought the Germans and their allies. Dobrowolska recalled that later Polish Scouts produced a map showing how to move underground via the cellars, while noting which streets were under fire. It was difficult to move this way as one could not walk upright, as one might on the street, but had to crouch, owing to the lack of headroom. (Dobrowolska is not the tallest woman in the world, therefore for taller men or women moving around this way must have been very difficult and uncomfortable.) Luckily Dobrowolska had had the foresight to take some sugar and bread from the table when they had fled the flat, and that was their food for the two-day trip. They overnighted at a position not far from Marszalkowska and eventually made it home. Once there, Dobrowolska learnt that her father had been wounded in the fighting for the PAST building and had since died.

Dobrowolska relates that Śródmieście was the most difficult area of Warsaw to hold, while the situation in Wola was also very difficult. This was not only because of the fighting but because the Germans had been able to enter the area, take everybody they could find and shoot them. Living in a besieged city is always appalling and Warsaw in the summer of 1944 was no different. Dobrowolska said that where she was living many people seemed to be bearing up better than in other districts, but even so there was much shooting in the district. Her home bore the scars of shooting and shelling, with parts in ruins but the stairs remained intact, which meant that Dobrowolska could go to other flats to see what was happening outside. Naturally there was shooting and explosions as the fighting continued, but a curious thing happened: every day between 13.00 and 15.00 there was a lull in the shooting. It seemed that the Germans took a regular break, perhaps for a meal. This allowed Dobrowolska and her mother to prepare their own meals in peace and quiet during these unlikely periods of calm. However like all teenagers, Dobrowolska was curious about what was happening outside, while her mother continuously told her to keep away from the windows: sound advice as on the rooftops were *głoby*, snipers or "pigeons". Dobrowolska maintains that these snipers were *Volksdeutscher* and not Ukrainian sharpshooters, as many claim. Once she was nearly hit by a sniper when, amazingly, she decided to sweep broken glass from her window and was shot at. Luckily the sniper's bullet struck bricks above her head; perhaps it was a *Volksdeutscher* and not a Ukrainian sharpshooter!

Dobrowolska and her mother were extremely reluctant to think of moving from their precarious situation on the third floor of their apartment block despite the firing around them, because many people who had taken to the cellar felt as if they had already been entombed. Her mother had twice been there. However, after the third week of the uprising, Dobrowolska and her mother made their way to the cellars as life was becoming too dangerous to be above ground. It was then that Dobrowolska took up duties as a medical orderly. It was the beginning of a long career, which was to see her become an academic in the world of medicine. It was also here that for the first time the full impact of the uprising and its consequences for so many people were to hit her. By the time Dobrowolska entered service, a good deal of the medical supplies had already run out but casualties were continuously mounting; many of these casualties were caused by shrapnel as shells and bombs fell on the city. All around her people died in the cellars and there was little that the medical staff could do to help those who were coming into the makeshift subterranean hospital. By the fourth week there was nothing left, no bandages, operations were done by candlelight as there was no power, while medical alcohol was being used as a disinfect. Meanwhile the Germans furthered their murderous and illegal reign of terror by threatening to bomb hospitals, which obviously terrified people. Many of the wounds were extremely serious; Dobrowolska clearly recalls a young girl who had had the top of her head cut away by flying shrapnel, which had left her brain exposed. This girl would probably not have received the medical attention she should have had and no doubt died as a result of her horrific injuries.

In her testimony Dobrowolska confirms the atrocities committed by the Germans and their allies. The use of snipers against civilian targets and the threat to destroy hospitals have already been noted – indeed many Polish hospitals had already been destroyed, complete with their staff and patients. She maintains that the second half of the uprising was the worst which of course it was as it was obvious that the Poles were losing. As the situation in Warsaw deteriorated civilian morale plummeted and supplies began to run out: there was a constant worry in the second half of the uprising about how to feed people, with mothers and children suffering most. Ordinary people were becoming more and more tired as they were sleep-deprived because of the fighting, continuously anxious as a result of the situation and of course lacking the basics of life, such as food and shelter. Other horrors witnessed by Dobrowolska included German armoured columns continuously used Polish civilians as human shields as they advanced against AK positions, while every area as far as she could see was on fire. Fire was the principle weapon used by the Germans as, while clearing passage for the deployment of tanks, it inspired fear amongst Polish civilians as well as depriving them of shelter and safety.[20]

The cost in civilian lives is the most controversial aspect of the Warsaw Uprising. Even though it cannot be claimed that the AK killed these people – clearly it was the Germans and their allies who committed these atrocities –it was the AK who had made the situation possible. Their recklessness and lack of thought and imagination failed to take into account what might happen to a defenseless civilian population in the time of a revolt. The Jewish revolt of the previous year should have served the AK as a lesson and an example in what might happen if there was a localized revolt anywhere in Poland. A national uprising might have produced a different result. If they had waited until the Germans eventually left Warsaw, as they would have been forced to do once the Red Army went on the offensive, and then attacked the German forces in the countryside, it would have served Poland and its people better.

Hoch is probably right that the Warsaw Uprising was a mistake. Anders later condemned the conduct of the uprising and without doubt Sikorski would have forbidden it. It was a desperate and crude coup attempt with little thought behind it. But this is to reach the end before time and to ignore the fact that the uprising was only due to last a few days before being relieved by outside forces. The crime committed by AK Command in Warsaw was that of willful ignorance – did they seriously believe that they would receive support from the Red Army? This was at a time when Stalin was already making sure that AK units that fell into the hands of the Soviet authorities were liquidated, losing the ability to fight for an independent Poland as their officers were usually murdered by the Soviet security forces and AK troops press-ganged into pro-Soviet forces. Instead of rising up against the Germans, the AK should have done nothing but let the Germans withdraw from Warsaw and then picked them off in the Polish countryside, where the AK ruled. The Red Army would have stopped at Praga and then eventually entered the capital but with no AK to destroy. It would just have been a city full of civilians, while the Polish government-in-exile maintained its "Home Army" as well as having two further armies, First Polish Corps and Second Polish Corps in the West. It was the fact that there was no substantial Polish Army in Poland after October 1944 that allowed the Red Army to overrun the country.

---

20   Dobrowolska.

8

Warsaw Abandoned and the Consequences of Failure

Despite the gigantic American airdrop over Warsaw on 18 September 1944, which had the effect of lifting the morale of the AK fighters and the remaining citizens, the situation in the city was dire. The following day there was further cause to consider if perhaps the uprising might succeed after all, as there were unconfirmed reports that infantry reinforcements were being sent to Praga, Warsaw's eastern suburb, which necessitated the fording of the River Vistula bisecting the capital. The reports suggested that a battalion from the Soviet-backed Berling Army was to cross the Vistula at midnight, 19 September. On 19 September it was further reported that for the first time the Luftwaffe was not bombing owing to the strong presence of Soviet fighter aircraft, while the German Army was being heavily shelled by the Red Army. Furthermore on 20 September the AK Commander in the Zoliborz area reported artillery duels across the Vistula, with Soviet artillery being directed by the AK.[1]

On the same day General Tadeusz Bór-Komorowski, the Warsaw AK commander, reorganized the entire AK command structure in the city. This served to reflect the dire situation of his forces, which were under-armed and undermanned. The commander of the Mokotów area added some flesh to the skeleton of Bór-Komorowski's reorganization as he made the following report: "Owing to the exhaustion of his men and the lack of food and ammunition, the Commander of Czerniakow today began at zero hour (midnight) to evacuate to me via the sewers. The Berling force left on the river bank is in a state of disorganisation."[2] Therefore from a single report it is clear that the AK was losing ground and could not move overland. It had to endure the discomfort of a sewage system in order to move around Warsaw. Equally it was obvious that little was to be gained from the Berling Army.

The problem for the Berling Army was the negative Soviet attitude towards it and towards Poles in general. The commander of 27th Infantry Division (Lublin District) reported that his division, during the "Tempest" action (an operation in eastern Poland which had preceded the Warsaw Uprising), had placed themselves tactically under the Red Army. They were ordered to march with a Soviet Army Corps to Warsaw: however they were drawn into a Soviet ambush, disarmed and taken to another concentration point.[3] No doubt it was one that suited the Soviet offensive rather than the major AK concern: Warsaw.

Bór-Komorowski had issued an order on 14 August commanding provincial AK units to move to Warsaw and assist in the fighting. A Soviet Order of the Day on 24 August, though, quoted this order, and commanded Soviet troops to prevent AK units reaching Warsaw by cutting roads, searching all vehicles, confiscating all arms found and arresting those carrying weapons. A further example of Soviet malpractice was that AK units moving from Rzeszów, in south-east Poland,

---

1   Pomian, op.cit. p.28.
2   Ibid. pp.28-9.
3   Ibid. p.29.

were not only disarmed but were also conscripted into the Berling Army. The Soviet order had been issued despite the fact that the British Military Mission in Moscow had previously informed the Soviet government of the serious situation in Warsaw.[4] The same communication observed that the uprising was the strongest manifestation of the Polish will for freedom and independence – the very reason why the Soviet government was anxious to see the rising fail.[5]

Previously the city of Wilno (claimed by Poland but today as Vilnius quite correctly the capital city of independent Lithuania), was liberated in a joint action between local AK units and the Red Army. This had caused acute discomfort for the Soviet government, for it could see that if there were any further similar successes involving the AK, the Soviets might have to admit that the AK was a genuine fighting ally and should be treated as such. Therefore the Soviet government, or more likely Stalin, sought to ensure that the AK was not to enjoy any further successes, especially the liberation of Warsaw. Soviet inactivity continued in and around Warsaw; at all times it should be remembered that any Soviet activity would not have been for the benefit of the AK but for the benefit of the Soviet Union, including the destruction of the Polish underground state wherever it endangered Soviet policies.

On 21 September two Soviet military officers parachuted into central Warsaw. They landed with broadcasting apparatus, which was to be used to try to establish contact with Marshal Rokossovsky, the Soviet Commander in Warsaw. There were other attempts by the Red Army to try to link up the fighting, as a single Red Army battalion crossed the Vistula at Żoliborz but was thrown back by the enemy. There was also news of an infantry battalion from the Berling Army, which had been fighting for several days in Czerniakow. The problem with the Berling Army was that even though its members were well equipped by the Soviets, their training and preparation was poor. They were often pitched into the front line after only three weeks of training, and as a consequence suffered heavy casualties. The battalion at Czerniakow had become cut off but had been able to withdraw via the sewage system to Mokotów, leaving a single company behind.[6] The Warsaw sewerage system (designed by William Lindley, a British engineer, in the nineteenth century), was never intended to become a major system of transportation or communications, let alone a battlefield. By late August the AK was obliged to rely upon it for moving around Warsaw, while the Germans were determined to prevent them from doing so. At the end of August the sewage system allowed 6,000 people to retreat from the Old Town to the city centre, while a further 1,000 escaped from the Żoliborz area.

Later, in talks with the AK as they negotiated for surrender, General von dem Bach-Zelewski admitted that he had not realised the potential of the city's sewage system as a means of transportation and communications between Warsaw's various districts. It was only when the defenders of the Old Town "disappeared" that the Germans finally realised that the sewers were being used in this manner, and represented a substantial danger to the German campaign to seize back the Polish capital. Zaleski admitted that from that time onwards the German armed forces and their allies in the city became quite fearful of the sewers, and "sewer paranoia" took over. This manifested itself so much that the Germans seemed to be in constant fear that the AK might emerge unexpectedly from the sewers and strike to the rear of German positions.

The Germans were never able to overcome this aspect of fighting, and so the AK remained more or less in control of the sewage system. Indeed, the Germans did not succeed in cutting off the sewer system located in Żoliborz from that of the Old Town. Part of the reason for this was

---

4   PISM: LOT A.V. 11/2a, A. Earle, Secretary Chiefs of Staff Committee to General Sosnkowski, C-in-C, Polish Armed Forces, 12 September 1944. See also Hanson, op.cit. p.161.
5   McGilvray, *A Military Government*, p.149.
6   Pomian, op.cit. p.29.

that the Germans were terrified of entering the system. Bach-Zelewski admitted that he had great difficulty in persuading his troops to enter the sewers and carry on the fighting from them. This was probably the reason why the Germans resorted to throwing grenades into manholes, while in Mokotów poisonous gas was released into the sewers by the Germans. The result of that particular attack was that the AK had to use indicator candles to check the purity of the air. So severe was the use of gas that the candles would not burn for several hours.

In spite of grim scenes in the sewer system, in this unorthodox setting the Poles began to develop a more sophisticated attitude and methodology of warfare against the Germans. Very quickly direction signs were placed under major road junctions and at sewer junctions, while food and medical supplies were secreted in wall cavities. The Germans made some tentative attempts to exploit the sewage system but these were limited because of an overwhelming fear, not just of the AK, but of the sewer system itself, with its tunnels and uncharted walkways and galleries in which they might become lost and die.

Intelligence gathering was one tactic employed by the Germans. Collaborators, usually ethnic Germans or Ukrainians, entered the city centre via smaller sewage channels and after infiltrating Polish-held areas would then return to German lines with intelligence reports. Not all of these spies managed to return, or they returned with fictitious reports. Some fell into AK hands: they were very careful about people found in the sewers. They guarded major entrances to the sewers and identity papers were checked. However operations in the sewers were extremely limited in scope, barely going beyond movement and communications. The sewers were deep; about twelve metres below the streets with tunnels that were high enough to permit people to move around freely.

The Germans eventually became aware of AK usage of the sewage system for military purposes, especially between the Old Town and Żoliborz. In response the Germans threw grenades into the system at this point, but still would not enter the tunnels. Another tactic used by the Germans was to lower listening devices into sewer shafts and sit patiently waiting for any sounds. This meant that all movement around the sewers had to be made with the utmost caution. Flashlights and conversation were forbidden but one wonders how a wounded fighter might have kept quiet all of the time. Walking in the sewers was extremely difficult as there were no flat surfaces and the tunnels were slippery and rounded. Those walking through this labyrinth had one hand on the person in front of them and their other hand on the sewer walls to keep their balance; such journeys lasted for several hours. Wanda Lesniewska recalled that at least one man, Dr. "Grom" Kujawski, carried a pregnant woman on his back through the sewers. In Dr. Kujawski's case it was his own wife, Krysia, who gave birth to their child later in a German prisoner of war camp. Stefania Hoch, who was also a midwife, delivered the child successfully.[7]

Passing under a manhole where it was suspected that the Germans were on the surface meant that people passed below singly and quickly, while resisting the temptation to fire up and into the Germans above them. The Germans did build a dam under the manhole cover on Muranówska Street, but it was after the evacuation of the Old Town, which took place during the night of 25-26 August. This dam was well constructed and blocked all traffic in the sewers. It also raised the water levels in sewers nearby. After two or three days following significant raising of the sewers' water levels, the AK decided to destroy this dam, which was done successfully. The AK conducted a similar operation in Żoliborz, while telephone communications were successfully laid through the sewers between Żoliborz and the city centre, but these were never used operationally as the Germans captured Żoliborz before they could be employed. Jan Rossman, "Wacek", a veteran of

---

7   Lesniewska.

the AK and of operations in the sewers wrote: "this struggle in the sewers is unique in the history of the Uprising. It is also probably one of a kind in the history of warfare."[8]

In a report to General von Vormann, commander of the German 9th Army, General von dem Bach-Zelewski wrote on 29 August:

> Despite the fact that the Polish resistance had undoubtedly inferior heavy weaponry, according to trustworthy reports, despite their death rate; the Poles were being constantly replenished by forces from all over Poland. After their formation and training, the newly formed units, which range from a company to a battalion, infiltrate into the city through a dense system of sewers and underground passages. The infiltration had even reached the Old Town district which is completely surrounded on the surface... This situation had led to the enemy (AK) in the south (Mokotów district) and in the north (Żoliborz district) becoming bold enough to go onto the offensive which are being repulsed but with difficulty.

Rossman provided a commentary on this report highlighting the most obvious consideration: the question of AK reinforcements. Evidence already examined proves that the German statement was not true, as a result of Soviet interception and detaining of AK units trying to reach Warsaw. Rossman wrote that the German claim was fiction and basically reinforced the notion that the Germans were terrified of the sewers to the point of being paranoid: overestimating the AK's ability to utilise this system. Rossman observed that the sewers provided a "significant psychological role in the fighting".[9]

Rossman's work also provides an interesting point about the fighting in Warsaw during 1944. He noted that during the Jewish revolt of April 1943, General Stroop, who had been charged with putting down that uprising, reported on 16 May 1943 that one of his first actions had been to flood the sewage system, thus preventing Jewish fighters from using them.[10] This then raises the question of why the German commanders in Warsaw in 1944 did not do the same. It rather smacks of incompetence and reduced Bach-Zelewski to exaggerating, if not lying, to General von Vormann as he tried to explain why the Germans had taken so long to defeat the Poles while enduring an unexpectedly high casualty rate. Bach-Zelewski was a second rate commander, and it was only circumstances which saved him from defeat. Meanwhile the misery of the Warsaw Uprising was beginning to come to an end.

The first line of German field fortifications west of Warsaw city centre were at Mlociny, Włochy and Służew, (today all destinations on suburban railway lines and the underground system) while Wilanów was occupied by the Wiking SS 5th Division, the Franconian-Sudeten 183rd Infantry Division and the Hermann Goering Division. It was obvious that the Germans remained heavily armed and could be easily reinforced. On 22 September the AK commander of the Mokotów Area reported unceasing artillery fire against the AK eastern sector of this district. He also reported that since 10.00 hours that morning there had been heavy movements of enemy transport, including tanks, lorries and horse-drawn vehicles. There were other enemy movements as they advanced to reinforce positions at Wilanów, while the main roads there and in Służew were strengthened with machine gun posts.

As it became increasingly important as a main route for communications and movement around Warsaw, the AK had begun to patrol the sewer system. Under Szucha Avenue one patrol found an obstacle in the system and a sapper unit was called to deal with it. It was at this time that

---

8　Jan Rossman, 'Wacek' 'In the Warsaw Sewers' *Zeszyty Historyczne* No. 109, www.warsawuprising.com.
9　Ibid.
10　Ibid.

Major-General "Monter" reported that a Soviet artillery officer, Alexander Chernukhyn, 2nd Artillery Regiment of the *Kaplyn* Brigade, had reported to him. Chernukhyn had been sent directly from Marshal Rokossovsky's staff to ask the following questions: what are the AK's requirements; what are the AK's views on Soviet operations outside Warsaw and of AK cooperation with these operations. The AK was also asked to identify targets for Soviet artillery in central Warsaw. The AK command certainly had views on the second questions and so transmitted the following reply to Marshal Rokossovsky:

> Lacking information on strength and possibilities, I cannot review operations between Modlin and Pilica, but only those directed against Warsaw. Warsaw is surrounded in the west by a ring of German field fortifications along the line Mlociny – Włochy, Służew – Wilanów, already garrisoned on the flanks. In the event of operations being concentrated on mastering Warsaw alone, the garrisons of this ring of fortifications may be increased, which will block the western exits from Warsaw itself and the enemy effort may be turned against these exits. In consequence of a bridgehead in the Warsaw area seems to require indispensably an exit from both flanks in the Pruszków area. To this end: a. On the north strikes from the Henryków-Jabłonna area through Izabelin, b. On the south from the Falenica – Otwock area through Kabacki Forest. For coordination of frontal attacks simultaneously in the direct (of) a. Żoliborz to Wilson Square, b. Vistula Embankment towards Ujazdowski Hospital and Wiejska Street. If the foregoing plan is adopted, we have the following possibilities of cooperating in the attack on the Kampinos Forest, our force of about one regiment in the Sieraków – Truskaw area can strike at the enemy on the western bank of the Vistula or cover the Red Army's operations in the southern part and western parts of the forest. Small partisan forces can cooperate in the attack on (the) Kabacki Forest. In the attack on Warsaw itself we can guarantee the cooperation of our forces holding Żoliborz, the city centre (southern part) and Mokotów in the direction of your lines.[11]

This single communiqué reveals the extent that the AK was willing to cooperate with the Red Army. It had even suggested a campaign strategy, which had every chance of success if only the Red Army had cooperated. However cooperation with the AK was anathema to the Soviets, and they delayed the liberation of Warsaw until January 1945.

While the AK command discussed strategy with Rokossovsky, fighting continued elsewhere in Warsaw. The commander in the Mokotów area reported on 24 September that his district had been under heavy artillery fire. This included eighteen Stuka dive-bombers and tanks, as well as heavy artillery. Both the AK and the Germans had taken heavy casualties: the AK had been able to destroy one tank and immobilise a further two. In Mokotów, the commander also reported that he had been slightly wounded but his deputy commander had been badly wounded. The action at Mokotów was a day of attack and counter-attack. The following day, 25 September, this commander sent the following message: "the enemy is using all his strength to achieve the liquidation of Mokotów. The situation is very serious. Lack of help from Soviet artillery. I shall defend the position on the ruins. Von dem Bach-Zelewski, General of Police, has sent an emissary with a proposal to let out the civilian population, as he is intending to make a concentrated attack and asks for a personal meeting with General Bór on neutral ground. I await the order on the civilian population."[12]

---

11   Pomian, op.cit. p.31.
12   Ibid. op.cit. p.32.

The British airman, Sergeant John Ward, in a dispatch from Warsaw to London described the situation at the beginning of September. He wrote on 2 September that practically every soldier who had not been killed had been wounded.[13] It was clearly an appalling situation to be in as unless the Soviets had a change of heart there was no hope of reinforcements or bettering the situation. On 11 September Ward reported that the enemy was trying to cut off and divide the AK in the south, with the position being split at Sikorski Avenue. At the same time huge fires burnt continuously. Ward also reported on the plight of the civilian population: he informed London that about 50% of the civilian population from northern parts of Warsaw were being pushed into a small area in the south of the city. This area was under heavy bombing attacks and artillery fire day and night, with very high losses. Ward reported that about 300,000 people were concentrated in this tiny area under terrifying conditions.

Ward was granted an interview with General Bór-Komorowski, the AK Commander in Warsaw, on 12 September. Interestingly the General refused to be drawn on whether he had called the uprising prematurely, but did say that it was unfortunate that there had been no coordination between the AK and the Red Army.[14] Bór-Komorowski should have been more politically astute about the real situation between the Polish government-in-exile and the Soviet government. Had he been, he would have realized that he was not going to enjoy any Soviet support. They only sent aid when it suited them and their ambitions for global expansion.

There was further evidence of inhumanity and the criminal attitude of the Germans and their allies in the battle for Warsaw as Ward reported that food supplies left by the enemy had been contaminated with strychnine. They knew full well that the Poles were starving, and would eat the food. Polish fatalities from this underhand method of warfare were recorded but not counted. The following day, 13 September, the Germans closed off the eastern side of Warsaw with the demolition of the Central Railway and Poniatowski Bridges over the Vistula. The old and narrow Kierbedz Bridge remained intact, as did the Old Northern Railway Bridge and a footbridge for access across the river, but Ward claimed that the AK had closed down the two destroyed bridges at the beginning of the uprising.[15] This seems unlikely, as the German Army had been able to operate over the river, travelling unhindered to and fro, which included moving trains across the Vistula directly under the barrels of Soviet artillery.

The question of the fate of the civilian population in Warsaw was one that refused to go away. It had interfered with the overall Polish military planning, such as it was, of the Warsaw Uprising. Adam Bień, a senior Polish politician from the Polish Peasant Party and heavily involved with the Polish underground movement (later sentenced by the Soviets in June 1945 to five years imprisonment for his role in the wartime Polish resistance), made reports back to London, like Ward. He reported that 12 September saw the beginning of a tacit agreement which led to the evacuation of several thousand elderly people, women and children from Polish lines over to the German lines. This was mainly the work of the Polish Red Cross, which had managed to reach an understanding with the Germans.

On the same day it was also reported that there had been aerial battles between the Luftwaffe and the Soviet Air Force. It was also reported that there had been no bread in Warsaw for the last ten days, and an insufficient water supply. Within days there was less bombing over Warsaw: the Soviet Air Force made it difficult for the Germans to launch air raids. There was also a steadying in morale amongst Poles in Warsaw once it was realised that the Red Army had finally captured Praga and the eastern shore of the Vistula. In a dispatch to Stanisław Mikołajczyk, the Prime

---

13   Ibid. op.cit. pp.38-52.
14   Ibid.
15   Ibid.

Minister in exile, Bień reported the terrible situation in Warsaw, including aerial bombardment and shelling, with hundreds of people buried under the ruins of the city. Again the spectre of starvation was raised as Bień observed that supplies dropped by the Soviets were negligible while there was a "catastrophic lack" of ammunition for the British and German weapons used by the AK. It was also noted that there had not been any recent drops by the Allies. Bień wrote that the Americans, when they had dropped weapons on 18 September, had raised morale but the lack of further drops had plunged both soldiers and civilians into depression and was a "monstrous" way to treat Warsaw.

On 20 September Bień summarized the situation. His overall premise was that the capital was in ruins, and he gave details. The Old Town had been completely burnt down and destroyed, as had the city centre as far as Sikorski Avenue. From there, heading south, the enemy was systematically burning down street after street, using artillery and aerial bombardment. In Mokotów, in what was described as a "quadrilateral" formed by Independence Avenue, Rakowiecki, Pulawski and Narbut Streets, every building was completely burnt out and all of the inhabitants apparently moved out to Pruszków, where their fates were uncertain. Bień said that owing to the destruction of the city tens of thousands of people had lost everything and were reduced to sheltering in cellars with other homeless people. These destitute people could not even move freely in the streets because of enemy artillery and aerial attacks, and so were travelling around the cellars, which interconnected under the streets and courtyards of Warsaw.

The situation of the civil population during September had gone from bad to worse. Bień made the point that after seven weeks of fighting people felt abandoned and were exhausted, owing to the lack of practical support from any of their allies. Already 20,000 people had left the city, while those who remained were "exhausted to uttermost limits". However, ordinary people were also acutely aware of their situation and asked the "tormenting question *what then?*' 'What then with Poland? with the Home Army? with state administration, with political and social life? What about acknowledgment by the Soviets of combatant rights for the Home Army?'"[16] This question was loaded against the Soviet Union rather than Nazi Germany. It was clear that Germany was the Polish enemy, but the Soviet Union even as an ally was less trusted than the German enemy: an incredible situation which only a Pole could understand. The western Allies failed to do so.

Bień was very clear in his observations of the Warsaw Uprising and understood that by the third week of September it could not continue for much longer without Allied support. He gave an accurate and well-judged report of the situation during that week:

> ... and that is the reason why further considerable and regular aid from the Allies in the form of ammunition, arms, food and medical supplies is indispensable, both for military and political reasons. The single lot of supplies dropped by the American force was sufficient for two days. I take the opportunity to draw your attention to the fact that the shortage of food is so acute now that it is causing starvation, that epidemics, dysentery are raging and that in view of the unbelievable distances we by ourselves will not be able to assume the minimum conditions of existence to tens of thousands of wronged people, lacking especially a roof over their heads, warm clothing and linen. As winter is approaching there can be no thought of rebuilding homes: we shall have to build barracks. Help from the outside is indispensable and that at once. And now you must make preparations immediately for action on this wide scale.'[17]

---

16   Ibid. p.69.
17   Ibid.

At a stroke Bień's statement disproved the original bluster of the AK when, following the American drop of 18 September, they said they needed nothing else until further notice. Two days is not long, but of course it did not mean that the Americans would have been in a position to make further drops. The lack of Allied help, especially from the Soviets, merely indicated to the Germans that Warsaw was of no importance to Allied war aims and so long as they treated the AK correctly as prisoners of war, they could more or less do as they liked, while the Soviets, an ally in the war against Germany, did not even have to treat AK fighters properly.

Between 24 and 27 September AK positions in Mokotów became the objective of an unrelenting German offensive. This offensive opened with a huge artillery barrage, in which it was claimed that the Germans deployed the entire arsenal of heavy artillery available to them. Despite this, the AK was able to fight off every German attack that day. However the German offensive continued into the night and the Mokotów AK began to lose territory as a result of the continuous attacks. Lieutenant-Colonel "Karol", the AK commander at Mokotów, decided to evacuate the region that very night and by 26 September the fighters had been withdrawn. The Germans, realizing that the Poles were using the sewers to travel by; began to block tunnels in the system. This caused the evacuation to be suspended until a new route could be found. On 27 September Mokotów surrendered, while AK fighters continued to defend themselves in the city centre and in Żoliborz. However, despite the acceptance of the AK as legal combatants, 120 AK soldiers who had got lost in the sewage system and exited into an area on Dworkowa Street occupied by the Germans were executed on the spot.

Following the fall of Mokotów, the Germans began a general offensive against Żoliborz on 28 September. This area was defended by 1,500 AK fighters but was attacked by over 8,000 enemy soldiers supported by armoured vehicles. It was at this point that Bór-Komorowski decided to open talks for terms of surrender. Talks finally began between AK envoys and the Germans at the German Headquarters on the morning of 30 September. By the afternoon of the same day Lieutenant-Colonel "Zywiciel" received an order from Bór-Komorowski to lay down his arms. At the same time the Polish delegation received consent from the Germans for a dawn to dusk ceasefire so the remaining Polish civilians could be evacuated from Warsaw. It was also reported on the BBC that Bór-Komorowski had been appointed C-in-C of Polish Armed Forces, following the dismissal of Sosnkowski from that post.[18] The removal of Sosnkowski as the Polish C-in-C had been long coming; the British establishment had never liked him and considered him to be second-rate. However his downfall was to issue his notorious Order of the Day No. 19 on 1 September. This order reflected his frustration with the Allies and their lack of help for Warsaw. Sosnkowski was extremely critical of the British Government and what he considered to be its pro-Soviet policy. This may or may not have been fair but did not serve to soothe the Soviet-Polish relationship. His removal was sought primarily by both Churchill and Eden.[19] The problem for Sosnkowski was that as with so many of the Polish émigré politicians who resided largely in Kensington which was also the seat of the Polish Government of Exile, they were out of touch with reality; the reality of their place in the alliance against Germany and even how they were perceived in their home country. Piotr Wandycz wrote, "émigré politics acquire after a while a certain aura of unreality and shadows replace substance".[20] Bór-Komorowski's appointment as C-in-C was probably the most foolish decision of the entire war and there had been a few. It was foolish because he

18   Warsawuprising.com

19   Edward Raczynski, *In Allied London*, London, Weidenfeld & Nicolson, 1962, diary entry, 20 September 1944, pp.235-6.

20   Matthew R. Schwonek, 'Gen. Kazimierz Sosnkowski's Order of the Day No. 19' *Journal of Slavic Military Studies*, 21, 2008, 364-376 quoting Piotr Wandycz, 'August Zalewski and his Times' *East European Quarterly*, 24, 1990, p.421. See also McGilvray, *A Military Government*, p.154.

was about to enter German captivity, thus leaving the Polish military effectively leaderless, but the decision to appoint him also served to further antagonise the Soviet government, which hated him even more than it had Sosnkowski.[21]

The Polish garrison of Warsaw surrendered on 3 October and the civilized world lamented its fall, but did nothing. Harold Nicolson, the British diplomat and diarist, noted on 4 October, "people are really horrified at the collapse of the resistors at Warsaw and feel that Russia has behaved abominably. Moreover the idea is gaining ground that Russia is seeking to establish herself in the Balkans and has given up all idea of fighting the Germans in East Prussia. Antony [Eden, British Foreign Secretary] does not share this pessimism. But nevertheless distrust of the Russians is universal."[22] Nicolson was wrong about the Russians not fighting in East Prussia but the sentiment regarding Russian or Soviet global ambitions was correct. There was little that the British or Americans could do about the Soviet Government's expansionist policies until Germany and her allies had been comprehensively defeated. Then and only then could the Allies challenge Stalin and the Soviet Union; meanwhile Poland had to be sacrificed.

Much of this work has dealt with how the Warsaw Uprising affected ordinary people. Not politicians or senior aristocratic officers seeking a return to the pre-war status quo, as if nothing had happened since 1939, but the people who had to live in Poland as best they could under German and Soviet occupations. It should be noted that other Polish resistance groups were reluctant to work with the AK as they were often viewed as *Panskie Wojsko*, a so-called "gentlemen's army" still linked to the pre-war Polish regime and seeking its return.[23] Up to a point the Germans behaved remarkably well, given how they had previously behaved in Poland and on the Eastern or Russian Front in general. AK surrenders were largely accepted with the minimum of fuss and documentation, while female AK members were given the choice of going to POW camps for women or accepting civilian status.[24] Women AK prisoners were pressurized by the Germans to drop their POW status and to become civilian workers. A large number refused and 1,721 were sent to a penal camp at Oberlangen in Holland; as the German government claimed that after October the former POW camp was disused , the International Red Cross did not know of the presence of the AK women there.[25] They remained at Oberlangen until April 1945, when the 10th Mounted Rifles, a regiment of the First Polish Armoured Division, acting on a tip off from local Dutch civilians, went to the camp and found their countrywomen. To be freed from captivity by Polish soldiers was like a miracle for these women AK fighters.[26]

General Bór-Komorowski, with his generals, walked to surrender to the Germans and they were driven away in German staff cars. As Davies notes, "most of them were never to see their native country again".[27] Bór-Komorowski was no mere prisoner of war but became a "*prominente*", a prisoner deemed by the German authorities to be of special value owing to perceived influence or valued connections. Between 5 February 1945 and 12 April 1945 he was held at the infamous Colditz prison camp before being taken away by the Germans.[28] Davies notes the pride with which

21   NA: CAB 65/48 WM (44) 130th Conclusion, Minute 3, Confidential Annexe, 2 October 1944. *The Manchester Guardian*, 3 October 1944. See also Raczynski, op.cit. diary entry 15 October 1944, pp.236-7.

22   *The Harold Nicolson Diaries, 1907-1963*, (ed) Nigel Nicolson, London, Weidenfeld & Nicolson, 2004, diary entry, 4 October 1944, pp.302-3.

23   Kochanski, op.cit. p.279.

24   Davies, *Rising*, p.434.

25   Kochanski, op.cit. p.424.

26   Evan McGilvray, *Man of Steel and Honour: General Stanisław Maczek. Soldier of Poland, Commander of the 1st Polish Armoured Division in North-West Europe 1944-45*, Solihull, Helion, 2012, pp.199-204.

27   Davies, *Rising*. p.435.

28   Gris Davies-Scourfield, *In Presence of my Foes: A Memoir of Calais, Colditz and Wartime Adventures*, Barnsley, Pen & Sword, 2004, 2nd Edition, pp.213, 218. Bór-Komorowski gave an account of his captivity and

AK fighter, male and female, marched out to surrender – their duty done, and it had been done. Between 3 October and 5 October 1944, 11,668 soldiers surrendered.[29] The fighters may have made an impressive sight when they gave themselves up to the Germans but there was another side of the surrender of Warsaw – the civilians and their plight was pitiful and was in total contrast to that of the AK. One can only wonder why Bór-Komorowski did not insist that the Germans took a more humane approach towards their civilian captives, but by that time he probably did not really care about their fate.

Civilians in Warsaw during the uprising suffered disproportionately to the AK fighters, not only because of the murderous attitude of the Germans and their allies but also because of the lack of care and preparation of the AK High Command. The state of these poor people as they left the ruins of what was their city was a disgrace, compared to the reasonably fit appearance of the AK fighters. Clearly the civilians had been neglected by their own people, quite apart from any actions of the Germans and the Soviets. Davies records the "dirty, exhausted, starving and bewildered", which had to march to two German transit camps between nine or twelve miles outside Warsaw. They were given no assistance and included all age groups. Many were wounded.[30] It must have been similar to the scenes in the film *The Killing Fields* in which Phnom Penh, the Cambodian capital, is evacuated by the Khmer Rouge and every person in the city whatever their state, medical or otherwise, was forced out without pity or help. Davies writes further, "these were the scenes which critics of the Rising would find hardest to forgive".[31] This was a major problem for the AK and the Warsaw Uprising; in so many respects there was little concern for the civilian population. It was very easy for the Soviets to criticize the uprising as the work of madmen and criminals, given the backgrounds of the leadership in Warsaw. It seemed that the Warsaw Uprising was an ill-advised and poorly judged attempt at snatching power by the former Polish elites. They continued to act in the same reckless manner as they had during the Second Republic, when between the wars Poland had been ruled with little concern for her own citizens. Civilian politicians, in the spring of 1944, demanded that the military elite leave politics. In an attempt to avoid this, the Polish Army in Poland (AK), relying on the naivety of their young fighters, gambled in an attempt to liberate Poland. They wanted to claim, as they had in 1918, that once more the Polish Army had freed the country, and thus legitimise their stake in political power in post-war Poland. This reckless gamble failed, and civilians paid the cost for the failure of the Warsaw Uprising.

Civilian suffering went beyond the scope of the war years and continued into the Communist era in Poland. The total cost in civilian lives was bad enough, while wounded casualties were probably treble the number of those who died. The civilian survivors were marched into captivity for an uncertain short-term fate and a long-term life of poverty if they lived through German imprisonment and returned to Poland. For some very good reasons such as being put on trial by the Communist authorities in Poland and possibly executed, most of the AK commanders who led the uprising did not return to Poland, and lived and died in exile in the west. Once more it was the "little people" who had to face up to the reality and consequences of the failure of the Warsaw Uprising. Davies notes that over 100,000 were sent to Germany as slave labourers, while tens of thousands were sent to concentration camps, including Ravensbruck, Auschwitz and Mauthausen.[32]

the circumstances of his release during the second half of April 1945 in Tadeusz Bór-Komorowski, *Armia Podziem NA*: 3rd Edition, London, Veritas, 1967, pp.360-4. He died in exile in London in 1966.

29   Davies, *Rising*, p.435.
30   Ibid. p.436.
31   Ibid.
32   Davies, *Uprising*, p.437.

Of the small group of ladies interviewed by the author during July 2012 not one left Poland, but their fates were different. Dr. Barbara Dobrowolska packed a haversack and walked to her family home in Łódź; it took her three days to walk to the city. During January 1945 the Red Army liberated Łódź, but her family had property seized by the newly arrived Communist authorities and her family home in the centre of the city was shared out between homeless families. This meant that Dobrowolska and her mother had to live in a single room while needy families were issued with the other rooms.

As already mentioned women who took part in the Warsaw Uprising could choose between being made prisoners of war, and treated as such, or accepting civilian status. Stefania Hoch and Wanda Lesniewska both opted to be taken as prisoners of war, where they were treated far better than their civilian counterparts. However this was not without incident, as initially the Germans tried to break the agreement covering the treatment of AK as prisoners of war. Upon accepting the AK surrender, the Germans took their prisoners to a convoy of lorries from where they were taken to a marshalling point and loaded on to trains. Lesniewska said that they were many wounded AK soldiers aboard the trains: however what is of great interest was the proposed destination of the prisoners. The Germans were taking them to Łódź. A German-speaking AK officer, Lieutenant-Colonel Szterelow, realised that the final destination of this convoy of AK prisoners was the punishment camp at Radogoszcz on the outskirts of Łódź. This was not a prisoner of war camp and was infamous for the atrocious treatment of its inmates, principally Jews and Poles, by its Nazi guards. Lieutenant-Colonel Szterelow argued with his captors that it was against the Geneva Convention to send the prisoners there, as they were prisoners of war and had to be treated as such. Eventually the Germans relented but the Poles spent three to four days on the train in Łódź, where local citizens, at great risk to themselves, provided them with food and water. Another stroke of luck had been that during the uprising Lesniewska's medical point had been caring for seven wounded German soldiers; as a result when the Poles surrendered, Lesniewska's people were able to take all of their medical supplies with them on to the train. They were able to continue providing a medical service, even when they were being transported into captivity. After their break in Łódź Lesniewska's convoy finally headed towards Germany: at first to the station at Jakobsthal and finally to Ehrenhain, a camp on the River Elbe. This was another example of German chicanery, as this camp was so filthy and infested with disease the Germans thought that their prisoners would soon die. Lesniewska recalls that in the camp there were prisoners of several nationalities, French, American and Italian, but by far the most numerous were Russian. They suffered most at the hands of their German captors and were in the worst condition when the Poles arrived.

The only way to survive this appalling cheating was to set to and clean up the camp. To this end the AK medical teams began their campaign and using their specialist skills managed to reduce infections and disease. There was at least one live birth at the camp and the baby lived to adulthood – it would not have happened if people like Wanda Lesniewska and Stefania Hoch had not been on hand to improve conditions there.

The Germans continued to be ill-disposed towards their prisoners. Later, when a Commission investigating the conditions of camps arrived from Berne in Switzerland, the Germans – under the pretence of looking for "dangerous people" – took one of the prisoners away to an undisclosed location. However this camp, which held about 2,000 people, protested to the Commission, with Mr. Milanowski, a leading pre-war local politician, acting as an informal spokesman for the prisoners. He pointed out that the camp they were in was already punishment enough – why should this individual be punished further? By this point of the war the Germans were aware that they had lost and were afraid of being accused of war crimes. The man was returned. Furthermore, thanks to the intervention of this commission, each prisoner was given some parcels of supplies. It was thanks to this that Wanda Lesniewska was able to exchange cigarettes from her parcel for a fur jerkin to go over her nurse's uniform, and so survive the winter of 1944-45. There were no further recorded attempts at foul play by the Germans at this camp, and in the spring of 1945 it was liberated by the Red Army.

Barbara Matys recalled that the day before the AK surrender in Warsaw was terrible, with urgent discussion about what they should do. Three options were put forward within her group: the first to make for the Vistula, the second to surrender, while the third was to fight to the death.[33] How serious the first and last suggestions were is not clear, but all the same many members of the AK must have wondered why they had bothered, having suffered and sacrificed themselves and their capital. At times senior commanders can be unfeeling and only make a sacrifice once they finally feel endangered. All the same, Matys and her colleagues surrendered as ordered and marched into German captivity. Matys found herself in a notorious POW camp in Lamsdorf (Stalag VIII-B – modern day Łambinowice, Poland). Even though the Germans had taken this group of AK as prisoners of war, they were again placing them in a camp with little medical care and a high death rate from disease if not neglect. A major problem was that many of the prisoners held at the camp were from the Red Army, and as the Soviet Union was not part of the International Red Cross movement the German authorities felt no obligation to treat their soldiers humanely. This meant, for example, that they did not receive Red Cross parcels containing cigarettes. These could be used as an alternative currency within the camp, perhaps buying small luxuries that might have meant the difference between life and death. Matys also says that the Germans hardly fed their Red Army prisoners at all, which – such was their wretched position – led to cases of cannibalism amongst the Soviet captives owing to the neglect and indifference of the authorities.

Once the AK nurses and other medical personal arrived in the camp, with their medical training and knowledge of hygiene, things began to improve. The Poles also began to help the Soviets with whom they had the most contact – with stolen, not issued medicine. Matys notes that typhus, malaria and tuberculosis were "conquered" in the camp. An Armenian soldier who had been serving in the Red Army and was now a prisoner wrote a "lovely letter" to Matys as she had nursed him back to health. This anonymous man wrote that even though he was in Russian (Soviet) uniform, she still saw him as a fellow human being. He enclosed a silver brooch, perhaps his only memento of his wife. This was passed through the wire of the compounds that separated the prisoners from each other. Matys knew nothing of his final fate.

By Easter 1945 the war was fast approaching its end. From the west, the Allies were already in Germany and from the east the Red Army was heading rapidly towards Berlin. Matys comments on this with a small yet significant incident. Easter Monday is known in Poland as *Śmigus-dyngus*, a time for throwing water over each other (this is done with good humour – and perhaps to settle a score with a rival). Apparently there was a German NCO called Holtz who persecuted the very sick in the camp. A group of Polish boys decided to pay him back for his behaviour; at dawn they soaked him with buckets of water.[34] Matys does not mention any German reprisal for this act of insubordination but one can be certain that only a year before people would have been shot for such an attack on a German soldier. What was concentrating the Germans' minds was the approach of the Red Army, the fear of defeat and of being arraigned as war criminals.

During May 1945 the Germans gave up their arms and the keys to every building and room in the camp, then most of them fled. The prisoners organised themselves and waited for the Red Army to come and liberate them. Once the Red Army reached the camp, preparations were put into place to return home. A Polish doctor, Dr. Jadwiga Beaupré made sure that the camp's medical team was kept together with a designated wagon for the sick and medical staff. Matys, with others, began to

---

33   Łukasz Modelski, *Dziewczyny Wojenne: Prawdziwe Historie*, Kraków, Znak, 2011, p.141.
34   Ibid. p.144.

think of the future and where she might want to go now that the war was over. Her father was in Britain and there was a chance that perhaps she might join him there, but she decided to return to Poland to her mother, brother and grandparents.[35] However Matys' war was not over as it was still active in Poland until about 1948-9.

Matys returned to study with the view of taking a degree in medicine but she also kept in contact with her comrades from the Warsaw Uprising, and continued to work for the Polish underground as it sought independence from the Soviet Union. There were two main arms of the underground, WiN (*Wolność i Niezawisłość* – Freedom and Independence) and NIE (*Niepodległość* – Independence. *Nie* is also the Polish for "No" – just what many people thought of the Soviet occupation of Poland). These had evolved from the remains of the AK after its dissolution by the government-in-exile on 19 January 1945.[36] In early January 1947, a few days before the elections which were to claim legitimacy (fraudulently) for the Soviet system of rule in Poland, after an equally flawed plebiscite held during the summer of 1946 that also sought to legitimize the imposition of Soviet rule in Poland, agents from the Polish secret police, UB (*Urząd Bezpieczeństwa*) took Matys in for questioning, as they were keen to discover about her suspected work with the underground.[37] It was all part of an intimidation campaign against suspected anti-Soviet activists and those who had fought in the Warsaw Uprising were treated with great suspicion by the Soviet authorities. Matys was briefly imprisoned and was subject to suspicion and periodic questioning by the UB for several years to come. She carried on her medical work in Warsaw until she retired. In her later years she was honoured for her wartime work and received the Krzyż Waleczny for her role in the fighting at the PAST building. She also received, early in the twenty-first century, one of the highest Polish orders, the Order of *Polonia Restituta* from President Lech Kaczyński, President of Poland from 2005 until his untimely and mysterious death in an air crash in Russia during 2010, which saw 95 other senior Polish political and military figures killed.[38] It is ironic that he was visiting the memorial to the victims of Katyń, the scene of the murders of Poles by the Soviet authorities in 1940. It is also interesting that women such as Matys could not be honoured for their service to their country until after 1989, when Poland was independent of the Soviet Union and had a president sympathetic to their cause. The Second World War and the Warsaw Uprising cast a long shadow. Taylor notes that the Soviet attitude towards Poland after May 1945 was that of "mild disapproval" but one of relief after the trial of sixteen AK leaders, including Stypulkowski, in Moscow – this can be inferred from the leniency of the sentences, from a few months to fifteen years imprisonment. The UK and the USA had also realised that they had little influence in Poland and pursued more realistic priorities as the Cold War began.[39] The Soviet authorities with their Polish Stalinist collaborators stayed their hand until after 1947, when there was a further wave of arrests of high profile AK officers who had continued to resist the Soviet annexation of Poland. This time several of these men were executed. The episode remains controversial in Poland, especially after 1989 when archives were fully opened and Polish collaborators

---

35   Ibid. Dr. Beaupré gives a detailed account of the time spent at Lamsdorf and after in a Polish journal article published in during 1974. She mentions Matys by name and gives her rank as Starszy *Sierżant* with Staff Sergeant being the approximate equivalent in the British Army. Sadly Beauprés account concludes with the fact that her eldest son had been arrested by the Germans in Kraków at the beginning of January 1945 only ten days before the Germans evacuated that city; he was never seen again. See: Jadwiga Beaupré, 'Relacja lerki z Zeithain' *Przegląd Lekarski*, 31 (1) 1974, 200-08.

36   McGilvray, *A Military Government*, p.167.

37   Modelski, op.cit. pp.145-6.

38   Ibid. pp.145-7. Matys.

39   Frederick Taylor, op.cit. p.226.

still living, often in good jobs or in receipt of good state pensions, were exposed. The arguments still rumble on.[40]

Barbara Gadomska was not taken as a prisoner of war. Instead she went with the evacuation of civilians to the Pruszków site, which was little more than a concentration camp. Gadomska recalls that the sight of the civilians was terrible, as they arrived with baggage and prams containing the little that they had after the rising failed, plus what they thought was necessary for the coming journey which was, in short, deportation. At Pruszków there was a very large hall made from concrete, and for two or three days people waited, sitting on the concrete floor. Eventually the Germans began to divide their captives into groups. They were mainly seeking workers who, in spite of earning a very small wage, were in fact to be slave labour for German war industries. Gadomowska is quite clear that she was assigned to a work camp rather than a concentration camp. From Pruszków she began a journey via Wrocław (formally Breslau a German city), and then to Berlin where she began work in an arms factory. By this stage of the war Gadomska noted that many Germans were distracted by the advancing Red Army, drawing ever closer; the result was that she and other prisoners were loosely guarded. Furthermore Berlin was suffering from heavy bombing by the Allies. This had caused great destruction and left many Berliners homeless, but incredibly many Germans showed sympathy and kindness towards the Poles. However they were cautious in their behaviour, as they were fearful of their own countrymen, not wishing to be denounced as being friendly towards enemies of Germany. Eventually the Red Army arrived in Berlin and in time Gadomska was able to return to Poland. She was reunited with her parents in Kreszowice near Kraków, where they had been living since the destruction and evacuation of Warsaw.[41]

From these case studies it can clearly be seen that the Germans, even though they claimed to be taking the AK as prisoners of war, failed to enter into the spirit of the agreement. The exception was in the case of the AK leadership, which was treated decently especially in view of the Germans' conduct at the beginning of the uprising when General Stefan Rowecki, the former head of the AK and in German custody since 1943, was executed on the first day. However what is clear as the case studies illustrate, is that the ordinary mortals of Warsaw suffered disproportionally as a consequence of the Warsaw Uprising being so ineptly handled by the Polish command. From day one it was clear that it was doomed to fail with little thought given to what might happen if it did. The consequences were horrendous, as civilians were slaughtered while gallant youngsters attempted to storm German strongholds armed with little except the zeal of youth. Warsaw itself was systematically destroyed while the AK was reduced to a mere shadow of its former self, thus allowing the Red Army to overrun Poland and annex it. It was not until 1989 before the goals of the Warsaw Uprising were achieved; its leaders had died in a frustrated exile but a handful of old ladies survived the trials and tribulations of that awful time and have given testimony of what they saw and endured.

I thank them and dedicate this book to them and their comrades wherever they are …

---

40   There is little, if any literature on this subject in English but for the Polish reader a recent interesting study is the case of Captain Witold Pilecki. Wiesław Jan Wysocki, *Rotmistrz Witold Pilecki, 1901-1948*, Warsaw, RYTM, 2012.

41   Gadomska.

Appendix

Nurses Who After the Warsaw Uprising Remained With Polish Wounded and Suffered Imprisonment as Prisoners of War in Germany mainly at Zeithain and other places

Babczyńska, neé Chmielniska, Daniela
Bobrowska, Krystyna
Bobrowska, Zofia
Borowicz, Anna
Borowska, Zofia
Chrobotko, Antonina
Dąbrowska, Wanda
Dąbrowska, Władysław
Dobosz, Stefania, (later Hoch)
Fabisiewicz, Alicja
Frankowska, Irena
Gacka, Irena
Germak, Ludwika
Gilewicz, Danuta
Górecka, Stanisława
Grawczyńska, Zofia
Iwaszko, Stanisława
Janus, Maria
Jarkowska-Krauze, Zofia
Jędraszko Wanda
Justyna, Jadwiga
Karpowicz, Irena
Keppen, Janina
Kędzierska, Barbara
Kłosóna, Maria
Kondracka-Bajer (Midwife)
Kotnowska, Halina
Kowalska Anna (later Marczyk) POW Camp – VI C Oberlagen Standbotel
Kowalska, Maria Teresa
Kralska, Janina Teresa
Krysiewicz, Wanda Stefania POW Camp – Altengrabow Stalag XI A
Księżopolska, Wanda
Kulczyńska, Jadwiga
Kurjowska, Naria
Kwiecińska, Władysława
Langer, Helena

Leszczyńska, Maria Anna POW Camp – Stalag IV B Lamsdorf
Lewińska-Rypel, Hanna
Lubieniecka-Babczyńska, Daniela
Łęczyn, Apolonia
Malinowska, Barbara
Malinowska, Leokadia
Manulik Stanisława
Matys-Wysiadecka, Barbara
Mazuraki Halina (Nursing Midwife)
Mizerska Janina Maria (Midwife)
Mrozowska, Jadwiga
Niemcewicz Aleksandra (later Ursyn)
Nowak, Józefa
Nowak, Katarzyna
Obertenna, Jadwiga
Ogonowska, Halina
Pawlowicz-Berka, Maria
Pawłowicz, Irma
Piekarz, Krystyna
Pniewska, I
Pniewska, Irena (Later Midwife)
Potocka, Kazimiera
Pytlakowska, Irena
Robakowska, Julia
Romanowska, Irena
Sańko, Danuta
Serini-Brodniewicz, Anita
Siczkówna, Joanna Helena
Skotnicka, Stefania
Sokół, Wladysława
Staniszewska, Barbara
Szmitkowska, Maria
Szymańska, Maria
Świątecka, Halina
Tryba, Olga
Trzaskowska, Janina
Tyczyńska, Janina
Walewicz, Alina

Walewicz, Anna   Zamorska, Stefania
Xsiężopolska, Wanda
Zajdel, Kazimierz

Based on Table 5a in Barbara Dobrowolska, *Materiały Historyczne: Pielęgniarstwa Polskiego, przyczynek do dziejów pielęgniarstwa Polskiego XX wieku*, Łódź, Oficyna Wysawnicza MA, 2013, pp.161-162.

Nurses killed During the Warsaw Uprising, 1944.

Abczyńska, Janina – *nom de guerre 'Julia'*   Gromulska, Wanda
Babicka-Zachertowa, Maria   Grzybowska, Jadwiga
Bagińska, Zofia   Hackiewicz, Halina
Baryła, Antonia   Halińska, Władysława
Biała, Anna   Janicka, Danuta
Bieniasz-Krzywiec, Antonia   Januszkiewicz, Irena
Bojarska-Wieczorkiewicz, Halina   Jarkowska-Krauze, Zofia
Borkowska, Wincenta   Jarkowska-Szelińska, Zofia
Brunner, Aldona   Jassonek, Zofia
Brzeska, Maria   Jaworska, Jadwiga
Budźta, Jadwiga   Jaxa-Bykowska, Klara
Bukaty, Jadwiga   Józwiakówna, Helena
Burkówna, Maria   Kaczorowska, Stefania
Burska-Toberowicz, Janina   Kaleńska, Iza
Buzalska, Rachela   Kamińska, Magdalena
Bykowska-Jaksa, Danuta   Kawecka, Jolanta
Chodakowska, Maria   Kieżun, Barbara
Cichocka, Ewa   Klarzyńska, Leokadia
Cieślak, Apolonia   Klocowa, Maria
Cytańska, Emilia   Kochanowska, Jolanta
Czechanowska, Maria   Kolarska, Ewa
Dąbrowska, Halina   Korzycka, Janina
Dynowska, Maria   Kosińska (Forename Unknown)
Erbichówna Ludmiła   Koskowska, Kazimiera
Etminis, Halina   Kossowska, Aleksandra
Fleisner, Wanda   Kostrzewska (Forename Unknown)
Frankowska-Gromza, Maria   Kowalska, Halina
Glomska, Janina   Kozal, Maria
Głowacka, Janina   Krassowska, Zofia
Goetzner, Janina   Krassowska, Zofia Halina
Grabicka, Bronisława   Krzeszkowska, Florentyna
Gramzowa, Maria   Kurażew, Katarzyna
Grochocka, Irena   Kurbisówna, Kazimiera
Grocholska, Barbara   Kutkowska, Irena
Grochowska, Janina   Kwaskowska, Stanisława
Grodzicka, Feliksa   Kwiatkowska, Irena

Lampicka, Dorata
Leńska, (Forename Unknown)
Leszkowska, Elżbieta
Likon, Oktawia
Likoń, Stanisława
Łach, Lachowska, Halina
Łukomska, Elwira
Machówna, Róża
Makowiecka, Maria
Maruszczak, Filomena
Marzecka, Stefania
Masłowska, Alicja
Matuszczak, Filomena
Matuszewska, Ewa
Mioduszewska, Maria
Moszkowska, Krystyna
Mrówczyńska, Wacława
Namok, Halina
Narbutt, Aleksandra
Narkoń, Stanisława
Nęckiewicz, Halina
Nowak, Helena
Oleszczakówna, Irena
Otocka, Wanda
Papieska, Bronisława
Pawłowicz-Berka, Maria
Pieśko, Irena
Pieślakówna, Józefa
Pietrulewicz, Krystyna
Pioterczykówna, Anna
Popławska, Hanna
Prześlakowska, Irena
Pszczółkowska, Halina
Puciłowska, Honorata
Radajewska, Maria
Radziwiłłowicz, Maria
Rankowska, Barbara
Redlińska-Jeske, Jadwiga
Rolińska, Władysława
Różycka, Maria
Rutkowska, Irena

Samiołkowska, Janina
Sapieżanka, Róża
Sidorowicz, Janina
Sikorowska, Janina
Sikorska, Aleksandra
Sikorska, Janina
Skarga, Zofia
Skaryń, Jadwiga
Smulewicz, Stanisława
Snopkiewicz, Natalia
Sopócko, Anna
Stabierska, Józefa
Stanulewicz, Stanisława
Stańczykowska, (Forename Unknown)
Sternlieb, Ludwika
Stępień, (Forename Unknown)
Szczepańska, Teresa
Szymańska, Stanisława
Ślęczkowska, Janina
Ślęzakiewicz, Halina
Ślęzakówna, Alina
Terpiłowska, Maria
Tyszkówska, Eryka
Walterowa, Eugenia
Wanatówna, Romana
Wardzyńska, Władysława
Wawrowska, Aleksandra
Wiefort, Adela
Wierzbicka, Władysława
Wiewiórowska, Natalia
Wiśniewska, Krystyna
Zaborowska, Wanda
Zakrzewska, Halina
Zakrzewska, Maria
Zarębska, Krystyna
Zdrodowska, Celina
Ziarko, Genowefa
Zielonkówna, Maria
Zwolińska, Wanda
Żmudzka, Małgorzata
Żylińska, Wanda

Table 11, Dobrowolska, pp.176-177.

Nurses Who Participated in the Warsaw Uprising, 1944.

Aleksandrowicz, Maria
Andruszkiewicz, Nella
Andrzejkowicz-Pracka-Węgierska, Zofia
Antczak, Apolonia
Banasiak, Helena
Bandurska, Halina
Barakowska-Kurkowska, Zofia
Barcikowska, Halina
Batycka, Jadwiga
Bedelek-Skonieczna, Jadwiga
Białowąs-Wysocka, Krystyna
Bielobradek, Romana
Bojarska, Zofia
Borowiec-Załęska, Walentyna
Brodniewicz, Anita
Bronicka, Franciszka
Budźta, Jadwiga
Bulińska, Halina
Bzowska-Fitkał, Maria
Chadaj, Bożena
Chanecka, Helena
Chocianowska-Przyłęcka, Janina
Chrzanowska, Danuta
Cybulska, Zofia
Czarnecka-Kłosowska, Jadwiga
Darska, Lucyna
Dawidowicz-Strzembosz, Maria
Dąbrowska, Wanda
Dmochowska, Anna
Dobosz-Hoch, Stefania
Dobrowolska, Barbara (Polish Scouting Movement)
Dobrzańska, Isia
Doellinger, Zofia
Dynowska, Maria
Dyrlacz, Anna
Dziedzic-Wrzoskowa, Aniela
Eichel-Wolańska, Zofia
Fryźlewicz, Katarzyna
Fudała-Sitkiewicz, Henryka
Gajewska-Tarnowska, Leokadia Wanda
Gałkowa, Danuta
Ginowicz, Janina
Glińska, Barbara
Glińska, Władysława
Glomska, Janina
Golińska, Maria

Grajewska, Helena Małgorzata
Grzelińska-Orlicka, Zofia
Idzikowska, Wanda
Iżycka, Jadwiga
Iżycka-Kowalska, Anna
Jabłońska-Sochańska, Aniela
Jabłońska, Krystyna
Jabłońska-Szklarewicz (Forename Unknown)
Janowska, Krystyna
Janus-Kurkowska, Maria
Jarkowska-Szelińska, Zofia
Jarzębowska, Helena
Jedlińska, Halina
Jurkowska-Krauze, Zofia
Justyna, Jadwiga
Kakiet, Anna
Kalinowska, Irena
Kalińska-Pater, Zofia
Karpowicz, Bronisława
Kelerowa, Wiktoria
Kilpert, Joanna
Kisińska, Stanisława
Kiźny, Maria
Kondracka, Jadwiga
Korabińska-Zatopiańska, Felicja
Kostrzewska, Aleksander
Kotarbińska, Anna
Kotnowska-Urbaniak, Halina
Kowalska-Gubrynowicz, Bronisława
Kowalska-Iżycka, Anna
Kowalska-Leśniewska (Forename Unknown)
Kozłowska-Gubrynowicz (Forename Unknown)
Kraińska-Fołtynowicz, Maria
Kręcisz-Sokołowska, Wanda
Królewskia, Aniela
Krzemińska-Fortuna, Barbara
Kubacka, Józefa
Kuroczyska, Władysława
Kurowska, Maria
Kwiecińska, Otylia
Lankajtes, Wanda
Lemańczyk, Maria
Lesiecka-Luboińska, Wanda
Lesień-Niznikowa, Helena
Leszczewicz, Monika
Lewińska-Rypel, Hanna

Lusińska, Maria
Łącka, Maria
Łukasiewicz, Kamila
Łyszczarz-Zdeb, Czesława
Maciejewska, (Forename Unknown)
Malkiewicz, Maria
Manulik, Stanisława
Markowska-Szuttenbach, Halina
Martin, Anna
Matusiewicz, Stanisława
Matuszewska, Ewa
Matiszewska, Maria
Maziołek, Helena
Michalak-Jedlińska, Halina
Michalska, Halina
Michałowska, Stefania
Michałowska-Szczepańska, Felicja
Modelska, Jadwiga
Moenke, Wanda
Moszyńska, Maria
Moszyńska, Wanda
Muszka, Zofia
Nabiałek-Konopińska, Irena
Nagórska, Helena
Niewiadomska, Stanisława
Niewińska, Aleksandra Julia
Nowak, Kazimiera
Ogińska, Wanda
Orlicka, Zofia
Owczarska-Jezierska, Barbara Maria
Oziębło, Helen
Paczkowska, Jadwiga
Pajewska-Tyszkiwicz, Jadwiga
Panek-Kraińska, Jadwiga
Paszkiewicz, Czesława
Pągowska, Maria
Pęczkowska, Apolonia
Pęska, Zofia
Pieśko, Irena
Płaczek-Tomaszewska, Janina
Pniewska, Irena
Pohorecka, Janina
Popiołek-Gorgas, Anna Maria
Potocka, Adela
Potocka-Ziembińska, Stefania
Poznańska, Wanda
Preizner-Nemec, Danuta
Rabowska-Witkiewicz, Helena
Raczyńska, Zofia

Radwańska-Cybulska, Hanna
Riedel, Aleksander
Rządkowska, Marta
Rzepisko-Kozikowa, Maria
Sasinowska, Helena
Selwańska-Truskolaska, Maria
Semilowa, Maria
Serini-Brodniewicz, Anita
Siczek, Anna
Siczek, Joanna
Siekielska, Zofia
Sierocka, Maria
Sikorska, Irena
Sister Anna (nun)
Siwicka, Romana
Słupiańska, Józefa
Smikalla, Janina
Smorońska, Maria
Sobiło, Maria
Sobota, Zofia
Sojka, Janina
Stareńga, Halina
Staręga, Halina
Stec-Traczewska, (Forename Unknown)
Stenpel-Kalinowska, Irena
Strzelczyk-Szac, Alicja
Suffczyńska, Jadwiga
Szelągowska, Michalina
Szełochwast, Anna
Szlagowska, Jadwiga
Szoc, Władysława
Szumska-Małecka, Maria
Szymańska-Woskowicz, Czesława
Święcicka-Pawlik, Zofia
Tincer-Zapoloska, Halina
Toporska, Zofia
Trafalska, Kazimiera,
Truskowska, Filomena,
Tyczyńska, Janina
Uniechowska-Dollinger, Zofia
Wadowska, Wanda
Walecka, Zofia
Walewicz-Pawlas, Alina
Warchoł-Rau-Olejniczakowa, Janina
Warda, Barbara
Wielowieyska, Anna
Wierzbicka, Alicja
Wilczyńska, Elżbieta
Wilkońska, Małgorzata

Wilkońska, Maria
Wiśniedwska, Irena
Wojewódzka-Dardas, Alicja
Wojlanis, Anna
Woźniak, Wanda
Wójcik, Halina
Wójcik, Maria Krystyna
Wysiadecka, Barbara

Zaborowska, Wanda
Zaczkiewicz-Biele, Wanda
Zadzerska, Maria
Zaleska-Leśniewska, Zofia
Żeromska, Natalia
Żmudzka, Małgorzata
Żołędziowska, Zofia

Table 14, Dobrowolska, pp.181-183.

Bibliography

INTERVIEWS

Dr. Barbara Dobrowolska, Łódź, 18 July 2012.
Stefania Hoch, Warsaw, 16 July 2012.
Barbara Gadomowska, Warsaw, 16 July 2012.
Wanda Lesniewska, Warsaw, 16 July 2012.
Barbara Matys, Warsaw, 16 July 2012.

UNPUBLISHED SOURCES

The Polish Institute & Sikorski Museum (PISM) Kensington, London

A.XII – Papers of the Ministry of National Defence.
LOT A.V. – *Pomoc Lotnictwa Dla Kraju 1941-1946*, (Aerial Support for the Homeland [Poland] 1941-1946).
KOL 24 – Marian Kukiel Papers.

National Archives of the United Kingdom (Kew)

AIR 8 – Air Ministry, Warsaw, RAF Assistance.
AIR 20 – Air Ministry, Assistance to Warsaw.
CAB 65 – War Cabinet Minutes.
CAB 80 – Chiefs of Staff Memorandum.
FO 371 – Foreign Office Correspondence.
FO 954 – Lord Avon (Eden) Papers.
GFM – German Foreign Ministry (Captured Papers).
HS4 – SOE (Poland).
HW1 – Intelligence Signals.
PREM 3 – Prime Ministers' Office.
WO 204 – War Office – Allied Force, Mediterranean Theatre, Military Head Quarters Papers.

Brotherton Library, University of Leeds

Map Room Messages of President Roosevelt, Reel 5.

Royal Air Force Museum Archives, Colindale, London, NW9

File X002-9271/002 appendix C. Sgt Ward, John George.

Imperial War Museum

IWM – 12787/03/41/1 Ralph Smorczewski – Reminiscences.

Głownego Archiwum Polskiego Towarzystwa Pielęgniarskiego, GAPTP (Main Archive Polish Nurses' Association) Warsaw

Typescript – Interview – Zofia Orlicka. (undated).
Wspomnienia z Powstania Warszawskiego (*Memories of the Warsaw Uprising*) 4 page manuscript – Barbara Gadomska, donated to author, 12 July 2012.

NEWSPAPERS

The Daily Telegraph
The Daily Worker
Dziennik Polski
The Evening Standard
The Manchester Guardian
The New York Times
Polish Fortnightly Review
Soviet War News
Soviet War News Weekly
The Times

PRINTED PRIMARY SOURCES

Danchev Alex, Todman Daniel, (eds) *War Diaries 1939-1945. Field Marshal Lord Alanbrooke*, London, Weidenfeld & Nicolson, 2001.
Dilks, David, (ed) *The Diaries of Sir Alexander Cadogan, 1938-1945*, London, Cassell, 1971.
Documents on Polish-Soviet Relations, 1939-1945, Volume 2, 1943-1945, London, Heinemann, 1967.
German War Crimes in Poland, Central Commission for Investigation of German Crimes in Poland, New York, Howard Fertig, 1982 (2 Volumes bound as a single volume).
Kliszko, Zenon, *Powstanie Warszawskie: Artykuły, przemówienia, wspomnienia dokumenty*, Warsaw, Książka i Wiedza, 1967.
Matusak, Piotr, (ed) *Powstanie Warszawskie 1944: Wybór Dokumentów*, 6 vols. Warsaw, Egros, 1997-2003.
Nicolson, Nigel (ed) *The Harold Nicolson Diaries, 1907-1963*, London, Weidenfeld & Nicolson, 2004.
Pomian, Andrzej, (ed) *The Warsaw Uprising: A Selection of Documents*, London, n.p. 1945.
Rutkowski, A. (ed) *The Report of Jürgen Stroop concerning the Uprising in the Ghetto in Warsaw and the Liquidation of the Jewish Residential Area*, Warsaw, Jewish Historical Institute, 1958.
Woodward, Llewellyn, (ed) *History of the Second World War. British Foreign Policy in the Second World War. Volume III*, London, HMSO, 1971.

PRINTED SECONDARY SOURCES (BOOKS & MONOGRAPHS)

Applebaum, Anne, *Iron Curtain. The Crushing of Eastern Europe, 1944-1956*, London, Allen Lane, 2012.
Bartoszewski, Władysław, *Abandoned Heroes of the Warsaw Uprising*, Kraków, Biały Kruk, 2008.
Bellamy, Chris, *Absolute War: Soviet Russia in the Second World War*, London, Macmillan, 2007.
Berling, Z, *Wspomnienia: Wolność na przetarg* (vol. 3) Warsaw, Polski Dom Wydawniczy, 1991.

Biddiscombe, Perry, *The SS Hunter Battalions. The Hidden History of the Nazi Resistance Movement 1944-45*, Stroud, UK, Tempus, 2006.

Bartelski, Lesław, M, *Mokotów 1944*, Warsaw, MON, 1971.

Bór-Komorowski, Tadeusz, *Armia Podziemna*, 3rd Edition, London, Veritas, 1967.

Bór-Komorowski, Tadeusz, *The Secret Army*, London, Victor Gollancz, 1950.

Bosworth, R.J.B. *Mussolini*, London, Bloomsbury, 2010.

Bruce, George, *The Warsaw Uprising, 1 August 1944-2 October 1944*, London, Rupert Hart-Davies, 1972.

Caddick-Adams, Peter, *Monty and Rommel: Parallel Lives*, London, Arrow Books, 2012.

Ciechanowski, Jan, C, *The Warsaw Uprising of 1944*, Cambridge, Cambridge University Press, 1974.

Clark, Alan, *Barbarossa: The Russian-German Conflict, 1941-1945*, London, Cassell, 2005.

Cornish, Nik, *Armageddon Ost. The German Defeat on the Eastern Front, 1944-5*, Hersham, Ian Allen, 2006.

Corrigan, Gordon, *The Second World War: A Military History*, London, Atlantic Books, 2010.

Davies, Norman, *Europe at War, 1939-1945: No Simple Victory*, London, Pan, 2007.

Davies, Norman, *Rising '44. The Battle for Warsaw*, London, Macmillan, 2003.

Davies-Scourfield, Gris, *In Presence of my Foes: A Memoir of Calais, Colditz and Wartime Adventures*, (2nd Edition) Barnsley, Pen & Sword, 2004.

Dobrowolska, Barbara, *Materiały Historyczne: Pielęgniarstwa Polskiego, przyczynek do dziejów pielęgniarstwa Polskiego XX wieku*, Łódź, Oficyna Wysawnicza MA, 2013.

Epstein, Catherine, *Model Nazi: Arthur Greiser and the Occupation of Western Poland*, New York, Oxford, 2010.

Erickson, John, *The Road to Berlin: Stalin's War with Germany, Volume 2*, London, Cassell, 2003.

Fisk, Robert, *The Great War for Civilization. The Conquest of the Middle East*, London, Harper Perennial, 2006.

Forczyk, Robert, *Warsaw 1944. Poland's Bid for Freedom*, Oxford, Osprey, 2009.

Grabowski, Waldermar, *Polski Administracja Cywilna 1940-1945*, Warsaw, Instytut Pamięci Narodowej, 2003.

Gross, Jan Tomasz, *Polish Society Under German Occupation. The Generalgouvernment, 1939-1944*, Princeton, Princeton University Press, 1979.

Hanson, Joanna K.M. *The Civilian Population and the Warsaw Uprising of 1944*, New York, CUP, 1982.

Karski, Jan, *Story of a Secret State: My Report to the World*, London, Penguin, 2011.

Kirchmayer, Jerzy, *Powstanie Warszawskie*, Warsaw, Ksiażka i Wiedza, 1959.

Kochanski, Halik, *The Eagle Unbowed: Poland and the Poles in the Second World War*, London, Allen Lane, 2012.

Kunert, Andrzej Krzysztof, Szarota, Tomasz, *Generał Stefan 'Grot' w relacjach i w pamięci zbiorowej*, Warsaw, Rytm, 2003.

McGilvray, Evan, *Man of Steel and Honour: General Stanisław Maczek. Soldier of Poland, Commander of the 1st Polish Armoured Division in North-West Europe 1944-45*, Solihull, Helion, 2012.

McGilvray, Evan, *A Military Government in Exile. The Polish Government-in-Exile, 1939-1945, a Study of Discontent*, Solihull, Helion, 2010.

McGilvray, Evan, *The Black Devils' March – A Doomed Odyssey – The 1st Polish Armoured Division, 1939-45*, Solihull, Helion, 2005.

Modelski, Łukasz, *Dziewczyny Wojenne: Prawdziwe Historie*, Kraków, Znak, 2011.

Paul, Allen, *Katyń. Stalin's Massacre and the Triumph of the Truth*, DeKalb, Illinois, North Illinois University Press, 2010.

Prażmowska, Anita, J. *Civil War in Poland, 1942-1948*, Basingstoke, Macmillan, 2004.

Puacz, Edward, *Problems of the Exiled Governments*, London, n.p. 1943.

Raczynski, Edward, *In Allied London*, Weidenfeld & Nicolson, 1962.

Roberts, Andrew, *The Storm of War. A New History of the Second World War*, London, Allen Lane, 2009.

Roberts, Geoffrey, *Stalin's Wars: From World War to Cold War, 1939-1953*, New Haven, Yale University Press, 2006.

Rozmysłowicz, Adam, *Gmach PAST-y w Powstanice Warszawskia 1944*, Warsaw, RTYM, 2008.

Sarner, Harvey, *General Anders and the Soldiers of the Polish Second Corps*, Cathedral City, Brunswick, 1997.

Snyder, Timothy, *Bloodlands: Europe between Hitler and Stalin*, New York, Basic Books, 2010.

Stafford, David, *Churchill & Secret Service*, London, Abacus, 1997.

Stypulkowski, Z, *Invitation to Moscow*, London, Thames & Hudson, 1951.

Sydnor, Charles W. Jr. *Soldiers of Destruction. The SS Death's Head Division, 1933-1945*, Princeton, Princeton University Press, 1977.

Taylor, Brian, *Barbarossa to Berlin: A Chronology of the Campaigns on the Eastern Front, 1941to 1945. Volume 2. The Defeat of Germany, 19 November 1942 to 15 May 1945*, Staplehurst, Spellmount, 2004.

Taylor, Frederick, *Exorcising Hitler. The Occupation and Denazification of Germany*, London, Bloomsbury, 2012.

Urbanek, Bożena, *Pielęgniarki i Sanitariuszki w powstaniu Warszawskim 1944r.* Warsaw, PWN, 1988.

Watson, Derek, *Molotov: A Biography*, Basingstoke, Palgrave Macmillan, 2005.

Werth, Alexander, *Russia at War, 1941-1945*, London, Barrie & Rockliff, 1964.

Wiatr, Jerzy, J. *The Soldier and the Nation. The Role of the Military in Polish Politics, 1918-1985*, Boulder, Westview, 1988.

Wysocki, Wiesław Jan, *Rotmistrz Witold Pilecki, 1901-1948*, Warsaw, RYTM, 2012.

Zagorski, W, (Lech) *Seventy Days*, Maidstone, George Mann, 1974, translated by John Welsh.

Zagorski, Waclaw, *Seventy Days. A Diary of the Warsaw Insurrection, 1944*, London, Frederick Muller, 1957, translated by John Welsh.

Zuławski, BR, *Powstanie Warszawskie*, Łódź, Wojska Polski, 1946.

JOURNALS

Beaupré, Jadwiga, 'Relacja lerki z Zeithain' *Pregląd Lekarski*, 31, 1974, 200-8.

Garliński, Józef, 'The Polish Underground State (1939-45)' *The Journal of Contemporary History*, 10, 1975, 219-59.

Lukas, Richard C. 'The Big Three and the Warsaw Uprising' *Military Affairs*, 39, 1975, 129-35.

Lukas, Richard C. 'Russia, the Warsaw Uprising and the Cold War' *Polish Review*, 20, 1975, 13-26.

Schwonek, Matthew R. 'Gen. Kazimierz Sosnkowski's Order of the Day No. 19' *Journal of Slavic Military Studies*, 21, 2008, 364-376.

ELECTRONIC SOURCES

Warsawuprising.com/.../dispatches_pri...accessed 30 March 2011

www.warsawuprising.com

www.deon.pl/druk/ZJGj3qVnZtGYdGqpag.html accessed 29 July 2012.

EMAIL CORRESPONDENCE

Major-General John Drewienkiewicz (British Army – Retired) to author, 24 October 2011.

TELEVISION

'The Cold War' BBC2, Broadcast, 26 September 1999.

Index

INDEX OF PEOPLE

INDEX OF PLACES

Note: All streets, districts etc. are part of Warsaw unless otherwise stated.

INDEX OF MISCELLANEOUS TERMS

INDEX OF MILITARY FORMATIONS & UNITS

Lightning Source UK Ltd.
Milton Keynes UK
UKOW06n1433100715

254953UK00005B/82/P